MATTERS OF LIFE AND DEATH

MATTERS OF LIFE AND DEATH

Psychoanalytic Reflections

Salman Akhtar

KARNAC

First published in 2011 by
Karnac Books Ltd
118 Finchley Road, London NW3 5HT

British Library Cataloguing in Publication Data

A C.I.P. for this book is available from the British Library

ISBN: 978 1 85575 801 8

Edited, designed and produced by The Studio Publishing Services Ltd
www.publishingservicesuk.co.uk
e-mail: studio@publishingservicesuk.co.uk

Printed in Great Britain

www.karnacbooks.com

To my uncle and aunt

Mr Abu Salim and Mrs Hamida Salim

with love and gratitude

CONTENTS

ACKNOWLEDGEMENTS

First and foremost, I wish to thank Dr Michael Vergare, the Senior Vice President of Academic Affairs and the Chairman of the Department of Psychiatry at Jefferson Medical College, for his kind sponsorship of my academic endeavours. I am also grateful to Drs Mitchell Cohen and Elizabeth Kunkel, the two Vice Chairs of the Department, for their support of my work.

A number of colleagues from the Psychoanalytic Center of Philadelphia helped me in the process of writing this book. Some suggested pertinent reading material, while others lent me clinical vignettes from their practices. Prominent among these individuals are Drs Jennifer Bonovitz, Ira Brenner, Abigail Kay, Mark Moore, Andrew Smolar, and George Wohlreich. My personal friends, the eminent nephrologist, Dr Naresh Julka, of Chicago, and Mr Nida Fazli, the renowned Urdu poet of Mumbai, also provided useful insights into the matters contained in this book. Drs Mona abu-Hamda, Rajnish Mago, Anujit Mukherjee, and Joseph Reppen also gave me meaningful input on certain aspects of this book. My son, Kabir, helped to find some important pieces of information. Ms Jan Wright, my assistant, prepared the manuscript with outstanding skill and diligence, helped me in library searches, and kept my language closer to the English idiom.

The love and support of my wife and fellow analyst, Dr Monisha Nayar, provided the holding environment essential for putting this book together. Her containment of my preoccupied states, intellectual input on earlier drafts of some of the chapters, and, above all, her generosity and friendship sustained me while I was involved in this work.

ABOUT THE AUTHOR

Salman Akhtar, MD, was born in India and completed his medical and psychiatric education there. Upon arriving in the United States in 1973, he repeated his psychiatric training at the University of Virginia School of Medicine, and then obtained psychoanalytic training from the Philadelphia Psychoanalytic Institute. Currently, he is Professor of Psychiatry at Jefferson Medical College and a Training and Supervising Analyst at the Psychoanalytic Center of Philadelphia. He has served on the editorial boards of the *International Journal of Psychoanalysis* and the *Journal of the American Psychoanalytic Association.* His more than 300 publications include eleven books—*Broken Structures* (1992); *Quest for Answers* (1995); *Inner Torment* (1999); *Immigration and Identity* (1999); *New Clinical Realms* (2003); *Objects of Our Desire* (2005); *Regarding Others* (2007); *Turning Points in Dynamic Psychotherapy* (2009); *The Damaged Core* (2009); *Comprehensive Dictionary of Psychoanalysis* (2009); and *Immigration and Acculturation* (2011)—as well as thirty edited or co-edited volumes in psychiatry and psychoanalysis. Dr Akhtar has delivered many prestigious addresses and lectures, including a Plenary Address at the Second International Congress of the International Society for the Study of Personality Disorders in

Oslo, Norway (1991), an Invited Plenary Paper at the Second International Margaret S. Mahler Symposium in Cologne, Germany (1993), an Invited Plenary Paper at the Rencontre Franco–Americaine de Psychanalyse meeting in Paris, France (1994), an Invited Keynote Address at the Annual Meetings of Division 39 of the American Psychological Association (1994), the Plenary Address at the Annual Meetings of the Canadian Psychoanalytic Association (2002), a Keynote Address at the 43rd IPA Congress in Rio de Janeiro, Brazil (2005); the Plenary Address at the 150th Freud Birthday Celebration sponsored by the Dutch Psychoanalytic Society and the Embassy of Austria in Leiden, Holland (2006); and the Inaugural Address at the First IPA–Asia Congress in Beijing, China (2010). Dr Akhtar is the recipient of the Journal of the American Psychoanalytic Association's Best Paper of the Year Award (1995), the Margaret Mahler Literature Prize (1996), the American Society of Psychoanalytic Physicians' Sigmund Freud Award (2000), the American College of Psychoanalysts' Laughlin Award (2003), the American Psychoanalytic Association's Edith Sabshin Award (2000), Columbia University's Robert Liebert Award for Distinguished Contributions to Applied Psychoanalysis (2004), the American Psychiatric Association's Kun Po Soo Award (2004), and the Irma Bland Award for being the Outstanding Teacher of Psychiatric Residents in the country (2005). Dr Akhtar is an internationally sought speaker and teacher, and his books have been translated into many languages, including German, Turkish, and Romanian. His interests are wide and he has served as the Film Review Editor for the *International Journal of Psychoanalysis*, and is currently serving as the Book Review Editor for the *International Journal of Applied Psychoanalytic Studies*. He has published seven collections of poetry, and serves as a Scholar-in-Residence at the Inter-Act Theatre Company in Philadelphia.

Introduction

Possessing neither the omnipotent ability nor the foolhardy desire to tackle the mysteries of life and death that have preoccupied philosophers, theologians, poets, and physicians for centuries, I have set my eyes on more modest goals. My focus in this book is only upon the intrapsychic vicissitudes of what it means to be truly alive and how death accompanies us at each step of our life's journey. Freud's life and death instincts are my guides. Loyal to his declaration that all living experience results from the opposition or combination of these two "basic instincts", I attempt to show that, psychologically speaking, death is always present in life and life in death. Dehumanization of living human beings and immortal renown of the dead are my divergent outposts. In between them is the territory that concerns me the most: what is emotionally central to being alive and how death and awareness of death—conscious or unconscious—silently colour our subjective experience.

In order to organize my thoughts on these matters, I have divided this book into three sections: Life, Death, and Life and Death. The first two parts consist of three chapters each, while the third part has the concluding chapter. Part I, dealing with life, opens with a chapter on human goodness. In this chapter, I offer evidence for the fact that psychoanalysis does have a perspective on human "goodness". Adding the pertinent notions of four later analysts (Melanie Klein, Donald Winnicott, Erik Erikson, and Wilfred Bion) to the life-affirming ideas hidden beneath Freud's avowed pessimism about human nature, I distil the attribute of a "good" person. These include: (a) rationality, restraint, and epistemic enthusiasm, (b) humility, gratitude, empathy, and reparative drive, (c) authenticity, concern for others, and playfulness, (d) trust, generativity, and care, and (e) truthfulness and faith. I address the objections that can be levelled against such a conclusion. Following this, I underscore that the role played by human "goodness" in the conduct of analytic therapy is by no means trivial. Eight different ways in which this is evident includes the analyst's (1) providing goodness to the patient; (2) behaving with good manners; (3) seeing goodness in the patient; (4) accepting the patient's goodness; (5) diagnosing and analysing false goodness; (6) interpreting the patient's defences against the analyst's goodness; (7) interpreting the patient's defences against his own goodness; (8) exploring the history and meanings of the words "good" for the patient.

This is followed by a chapter on the elusive concept of happiness. In this chapter, I summarize the views of Freud and subsequent psychoanalysts (especially Helene Deutsch, Bertram Lewin, Melanie Klein, and Heinz Kohut) on the concept of happiness. I also attempt to extract meaningful material from the writings of the contemporary Happiness Movement, as well as those of philosophical and microeconomic perspectives. Pooling these diverse sets of observations together, I suggest that the affects and experiences subsumed under the broad rubric of "happiness" belong to four different, though potentially overlapping, categories. These categories are pleasure, joy, ecstasy, and contentment. I then delineate ontogenetic roots, metapsychological correlates, and experiential building blocks for each of these categories. Finally, I demonstrate how the subjective experience of happiness (both in its broad sense and in its constituent categories) has an impact upon the conduct of psychotherapy and psychoanalysis.

The final chapter in this section is about playfulness. I regard playfulness as a character trait and/or interactional pattern comprising light-heartedness, spontaneity, pleasure experienced in the context of mutuality, and a transient suspension of the reality—

unreality boundary. I trace the development of playfulness back to the matrix of early parent–child relationship and even to certain "hard-wired" constitutional capacities of the child. Like any other mental capacity, playfulness is subject to the encroachment of psychopathology. This manifests in five different ways: (i) deficient playfulness, (ii) pseudo-playfulness, (iii) inhibited playfulness, (iv) derailed playfulness, and (v) malignant playfulness. Finally, I discuss the application of these ideas to the therapeutic situation.

Part II of the book, titled "Death", has chapters on mortality, graves, and orphans. The chapter on mortality juxtaposes two different vantage points on death and highlights the tension that exists between attitudes emanating from denial of death and those arising from its acceptance. Both perspectives have profoundly significant dynamic, structural, and existential functions. Indeed, one can discern psychic benefits of either pole of this dialectic (denial making it easier to go on living, acceptance making the experience of life richer and more textured). Extending such insights to the clinical situation, I underscore that the reality of one's approaching mortality has an impact upon the conduct of intensive psychotherapy and psychoanalysis in many important ways, including: (1) discerning the patient's concern with death; (2) exploring the patient's feelings and attitudes about his or her mortality; (3) helping the patient gain a more active role in his post-death destiny; (4) managing countertransference reactions to these difficult topics.

In the next chapter, I elucidate the psychological significance of human graves. I highlight the potential role of these "ultimate resting places" in facilitating mourning on the part of those left behind. With the help of recollections provided by friends, and by using clinical illustrations, I highlight the complex function of visiting graves of one's relatives. And, by taking the liberty to digress into some sociopolitical matters, I demonstrate how the desecration and destruction of graves become vehicles of "ethnic cleansing" and religious and racial hatred.

This is followed by a chapter on the multi-layered consequences of childhood parental loss. Employing the much avoided but direct and evocative designation "orphan", I elucidate the lifelong struggles and vulnerabilities of individuals whose parents have died early on in their lives. The realms in which long-term consequences of this trauma can be found include those of aggression, narcissism, love and sexuality, subjective experience of time, and attitudes toward one's own mortality. However, a more central issue is the intrapsychic relationship the "orphan" maintains with his or her lost parent. Never fully relinquished, this internal object-representation exerts a powerful influence on the individual, an influence that can be pathogenic (e.g., lifelong vulnerability to separation anxiety) or salutary (e.g., enhanced ambition and creativity). Clearly, the balance of outcome depends upon a large number of factors that include the age at which the loss occurred, the nature of relationship with the parent before he or she died, the constitutional talents of the child, the degree of love and reliability offered by the surviving parent and/or substitute parental figure(s), the availability of health-promoting role models, the monetary stability of the family, and the degree to which those around the child were willing and/or able to facilitate his mourning of the loss. This last mentioned factor cannot be overemphasized, since many adults feel uncomfortable in seeing a child sad and distract him from the work of mourning instead of helping him with it. All this has consequences for the treatment of adults who have lost one or both parents during childhood. A greater degree of "illusion" and "holding", validation of the tragic nature of the loss, clarification and interpretation of defences against mourning, unmasking of the defensive uses of the tragedy and of its consequences, and careful monitoring of the countertransference experience constitute the needed background for conducting psychotherapy and psychoanalysis with such patients.

The last section, titled "Life and Death", consists of the closing chapter. In this essay, I attempt to show that life and death are not as separate from each other as is generally considered. Mini- and micro-deaths on both biological and psychological fronts occur on a daily basis in life. And, death does not terminate the object-relational, psychic, and internalized impact we have upon others. Life and death turn out to be intermingled with each other. The value of accepting this shows up not only in greater attunement with those under our care, but also in keener appreciation of life and fuller acceptance of death.

The fundamental thrust of these socio-clinical meditations is to enhance appreciation of aspects of life that have been inoptimally addressed in psychoanalytic literature and to expand the view of death in ways that might be personally and technically enriching. Understanding these issues and putting them to use or, at least, grappling with them, might require (and result in) major conceptual shifts in minds used to the customary restrictions on psychoanalytic theory and technique. The effect might even be jolting. However, the agenda that I have put on the table here is a serious one, and ignoring it will preclude advances in our thought and praxis.

PART I
LIFE

CHAPTER ONE

Goodness

> "In youth and health, in summer, in the woods or on the mountains, there come days when the weather seems all whispering with peace, hours when the goodness and beauty of all existence enfolds us like a dry, warm climate, or chime through us as if our inner ears were subtly ringing with the world's security"
>
> (James, 1902, p. 269)

Freud's (1915b) wry observation that "most of our sentimentalists, friends of humanity, and protectors of animals have been evolved from little sadists and animal tormentors" (p. 282) is but one illustration of his pessimistic view of human nature. With a stoic ethic and sceptical intellect as his chief allies, Freud suspected that instinctual and pleasure-based motives underlay most, if not all, human endeavour. Vast swathes of humanity, in his eyes, were "good for nothing in life" (1905a, p. 263) besides being "lazy and unintelligent" (1927c, p. 7). Indeed, he went so far as to declare that "belief in the goodness of human nature is one of those evil illusions by which mankind expect their lives to be beautified and made easier while in reality they only cause damage" (1933a, p. 104). Freud's (1933b) discourse on why nations go to war also underscored his view that human beings were basically destructive and violent.

From a different perspective, Freud's (1912–1913) proposal of an actual, even if "pre-historic", murder of the primal father saddled man with ancestral "badness" and a sort of "original sin". His pronouncement that the "two great human crimes" (1916, p. 333) were incest and parricide had a similar result. Since wishes to commit these "crimes" were integral to the childhood Oedipal experience, and since no one ever fully gave them up, all human beings remained criminal at the bottom of their hearts. Actually, Freud (1927c) did say that human beings were "antisocial and anticultural" (p. 7) at the core of their beings. All in all, for Freud, the essential human nature was nothing to be celebrated. In fact, it was rather dismal.

Fiercely loyal to the founder of their discipline and avoidant, like him, of the moral shadows of religion, psychoanalysts adopted a naturalistic and sceptical view of man. They assiduously sidestepped the labels of "good" and "bad", and insisted that their clinical approach was entirely devoid of moral judgements. Writing of psychoanalytic technique, Hartmann (1960) declared that "Moral considerations are kept from interfering with it. This allows a minimizing of possible conflicts of valuation. The analytic therapy is a kind of technology" (pp. 20–21).

On the theoretical front, too, analysts strove to evolve a value-free terminology. Yet, a careful look at the corpus of psychoanalytic theory reveals numerous concepts with the prefix "good". Just take a look at the following:

- "good object" (Klein, 1930);
- "poor little good child" (Menninger, 1932);
- "too little good" (Riviere, 1937);
- "negative goodness" (Deutsch, 1942);
- "good analytic hour" (Kris, 1956);
- "good-enough mother" (Winnicott, 1960);
- "good dream" (Khan, 1962);
- "too good mother" (Shields, 1964);
- "The so-called good hysteric" (Zetzel, 1968);

- "on being good" (Balsam, 1988);
- "good-enough hate" (Harvey Rich, 1995, cited in Akhtar, 1999a);
- "false goodness" (Schafer, 2002);
- "defences against goodness" (Schafer, 2002);
- "good-enough death" (Shneidman, 2008).

But how is the word "good" being used here? Does "good" mean aim-inhibited? Sublimated? Developmentally appropriate? Ego-replenishing? Empathic? Well balanced between conscious and unconscious? Suitably representative of the polarities of drive and defence? The most likely answer to such questions is "all of the above, in varying permutations and combinations". In other words, it is along the economic, structural, adaptive, and topographic perspectives that the qualifier "good" is being used. There might be relational imperatives here, but no moral implication at all. Is this really the case? Or does psychoanalysis have something to say about human goodness?

The views of Freud, Klein, Winnicott, Erikson, and Bion

In search of the morality which might lurk underneath the judgement-free façade of psychoanalysis, and, more specifically, to unearth the discipline's stance on human goodness, let us take a fresh look at Freud and then at the pertinent notions in the works of Klein, Winnicott, Erikson, and Bion. Returning to Freud, one can safely conclude that the avoidance of the "great human crimes" at the behest of superego is the minimal criteria of being "not bad". To this, one might add the contribution of the "ego ideal"; this structure is a container of aspirations, positive familial and cultural legacies, and blueprints for the desired ways of being. As a psychic structure, the ego-ideal provides a yardstick for an individual's assessing how well he has met his expectations of himself. It is, thus, a counterpart of "superego", or the conscious. The ego-ideal exhorts and pushes, striving to diminish the gap between the self as it is and as it is desired to be. The superego, in contrast, criticizes one for transgressing inner moral injunctions. Failure to meet superego demands causes guilt. Failure to approach the ego-ideal's demands causes dejection and shame. Ego's striving for closeness with the ego ideal produces feelings of self-acceptance and goodness. A sense of being good also arises from appropriate instinctual aim-inhibition, sublimation, and the work of creativity. The structure responsible for these activities, the ego, is also the prime agent for rationality, perception, and reality contact. Moreover, "the ego is to be regarded as a great reservoir of libido, from which libido is sent to objects and which is always ready to absorb libido flowing back from objects" (1922, p. 257). Thus, loving and being loved enter the picture, and what is "goodness" without love?

If one thinks that this pretty much rounds off Freud's picture of human goodness, one is in for a big surprise. The dour theoretician who declared that the "aim of all life is death" (Freud, 1920g, p. 38) also posited the glorious concept of life instinct. This great force—with its subsidiary interests of sexuality and self-preservation—is responsible for combating the inherent self-destructiveness of human beings. More importantly, it puts a premium on growth, synthesis, and advancement. It presses for the establishment and maintenance of more differentiated and organized forms of mentation, behaviour, and social units. Forever striving for ego furtherance, life instinct contributes to the evolution of novel ways of thinking and new avenues of self-expression. Inherent and natural, this force contains and expresses what is best in human beings. It is life instinct that gives life to life. Knowledge is its partner; discovery and invention are its offspring.

While Freud's "punishing conscience" (Gay, 1988, p. 140) might have precluded his capitalizing on his own notion of life instinct and adding positive elements to his negative view of mankind, Klein tackled the subject of human goodness head on. In clearly expressed or subtly implied views over the course of several contributions (Klein, 1933, 1935, 1937, 1940, 1957, 1960), she delineated "goodness" as perceiving others as whole objects, experiencing concern for them, acknowledging gratitude for the libidinal supplies and aggressive containment one has received from others, and acting with reparative intent and generosity towards them. Working through of "manic defences" (idealization, denial, and omnipotence) was necessary for this to occur; it resulted in modesty, mastery over envy, acceptance of the blemished and finite nature of life, and patience. According to Klein, the child's psyche arrives at such a constellation only after becoming capable of recognizing and bearing the fact that he himself has attacked, extracted supplies from, and damaged the "good" (i.e., giving) breast. Such ownership of aggression affords the hitherto "purified pleasure ego"(Freud, 1915c) a measure of modesty and remorse. If these deflating affects and self-views are not dissipated or split-off, efforts at reparation can begin. A shift from "paranoid" to "depressive" position has now taken place. This developmental achievement, once adequately structuralized, remains available as a psychic backdrop for perception, affect processing, and action. Humility, gratitude, and reparation are its cornerstones. However, Klein emphasized that to be genuinely considerate of others, one must be able to put oneself in the mind-set of the other. In her own words "this capacity for identification with another person is a most important element in human relationships in general, and is also a condition for real and strong feelings of love" (1937, p. 311).

Such capacity for concern, along with authenticity and a robust "area of intermediate experience", constituted the three central features of a well-evolved personality for Winnicott (1953, 1960, 1962). While all three require the participation of early care-takers for their proper consolidation, they originate from the depth of the infant's psychic core. Authenticity, in the form of psychosomatic unity and "going-on-being", underlies Winnicott's (1960) concept of "true self". In Buddhist metaphor, this is "one thought–one action". The mind–body axis is conflict-free and action is not reactive in nature. It emanates from within, has an element of spontaneity, and reflects the "essence of living" (Winnicott, 1960, p. 144). The second element emphasized by Winnicott has echoes of the Kleinian discourse noted above. This pertains to the capacity for concern. Unlike Klein, who regarded such capacity to emerge from the dawning awareness on the child's part that he has damaged the breast (mother) in phantasy, Winnicott (1962) attributed the origin of this capacity to the ability of the mother to "survive" the child's age-specific "ruthlessness". One can, therefore, say that the capacity for concern is not really "inherent" to man; it is a developmental achievement. Strictly speaking, this would be correct. However, the nature–nurture dialectics, interaction, and conflation during infancy and childhood make it hard to surgically tease apart these things. For instance, the mother might be more able and willing to "survive" the ruthless demands of one child and not those of the other, depending upon the child's temperamental qualities, and so on.

The premium on authenticity and concern in Winnicott's perspective is matched, if not overshadowed, by the importance he placed upon the value of the "intermediate area of experience". This involves that aspect of the mind (a) where reality and unreality coexist, (b) which is both simple and contradictory, (c) which can be observed, but is largely a matter of experiencing, and (d) about which there is a "gentlemanly agreement" that permits its origins and nature to remain private. Also called the "transitional space", or "transitional realm", (Winnicott, 1953), this domain of subjectivity is where imagination is born and paradox reigns supreme. It is the location of cultural experience at large. Poetry, games, fiction, movies, love, affiliation, spirituality, and religious experiences populate this area (Winnicott, 1971). When this area is underdeveloped, personality acquires a rigid and unimaginative quality. When this area is well developed, personality displays the capacity for spontaneity, playfulness, metaphorical thinking, and creativity. Although the initial impetus for it emanates from within the child, its consolidation depends upon the mother's capacity to go along with the child's spontaneous gesture.

Such structure-building role of early mother–child interaction also underlay Erikson's (1950, 1959) notion of "basic trust" and healthy optimism towards life. However, his deeper notions of human goodness involve developmental events that take place long after childhood. Arriving at middle age, the individual encounters the possibility of guiding the next generation. Merely having children, nephews and nieces, junior employees, or students is not enough. It is the intrapsychic capacity to treat them with benevolent support, to grant them autonomy, and to facilitate their own pursuits that constitutes the essence of "generativity". Self-interest recedes to the background and altruistic concern prevails. Ego interest expands beyond the act of generation to that which is being generated. A certain "belief in the species" (Erikson, 1968, p. 138) makes the next generation appear a welcome trust. To safeguard its future, individuals create civic institutions, and these, in turn, codify the ethics of generative succession. Capacity for genuine "care" now appears on the horizon. This involves the attitude (and practice) of supporting societal structures and rituals, as well as protective tenderness towards the animal and plant kingdoms. Man acquires "goodness" by his connection not only to his ancestors and progeny, but to the universe at large.

The near-spiritual cadence of these notions leads one to consider what Bion (1965, 1967a, 1970) implies about human goodness. The points he seems to underscore include truthfulness and the capacity to have faith. For Bion, truth is pre-existing and denotes the thing-in-itself, which is immeasurable. This truth is out there, waiting to be found by a receptive mind that has emptied itself of pre-conception, memory, and desire. Acquired knowledge can prepare the platform from which a leap of faith is taken. But, it is leaving knowledge and experience behind that actually constitutes a step towards "O", the absolute truth of the moment. (Bion's choice of the letter "O" in this context remains mysterious. At least three explanations have been offered: (1) Lopez-Corvo (2003) thinks that the letter "O" is taken from the word "origin" and is "related to the same term used to designate the centre of the Cartesian coordinates that correspond to the point where the X and Y axes intercept; however, it could have also been taken from the concept of 'origin' in Zen Buddhism" (p. 197); (2) Symington (2008) believes that the "O" stood for Ontos in Bion's mind, since he often used Greek letters to designate psychological realities and both "O" and Ontos denote ultimate reality and absolute truth; (3) I (Akhtar, 2008a) propose that Bion's "O" is a truncated form of Om, the Sanskrit word for the Omnipresent Creator; this is likely in light of the fact that Bion grew up until the age of eight in India, where he was taken care of by a Hindu maid, who presumably took him to many Hindu temples and exposed him to the chants of the word Om.) Take, for instance, the Oedipus complex or, for that matter, the mathematical equation, $E=mc^2$; these truths existed long before Sophocles', Freud's, and Einstein's discovery of them. In other words, the supreme godhead of veracity pre-existed the human capacity to think it. This leads to the related notion of faith in Bion's work. For Bion, faith is not a product of knowledge, experience, and thought. Turning conventional wisdom on its head, he declares that it is not *thinking* but *not thinking* that creates the possibility of discovering truth and, hence, developing faith in the universe around us. Uncrowded by thought and cleansed of "memory and desire", the mind becomes concerned "neither with what had happened nor with what is going to happen but what is happening" (1967, p. 271). Such immediacy of experience reveals truth and creates faith in the order that exists out there.

Having briefly surveyed the view of human goodness in the writings of Freud, Klein, Winnicott, Erikson, and Bion, we are now ready to pool their observations and draw a composite picture of it all. Assuming our deductions about their views to be true, a good human being (from a psychoanalytic perspective) would possess the following qualities:

- rationality, restraint, epistemic enthusiasm, and striving for synthesis (Freud);
- humility, gratitude, empathy, and reparation (Klein);
- authenticity, concern for others, and playfulness (Winnicott);
- trust, generativity, and care (Erikson);
- truthfulness and faith (Bion).

Three objections can be raised against such a conclusion. The first would declare the choice of the five theorists cited here to be idiosyncratic. A corollary of this line of thinking would be the proposal of additional or alternative psychoanalytic views in evolving the picture of human goodness. Hartmann's (1960) "health values", Loewald's (1960, 1970) generative vision, Anna Freud's (1963) developmental lines, and Kohlberg's (1984) hierarchy of moral development would certainly be significant contenders in this context. The second criticism would be that some of the qualities listed above seem contradictory; rationality and restraint especially stand in contrast to authenticity and playfulness. The third criticism that might be hurled at the portrayal of human "goodness" above is that it merely represents healthy development; there is nothing "good" or "bad" about it at all.

In response to these objections, the following can be said. First, the picture drawn here is a sketch, not a finished painting. However, by drawing (pun unintended) upon the work of Freud and four highly respected contributors to the field, the message does carry some weight. Adding other perspectives only enriches what has been summarized above. Second, the seeming contradictions in the qualities listed above are readily resolved in a harmonious manner by the ego function of synthesis and "fitting together" (Hartmann, 1939). Finally, as far as the point about the qualities enumerated above being merely developmental and not moral in any way is concerned, the rejoinder might be that indeed these are developmental achievements, but with ethical implications. Together, these characteristics transcend the plebeian parameters of psychic development alone. Generativity is at a higher level of abstraction than genital primacy. Humility, truthfulness, and care are more inclusive than, for instance, the satisfactory resolution of the oral or anal phase. Concepts involved in the above-mentioned description of human goodness have a life enhancing, world-enriching, and "anagogic" (Silberer, 1914) quality about them. They sustain love, meaning, history, relatedness, and legacy.

Now, whether such human "goodness" is inherent or acquired still remains unanswered. Since all its attributes can be traced to Freud's "life instinct", which, by definition, is an inherent force, it would appear that human goodness is also "hard-wired" at its base. Parallel to the destructive forces of the "death instinct", the psychosocially enriching activities and qualities of the "life instinct" also emanate from the most fundamental tissue of human nature. To be more precise, though, both "goodness" and "badness" appear essential components of human nature that can be exaggerated, diminished, re-directed, and modified by early environmental stimuli. However, to return to the main topic of our concern, it seems safe to assume that "goodness" (like "badness") is intrinsic to human nature.

Observational data from ethology and neonatology support such a conclusion. The former offers convincing evidence that qualities of attachment, concern, altruism, co-operation, and even forgiveness are amply evident among animals (Cheney, Seyfarth, & Silk, 1995; de Waal & van Roosmalen, 1979; Hrdy, 1999; Ren, Yan, & Su, 1991; Silk, 1998). The latter demonstrates that smiling, social referencing, reciprocity, affect attunement, empathy, and pleasure in finding new insights all have origins in earliest infancy and emanate from a state of biological preparedness (see Emde, 1991, for a comprehensive survey of this literature). Putting the ethological and infant-observational data together leads one to conclude that seeds of "goodness" are sowed by nature itself.

Seelig and Rosof (2001), who have comprehensively reviewed the pertinent literature, conclude that, at its roots, human altruism is "hard-wired", as it is conducive to the survival of the species.

Having thus traced the capacity for "goodness" to the most basic "animal" core of human being, one needs to consider the myriad affective and behavioural manifestations of this substrate as these appear in that most human of endeavours, the psychoanalytic relationship.

Eight ways in which "goodness" plays a role in the clinical situation

Contemporary psychoanalytic practice widely recognizes that the analyst's non-judgemental attitude is invariably coupled with his earnest interest, compassion, and sensitivity to the analysand's developmental potentialities. Terms such as "technical neutrality" (Kernberg, 1976) and "interpretive neutrality" (Gill, 1994) emphasize one pole of this dialectic and "compassionate neutrality" (Greenson, 1958) and "benevolent neutrality" (Stone, 1961) the other pole. Regardless of the emphasis, both camps concede that departures from strict neutrality are often necessary in situations that constitute emergencies for the analysand, emergencies for someone vulnerable to the analysand's destructiveness, and emergencies for the analyst, including threat of physical violence (Hoffer, 1985). And, it is at this juncture that technical and moral decisions become blurred, though challenges to retain a value-free approach can be posed by more subtle situations as well (Klauber, 1968; Meissner, 1996). The clinician's pride in his morally neutral approach comes undone in his encounter with liars, philanderers, embezzlers, racists, rapists, child abusers, and even those with sharply different sociopolitical views. This is only natural. However, in its concern with "problems of imposition, persuasion, and coercion", psychoanalysis has not accorded a proper place to "the idea of a benign, or perhaps helpful, use of the analyst's moral framework" (Hagman, 2000, p. 69).

Hartmann's (1960) protestations to the contrary notwithstanding, the fact is that moral values do enter the clinical work of psychoanalysis. We psychoanalysts do not leave our sociopolitical world view and ethical yardsticks at the door of our offices, nor do our patients. In the words of Klauber (1968)

> Analyst and patient are not only analyst and patient; they are also individuals with highly integrated, and to a large extent unmodifiable, systems of values, and the attitude of one to another expresses not only transference and countertransference but views which remain ego-syntonic and firmly held on reflection. A theory of technique which ignores the immense influence on the psychoanalytic transaction of the value systems of patient and analyst alike ignores a basic psychic reality behind any psychoanalytic partnership. What has to be taken into account is what the Greeks might have called the ethos of patient and analyst—a word meaning originally an accustomed seat—in addition to the *pathos* of more labile reactions. [p. 128, original italics]

While technical errors originating in "moral countertransference" (Mills, 2005) attract greater attention, the helpful role played by human "goodness" in the conduct of analytic treatment is by no means trivial. Before a prudish idealization of neutrality makes the reader gasp, a clarification seems necessary: "goodness", in this context, means nothing else except the way it has been defined in the preceding section of this chapter. Such "goodness" seems to have a multi-faceted impact upon the day-to-day work of the psychoanalyst. Eight different ways in which this is evident include the analyst's (1) providing goodness to the patient; (2) behaving with good manners; (3) seeing goodness in the patient; (4) accepting patient's goodness; (5) diagnosing and analysing false goodness; (6) interpreting patient's defences against the analyst's goodness; (7) interpreting patient's defences against his own goodness; and, (8) exploring the history and meanings of the word "good" for the patient. These technical measures are commented upon in some detail below.

Providing goodness to the patient

Regardless of whether he conceptualizes it as such or not, the practising psychoanalyst regularly provides "goodness" to those under his care. He delves into the irrational, but remains rational himself. He controls his impulses. He puts a premium on knowing more and more about the individuality and dialectics of the two minds in clinical interaction. He also constantly makes efforts to organize the material at increasing levels of abstraction and sophistication. He does not act with undue certainty, and feels gratitude for the patient's willingness to trust him with his innermost experiences. He strikes a balance between authenticity and responsiveness, and between deliberate restraint and imaginative playfulness (see Parsons, 2000, especially in this regard). He is generative and truthful. He sustains hope, even (and especially) when the patient may not have much reason to be optimistic.

The analysand's encounter with such attributes of the analyst on an ongoing basis results in his or her internalization of them. The analyst's "goodness" also serves as a screen on which the projections and externalizations of the patient's "badness" can be witnessed, understood, and interpreted. Offered in a manner that is neither loud nor maudlin, it does not make the patient worry about his imagined "badness". Essentially, the analyst's "goodness" represents an aspect of the wider concept of "caring" described by Tahka (1993).

> Caring is an attitude, not necessarily anything one does. It is a form of interest in another human being that has its roots in the parents' phase-specifically adequate attitudes towards their children at the latter's changing developmental stages. The capacity and motivation for caring for other people seem more likely to be gradually acquired through identifications with the developmental object's caring attitude toward oneself, than simply as a result of reaction formations against and modification of early feelings of guilt. Caring for the patient becomes mobilized by the analyst's phase-specific, complementary, and empathic responses to the patient's verbal and nonverbal cues and messages. [p. 345]

In this context, the following reminder by Stone (1961) is highly pertinent.

> Most important attitudes are imparted nonverbally—by the timing and duration of silences, by tone of voice and the rhetorical nuances in interventions, by facial expression at the beginning and the end of

> hours, and by the mood in which realities are dealt with: hours, fees, absences, intercurrent life crises, or other important matters. [p. 167]

In other words, the analyst does not have to do anything "extra" to be good to his patient; his unhurried and non-judgemental but deeply interested attitude is in itself the carrier of "goodness" that the patient has lacked, repressed, or destroyed within himself.

Behaving with good manners

The analyst behaves in accordance with good manners. This seems too elementary a point to make, but the need for doing so arises because hardly any discussion of technique explicitly mentions it. The novice, especially, needs to know that, by and large, it is appropriate to say "thank you" when the patient hands over his payment or agrees to a schedule change requested by the analyst. Similarly, it is only decent to express sympathy at the death of someone close to the analysand and offer congratulations at a major success or achievement of the analysand. And it can certainly come across as self-serving and inconsiderate to present a bill to the patient on the first day of resuming analytic work after a long vacation.

Three qualifications must be added, however. First, the exercise of "good manners" must be tailored to the individual idiosyncrasies and sensitivities of each dyad. Some patients can hear "I am sorry" or "Thank you" from their analysts and then go on with the usual free-associative work. Others are unable to retain equanimity in the face of such expressions; these acquire greater affective valence for them and, therefore, complicate the analytic process. Well-attuned titration of the analyst's "goodness" is the key here. Second, the display of "good manners" by the analyst is not done in a shrill and exaggerated way; it is subtle and integral to the "waking screen" (Pacella, 1980) of his discourse with the patient. Third, "good manners" vary from era to era and from region to region. Thus, shaking hands at the beginning and end of each session is customary in some cultures and not in others. Therefore, what are "good manners" at one place might be experienced as intrusions at another; this acquires a far greater significance when the analyst and analysand are from different cultures (Akhtar, 1999b; Perez-Foster, Moskowitz, & Javier, 1996).

Seeing goodness in the patient

Like the sculptor who can envision the statue hidden in a rock, the analyst sees the potential strengths of his patient. This has a developmentally salutary impact upon the patient who strives for correspondence and proximity with the analyst's "vision" of him. In Loewald's (1960) words,

> The parent–child relationship can serve as a model here. The parent ideally is in an empathic relationship of understanding the child's particular stage in development, yet ahead in his vision of the child's future and mediating this vision to the child in his dealing with him. This vision, informed by the parent's own experience and knowledge of growth and future, is, ideally, a more articulate and more integrated version of the core of being that the child presents to the parents. This "more" that the parent sees and knows, he mediates to the child so that the child in identification with it can grow. The child, by internalizing aspects of the parent, also internalizes the parent's image of the child—an image that is mediated to the child in the thousand different ways of being handled, bodily and emotionally. [p. 229]

The caveat that needs to be entered here pertains to the fact that the analyst's vision must be primarily guided by his empathic knowledge of the patient and not by his falsely generative hunger for clinical offsprings. Assessment of "analysability" and—on the other temporal pole of the clinical scenario—of readiness for termination provide two clear instances where the analyst's impartial and yet developmentally informed vision plays a significant role in technique. *Vis-à-vis* patients' inherent "goodness" *per se*, however, the concept of "anagogic interpretation" (Silberer, 1914) is far more apt. This refers to a mode of decoding symbolism that brings out its universal, transcendent, and ethical dimension. Unlike the usual psychoanalytic tendency to decipher symbols along personal and sexual lines, *anagogic* (Greek for "to bear upwards") interpretations elevate the concrete into the spiritual. For instance, from a traditional analytic stance, a dream of buying a big house might be seen as related to a competitive wish, a desire to expand one's family, or a soothing defence against feelings of inferiority in other realms of life, and so on. From an "anagogic" perspective, however, the same dream can be seen as expressing a desire to expand one's mind so that one can include concerns and problems faced by others; the dream will be viewed as a statement of blossoming civic-mindedness.

Less high-minded, and yet pertinent to the analyst's seeing "goodness" in the patient, are Winnicott's (1956) and Casement's (1991) views on antisocial tendency and unconscious hope, respectively. These perspectives impel the analyst to discern a streak of optimism and search for redress in provocative behaviour. As a result, what seems phenomenologically "bad" turns out to be developmentally "good".

Accepting the patient's goodness

A closely related issue is that of the analyst's capacity and willingness to gracefully receive the patient's "goodness", which comes to him in many forms. The following list, though by no means exhaustive, includes the most common day-to-day manifestations of the patient's "goodness".

- Patient saying "thank you" when the analyst accommodates his need for a schedule change.
- Patient's willingness to change his schedule in accordance with the analyst's needs.
- Patient's agreement to a fee increase proposed by the analyst.
- Patient's wit, clever turn of phrase, and telling a nice joke.
- Patient's expression of sympathy upon hearing of analyst's illness or other misfortune.
- Patient telling the analyst about a good book he has recently read, or a film that he has just seen.
- Patient expressing a desire to read papers and books written by the analyst.
- Patient giving the analyst a gift at an appropriate juncture in their work (e.g., termination, patient's return from his home in a foreign country). (Taking something from an analysand is regarded as a collusion with the latter's instinctual agenda and a gratification of his id pressures or superego commands. It is supposed to contaminate transference, since all sorts of unspoken wish–defence–fantasy constellations might get smuggled out (of analytic scrutiny) along with the "gift". The

mainstream position is to decline the patient's offer of a gift, and instead analyse what gives rise to such a wish. Gifts that are too instinctual (e.g., expensive, edible, sexual) and/or are likely to corrupt the analyst's "work ego" are especially to be declined. Gifts that are minor and understandable tokens of gratitude at termination, for instance, might pose less threat to the integrity of the analytic process. The overt "magnitude" of a gift is, however, less important than its true meanings within the context of the real and transference relationship the patient has with the analyst. While it is generally better to err on the side of "abstinence", it needs to be kept in mind that "rejecting gifts can increase the asymmetry of the dyad to a painful extreme and the consequences might sometimes be irremediable" (Thoma & Kachele, 1994, p. 301). The considerable literature on this topic has been skilfully summarized by Smolar (2002, 2003).)

- Patient's expression of gratitude for the analyst's tolerance of his affective turmoil, or for the analyst's helping him to gain new insights into himself.

To be sure, all these behaviours can contain material for analytic exploration. Worse, they might result from reversals of subterranean hostility and are "good" only on the surface. This would certainly require interpretation. However, undue scepticism *vis-à-vis* the patient's decency is hardly commendable. To rationalize that credulously "accepting" the patient's goodness bypasses deeper analysis and is disrespectful to the patient overlooks that excessive questioning of the patient's gestures might be equally detrimental to the analytic process. This is especially true regarding gifts from the patient (Smolar, 2002). Categorically rejecting all such offerings used to be the recommended practice in the days when Lowenstein (1958) spoke of having shocked a trainee by telling him that he ought to have accepted the gift offered by his patient. The view that accepting gifts derails the analysis of such a gesture needs to be tempered by remembering that "rejecting presents often prevents analysts from recognizing their true meanings" (Thoma & Kachele, 1994, p. 301). Transference is affected as much by deprivation as it is by gratification. The important point is to avoid "superfluous iatrogenic regressions attendant on superfluous deprivations"

(Stone, 1961, p. 170). Manifestations of "goodness" on the patient's part sometimes need analytic exploration and sometimes plain and simple acceptance. The importance of "the capacity to have pleasure in one's patient's pleasure" (Treurniet, 1997, p. 621) can hardly be overemphasized.

However, matters do not end with "accepting" the patient's goodness; one also has to deal with the thorny issue of reflecting and explicitly acknowledging what is good in the patient at a given moment. Analysts dread "praising" their patients for all sorts of technically correct reasons. However, approvingly underscoring ego advancement in an erstwhile conflictual realm is different from praise for an achievement in external reality. This aspect of analytic technique has received inoptimal attention. As a result, no one has raised the question of whether the "admission", towards the end of the treatment, of the patient's having been a burden (Winnicott, 1947) has a counterpart in the analyst's acknowledging, at termination, that he has been a psychological beneficiary of the patient's goodness over the course of their work. This requires more thought.

Diagnosing and analysing false goodness

Yet another manner in which the notion of "goodness" enters clinical work is when the patient begins to display "false goodness" (Schafer, 2002) towards the analyst. The patient becomes overly solicitous, obsequious, agreeable, and nice. He brushes off the analyst's clinical errors, lapses in tact, and lateness for sessions with surprising affability. If the analyst sneezes or coughs even a little, the patient worries whether he should "burden" him with his trivial worries. A careful scrutiny of the patient's affects and their resonance in the countertransference, however, leads to the suspicion that all is not well here.

> What will not be in evidence at such times is the cluster of affects surrounding mature interest in and concern for the object. Consequently, to the extent that the analyst is not taken in by this simulation of goodness, he or she begins to feel up against a ruthless "do-gooder" who is likely to get uneasy, reproachful, and self-critical in response to a perception that an "offering" is not being gratefully received. [Schafer, 2002, p. 14]

Such "false goodness" often emanates from the projection of neediness and weakness upon the analyst. There is a quality of narcissistic rigidity about the patient's solicitousness that makes the analyst feel stifled, not loved. The emphasis upon such transference–countertransference phenomena should not lead one to overlook that "false goodness" might suffuse the patient's character and object-relations in general. Psychoanalytic literature is replete with descriptions of phenomena like "pseudohumility" (Jones, 1913), "pseudosublimation" (Kernberg, 1975), and "pseudoforgiveness" (Akhtar, 2002), all of which constitute aspects of "false goodness". An implication of such broadened perspective on "false goodness" is that discerning and interpreting it is no longer restricted to the transference realm; its extra-transference interpretation is also possible and might even be necessary.

Interpreting the patient's defences against other's "goodness"

For individuals with much childhood neglect and trauma, starting psychoanalytic treatment is a profoundly significant experience. The availability of someone empathic, reliable, non-judgemental, patient, and constant is often an entirely new experience for them. It stirs up a wide gamut of intense, often contradictory emotions: disbelief and excitement, anaclitic yearnings and anxious withdrawal, hate transferred from early frustrating objects and hope that such hate will not destroy the new object, and so on. One frequent transference manifestation is the individual's inability to tolerate the analyst's "goodness"; it stirs up affects and longings that are truly difficult to bear. Encounter with his "goodness" mobilizes desperate hunger for more such experiences and the fear that one would deplete the analyst and therefore be rejected. Envy (of the analyst's soothing and containing capacities) also gets stirred up. And, to ward off the uncomfortable feelings of greed and envy, the patient utilizes all sorts of defensive manoeuvres, including cynicism, scorn, and mistrust, or over-idealization, which is based upon the mechanism of "denial by exaggeration" (Fenichel, 1945).

Clearly, the patient's intolerance of goodness can extend beyond the clinical situation. He might show an inability to appreciate others' kind gestures towards him, defensively withdraw from their love, and be peculiarly resistant to accepting compliments and receiving good news.

Clinical vignette 1

> Dan Schwartzman, a forty-five-year-old piano teacher who had fallen on hard times, was in psychotherapy for chronic feelings of inferiority, irritability, and rage. He loved his wife and acquiesced to seek help since she was becoming concerned about his increasing reliance upon alcohol to soothe himself.
>
> Dan's main difficulty revolved about the rage he felt at his father, who had always belittled and mocked him. His father was a hugely successful businessman who had just turned eighty. On one hand, Dan wanted to cut off ties with his father. On the other hand, he kept hoping that the old man would die and leave him a few million dollars. As a result, he sheepishly showed up at the weekly lunch his father arranged in lavish restaurants in town, where he regularly insulted Dan and showed a starkly preferential behaviour towards Dan's sister. Their mother had passed away. While secretly hating the cantankerous old man and praying for his death, Dan feared that, at the slightest whim, his father was capable of disinheriting him and leaving all the estate to his sister. He wanted to be nasty to his father, but kept his mouth shut. He was, thus, on a tightrope stretched between pleasure of revenge and the haven of monetary security.
>
> Dan began one of his sessions by telling me that the previous evening, he had received a phone call from his uncle, his father's brother, saying that he was aware of Dan's financial distress and had left him a considerable sum of money in his will. Dan went on to say, "As soon as I heard this, I said to myself, 'Shit, Uncle Bob is doing this because he has found out that my father has disinherited me!'" Upon listening to this, I said the following to Dan, "It is striking that, when your uncle told you that he has left you a lot of money, your first thought was not about his kindness towards you but about what it might (or might not) have implied about your father's cruelty towards you. For some reason, it seems, you were just not capable or willing to celebrate your uncle's goodness even for a minute, or, for that matter, your own sense of relief. Why?"

Anxiety seems to play a great role in such "inability" to register others' goodness, since doing so would automatically lead to a changed world view and tax the ego's adaptive capacities. Moreover, in accepting that others are being good towards one, one is compelled to renounce the pleasures of self-pity and the associated sadomasochism. Passively ignoring others' goodness seems a less risky pathway. Then there are more active efforts to thwart and spoil others' goodness. Intolerance of compliments from others is often based upon such dynamics.

Clinical vignette 2

> Catherine McCarthy, a thirty-seven-year-old attorney with a pronounced tendency to be flirtatious that arose from a powerful Oedipal fixation, narrated the following incident during one of her analytic sessions with me. She said that the previous evening, she had given a compliment to her highly successful and narcissistic husband regarding his handling of the family dog. "You are far better with Jake [the dog] than I am," she had said. With disbelief and pain in her voice, she then told that he responded to her admiring comment by saying, "Darling, I am better than you in most things."

Whether one chooses to say anything about this remark or not, it seems clear that my patient's husband had difficulty accepting and enjoying his wife's "goodness" towards him. Her comment stirred up greed instead of gratitude in him; envy of her capacity for kindness perhaps also played a role in his devaluing remark. More intense forms of this dynamic are typical of malignant narcissists (Kernberg, 1984; Weigert, 1967). Keeping all this in mind would encourage the analyst to interpret the patient's defences against goodness in the extra-transference realm.

When such attacks on his goodness are directed at the analyst himself, he must avoid succumbing to their surface brutality. He "must assume that an analysand of this kind is fundamentally ambivalent in relation to goodness, not merely negative toward it" (Schafer, 2002, p. 7). Awareness of this deeper current in the patient's attitude and verbalizations helps the analyst to sustain interpretative work and avoid unhelpful degrees of negative countertransference.

Interpreting the patient's defences against his own "goodness"

Although the reasons for it vary greatly, hiding one's goodness from oneself and others is hardly a rare human phenomenon. Many individuals undergoing analytic treatment show evidence of it. They seem oblivious to all that is good inside them. They disown their creativity or attribute it to external sources. They minimize or mock their acts of kindness and feel somewhat depersonalized when others notice them. Acknowledging the existence of inner goodness is laden with dangers for them. Prominent among such dangers is the fear of stirring up envy in others. This, in turn, gives rise to the unpleasant expectation that others (including the analyst) will make fun of one's goodness and attack it. The subsequent negation, repression, or even destruction of their own goodness thus turns out to be a pre-emptive defence. This explains why "many who live normal and valuable lives do not feel they are responsible for the best that is in them" (Winnicott, 1935, p. 133).

Some of these individuals deposit their goodness into others for safe keeping. Such use of "positive projective identification" (Hamilton, 1986) has interesting consequences within and outside the clinical situation. In the former setting, it can give rise to a joyous and noticeably more creative feeling in the analyst during his sessions with that particular patient (Kramer & Akhtar, 1988); it is only gradually that such countertransference vitality recedes, revealing its origins in the patient's repudiated sense of his goodness. Outside of the treatment situation, one comes across this phenomenon among the "shy narcissists" (Akhtar, 2000), who live out their ambitions vicariously by playing "second fiddle" to someone whose success they have themselves silently engineered. At other times, such "depositing" of one's goodness into others results in a distorted view of oneself and an idealized view of others.

Clinical vignette 3

Jack Lieberman, a deeply traumatized but highly successful businessman in his mid-sixties, suffered from chronic self-loathing and from uncertainty despite frequent accolades from esteemed others and

> almost daily hob-nobbing with renowned members of society. He had grown up with constant ridicule and abuse by his somewhat sociopathic older brother who, in Jack's perception, was secretly admired by his parents. Moreover, Jack never felt truly appreciated by his parents, no matter what he achieved or accomplished. As an adult, he often derided himself as being inferior to others, unable to love, have empathy for this or that person, and forgive others for their blemishes. He dismissed his own cognitive and linguistic talents, especially in the realm of administration and business negotiations, with an air of nonchalance, if not derision. He experienced disbelief when his wife praised his appearance and called him a "good man".
>
> In one of his sessions, Jack reported the following incident. He was taking a stroll on the boardwalk and caught a glimpse of some teenage boys and girls playing volleyball on the beach. The girls were nubile and skimpily dressed. Jack thought that he would want to "fuck them right there", while the boys who were playing with them seemed to be devoid of such lust; they seem to be innocently playing volleyball. Jack was filled with a wistful longing for the simplicity of the heart he felt he had lost along the way and also with contempt for himself. As he narrated this experience, I found myself empathizing with both: what appeared to be his sexual (and oral) greed as well as his superego attack against his libidinal impulses. However, to my mind, a more important aspect of the entire experience was his capacity to "read" the boys' innocence. As I thought more, it became clear that this was based upon an admixture of (a) intact reality testing and plausible perceptions; (b) empathic resonance with the experience of those boys, and (c) a projection of his own repudiated "goodness" into them. Therefore, I said, "I can sense your wistfulness and, to a certain extent, understand your criticism about your hunger. What puzzles me, however, is that you say nothing about how you were able to recognize those boys' 'goodness' from afar. What do you think made that possible?"

In making this intervention, I was attempting to help Jack become cognizant that the innocence he had attributed to the boys on the beach was, at least in part, his own repudiated inner goodness. My conjecture found strength by the fact that Jack had not allowed any possibility that even one of those boys might be experiencing lust and sexual greed. They were "all good" in his inner experience.

Exploring the history and meanings of the word "good" for the patient

The foregoing discourse shows that the idea of "goodness" flourishes in psychic reality and gives colour and direction to organizing unconscious fantasies. Here, it is useful to keep the following reminder by Hartmann (1960) in mind:

> Not only does every human being start by attributing goodness, in a still undifferentiated way, to objects and actions in the measure they provide satisfaction. This linkage of satisfaction with goodness does in a way persist although the pleasure conditions have changed and pleasure in moral behavior has evolved and become differentiated from that which characterizes instinctual gratification. But we learn not to attribute greater value to what provides us with more immediate or more intense gratification. Certain pleasures gradually become linked not to "good" but to "bad." We also learn to differentiate between "morally good" according to our own scale of values and "morally good" according to the scale of values of others. [pp. 47–48]

Clearly then, the word "good" has mental reference points and meanings that are multi-faceted and multi-layered. It is, therefore, useful to explore the ways in which it is used by the analysand. When did he first hear the expression? In what connection? From whom? What sort of things, people, events, and activities does he consider to be "good"? Why? How does his definition of "good" resemble, or differ from, those of his parents and siblings? Exploration along these lines often proves to be analytically productive. Doing so helps the analyst

> . . . construct a fuller moral, ethical, and object-related account of the analysand's history and present status. . . . Among the ego psychological prototypes [of this line of exploration] are the genealogy of specific defenses and sublimatory efforts. In functioning this way, the analyst remains an investigator of language usage and the interpretations it allows and blocks. [Schafer, 2002, p. 18]

It must also be noted that, at times, it is the manner in which the word "good" is uttered by someone that gives a clue to his or her inner difficulties in the realm of goodness.

Clinical vignette 4

> Jack Lieberman (mentioned above in Clinical Vignette 3) was once talking about his business firm's giving a large sum of money towards helping college students from low income families and disadvantaged backgrounds to obtain higher education in the fields of commerce and business; the idea was that, with qualifications from more prestigious schools, they would have a greater chance of getting a foothold in the highly competitive world of business. In an earnest, if not solemn, voice Jack said, "I want to do good for others." However, as soon as the words came out of his mouth and he became aware of what he had said, he repeated the sentence with an entirely different cadence. This time, he uttered the word "good" with an ironic and self-mocking inflection. When I pointed this out, Jack resorted to the rationalization that most people, including doctors he said, would admit of their good intentions only in such deliberately caricatured ways; doing otherwise appeared self-indulgent and a bit silly. However, both of us could see what was actually going on here. Jack had become embarrassed (and frightened) at the declaration of his goodness and was perhaps concerned that I would not appreciate it (like his parents) or, worse, make fun of it (like his brother).

In observing the use of the words "good" and "goodness", therefore, the analyst not only has to take into account their context, their history, their proximity or distance from the customary familial usage, but also the affect that accompanies their utterance and the psychic processes that precede and follow once these words have been spoken.

Concluding remarks

This brief essay on the technical implications of "goodness" constitutes a preliminary communication. The steps and strategies delineated here await criticism, debate, and refinement. To begin with, these guidelines have to be "individualized" in the language of each clinical dyad. They also need to be "softened" by the "incorporation of the non-ideal, of 'objective' reality, of the value of 'good enough' into the analyst's conscience" (Treurniet, 1997, p. 623). Goodness on the part of both parties ought to have the leeway that comes with being human. An occasional slip up of restraint does not hurt in the long run and a sense of humour almost always helps.

It should also be noted that in focusing upon "micro" processes, the foregoing discourse has given short shift to "macro" ways in which the "goodness" concept affects the analyst–analysand dyad. To cover the latter, albeit briefly, one has to note the following set of observations. The analysand brings his own morality and his need to be connected with what he sees as good in life; superego harshness and ego-ideal pathology notwithstanding, the healthy aspects of the analysand's ego ideal also populate the chamber of analytic dialogue. The analyst is no exception. He, too, is affected, in his listening and intervening, by his "moral framework" (Taylor, 1989). Even his capacities to care and be empathic rest (at least partly) upon his considering such attributes to be "good". The following statement by Meissner (1996) eloquently addresses this very point.

> The good analyst's participation in the process may involve value elements that he can not be expected to exclude, nor would it be in the interest of analytic work and of benefit to the patient to do so. By the same token, ethical values of understanding, authenticity, the centrality of self-knowledge and so on are embedded in the very structure of the analytic process and can not be expunged without destroying its very nature. [p. 210]

On the level of his professional development and work-related identity, too, the analyst is deeply affected by what he has been taught and/or has come to consider "good technique", who he regards (and/or has regarded) as "good analysts", "good supervisors", "good supervisees", and, why not, even "good institutes". Taking this one step further, Goldberg (2007) argues that the psychoanalytic profession upholds unrealistic and almost 'saintly' ideals for its members' identities and even social conduct. He urges that a softening of this is needed, though of course, the respect for therapeutic frame and boundaries has to be maintained. Such matters have also attracted the attention of George Hagman (2000), who asserts that

> . . . it is time to place the problem of values and morals at the center of our clinical theories. Moral frameworks are not simply projected by people onto the world. These frameworks *are* the human world;

> they are not reducible to something nor can they be compartmentalized or made external to our "selves." When we examine our own or others' emotional lives, we are compelled, not by choice or inclination, but by necessity, to make judgments, to discriminate, to evaluate according to a moral framework. Human life can not be understood on any other terms. In other words, the analyst's experience of self and others has a pervasive and deep moral orientation. The practicing analyst defines his or her professional selfhood within a complex, multifaceted community that offers various moral and intellectual frameworks. He or she defines not only what an analyst is, but also what a "good" analyst is. [pp. 80–81, original italics]

Now, in so far as all analysts strive to be "good analysts", master the principles of "good technique", and do "good" by their patients, the notion of "goodness" seems integral to their enterprise at a most basic and emotionally felt level. Whether they recognize it as such or not depends upon their theoretical orientation, their openness to new ways of looking at familiar data, and, ultimately, their overall comfort with goodness, be it their patient's or their own.

CHAPTER TWO

Happiness

"The happiness that is genuinely satisfying is accompanied by the fullest exercise of our faculties and the fullest realization of the world in which we live"

(Russell, 1930, p. 74)

We psychoanalysts are a little wary of happiness. Deeply influenced by the pessimistic world-view of the discipline's founder, Sigmund Freud, we approach moments of joy with trepidation. We remain alert to their transient nature and doubt even their veracity; the repudiated anguish or warded-off anxiety that we suspect lurks underneath them is our prime concern. This is especially true of our professional lives. For us, a patient's jovial banter is merely a defensive cloak for the darkness in his heart, his good mood a thin veil over inner sadness. Let me put it bluntly: we are clinicians of despair, and misery is the mother tongue of our profession.

However, it is also true that, in our personal lives, we seem capable of relaxing and of experiencing happiness. Making love, having a lively dinner conversation with friends, playing with our dogs, reading a good book, watching our grandchildren grow, and receiving the news that something we wrote has been accepted by a prestigious journal are all capable of stirring up the sort of pleasurable feelings in us that we associate with happiness. Come to think of it, there are moments in our clinical work also that bring us deep satisfaction and a gratifying sense of mutuality and grace. Despite all this, our literature on the phenomenology, origins, metapsychology, and technical significance of happiness is meagre.

In this chapter, I attempt to bring the scattered writings on this topic together with the aim of developing a well-anchored and comprehensive understanding of the phenomena that fall under the rubric of happiness. I begin with Freud's views and then move on to subsequent psychoanalytic (and a few non-psychoanalytic) contributions. Pooling the various observations together, I categorize the feelings of happiness into four subtypes and elucidate their nature, as well as the overlaps between them. Following this, I discuss the technical implications of these findings. I conclude by making a few summarizing remarks and pointing out areas that warrant further attention.

Freud's views

Freud used the word "happiness" 130 times in his written work (Guttman, Jones, & Parrish, 1980). More than a third—forty-five to be precise—of these usages are contained in *Civilization and Its Discontents* (Freud, 1930a), a text devoted to investigating the relationship between societal constraints on pleasure-seeking, and the consequent unhappiness and search for happiness. Early on in this book, Freud laid down his definition of happiness. He said that "what we call happiness in the strictest sense comes from the (preferably sudden) satisfaction of needs which have been dammed up to a high degree, and it is from its nature only possible as an episodic phenomenon" (*ibid.*, p. 76). The implications that the discharge of a "dammed up" impulse produces greater happiness becomes clear when, a little later in the text, Freud identified happiness as "a problem of the economies of the individual's libido" (*ibid.*, p. 83) and declared that "The feeling of happiness derived from the satisfaction of a wild instinctual impulse untamed is incomparably more intense than that derived from sating an instinct that has been tamed" (*ibid.*, p. 79).

The instinct theory that pervades these comments tempts one to regard Freud's views on happiness in simplistic terms: instinctual discharge causes happiness and instinctual tension causes unpleasure. The fact is that Freud's take on happiness is complex and multi-faceted. And, it cannot be properly understood without taking into account what he regarded as the unavoidable sources of unhappiness in man's life: (a) the ongoing, even if slow, decay of the human body, (b) the unfathomable challenges and disasters caused by nature, and (c) the pain and suffering that is inherent in interpersonal relationships. "We are never so defenceless against suffering as when we love, never so helplessly unhappy as when we have lost a loved object or its love" (*ibid.*, p. 82), Freud stated.

Mired in pervasive vulnerability to unhappiness, man, none the less, valiantly seeks happiness. In Freud's own words, "the programme of becoming happy, which the pleasure principle imposes on us cannot be fulfilled; yet we must not—indeed cannot—give up our efforts to bring it nearer to fulfilment by some means or other" (*ibid.*, p. 83). There are many pathways to arrive at happiness, according to Freud. However, since happiness is "something essentially subjective" (*ibid.*, p. 89), the roads taken by one individual differ considerably from that chosen by another ("There is no golden rule that applies to everyone" (*ibid.*, p. 83)). Freud's list of the various ways in which people seek happiness included (a) use of intoxicants, (b) enjoyment of beauty, (c) devotion to work, and (d) friendships, and, paradoxically, (e) withdrawal from human relationships.

Freud reiterated the ideas he had expressed in an earlier monograph, *The Future of an Illusion* (1927c), dealing with religion. He stated,

> A special importance attaches to the case in which the attempt to procure a certainty of happiness and a protection against suffering through a delusional remoulding of reality is made by a considerable number of people in common. The religions of mankind must be classed among the mass delusions of this kind. [1930a, p. 81]

Regardless of whether it is drugs or work, beauty or religion, friendship or a hermit-like withdrawal, nothing seems to offer sustained happiness to man. Each method provides only momentary and partial relief from the unhappiness that gnaws at the human soul. Pertinent in this regard is Thompson's (2004) reminder that "Freud's conception of pleasure is more than a theory of affect, an ontological category that is concerned with a much larger question: what it means to be human" (p. 142). It is in this context that the problem at the core of *Civilization and Its Discontents* becomes clear: the very institutions that make man human are the source of his inescapable anguish. They force him to choose between his pleasure and his contributing to the stability of the society.

> The development of the individual seems to us to be a product of the interaction between two urges, the urge towards happiness, which we usually call "egoistic", and the urge towards union with others in the community, which we call "altruistic". [Thompson, 2004, p. 140]

The restrictions posed by civilized society upon man's coprophilic, sadistic, and incestuous tendencies also take a huge psychic toll. The need to relate to fellow human beings—even depend upon them—adds to the possibility of frustration. The neurotic resorts to playing it safe, withdraws into fantasy, and thus minimizes his risk of disappointment. But psychoanalysis

> . . . offers the neurotic a second chance at happiness, by coming out of his self-imposed exile and placing his future prospects at risk . . . Implicit in Freud's technical writings is the view that to increase our chances of happiness, we must place ourselves at risk, including our chances at love, the risk neurotics fear most. From this angle, happiness depends not on the growth of our success but on the satisfaction derived from knowing that we are willing to be at risk, in the first place, win or lose, or as Plato put it, to simply be "in the game". [*ibid.*, p. 151]

Lest the focus on Freud's 1930 monograph leave the reader with the impression that ideas expressed in it exhaust what Freud had to say about happiness, the following important observations from some of his other writings should work as a corrective.

- *On money and happiness*: "Happiness is the deferred fulfilment of a prehistoric wish. That is why wealth brings so little happiness; money is not an infantile wish" (1898, p. 244).
- *On concurrence of childhood and happiness:* There is reason for "some doubt in regard to the happiness of childhood as it has been constructed by adults in retrospect" (1900a, p. 130).
- *On physical well-being and happiness*: "Under the influence of joy, of 'happiness', we find that our whole body blossoms out and shows signs of a renewal of youth" (1890a, p. 287).
- *On the availability of love object and happiness*: "The subject was healthy as long as his need for love was satisfied by a real object in the external world; he becomes neurotic as soon as this object is withdrawn from him without a substitute taking its place. Here happiness coincides with health and unhappiness with neurosis" (1912c, p. 23).
- *On the relationship between phantasy and happiness*: "The best known production of phantasy are the so-called daydreams . . . Imagined satisfactions of ambitious, megalomanic, erotic wishes which flourish all the more exuberantly the more reality counsels modesty and restraint. The essence of happiness of phantasy—making the obtaining of pleasure free once more from the assent of reality—is shown in them unmistakably" (1916–1917, p. 372).
- *On foetal life and happiness*: The idea of "intrauterine happiness . . . is far fetched" (1926d, p. 136).

In summary, Freud's views on happiness underscore the following points: (a) happiness results from satisfaction of instincts, (b) the pleasure resulting from untamed instincts' gratification is greater than that associated with civilized sexuality, (c) happiness is always episodic and incomplete, (d) it is difficult to be happy, because powerful forces causing unhappiness are inherent in being human, (e) happiness is subjective and there is great individual variation in seeking it, and (f) psychoanalysis cannot promise sustained happiness and it should be regarded as successful if it can transform "hysterical misery into common unhappiness" (Breuer & Freud, 1895, p. 305). What exactly were the constituents of this irreducible unhappiness were left unclear. Moreover, Freud was hardly alone in coming to the conclusion that a certain amount of suffering is inevitable in the course of life. Buddha's first Noble Truth comprised this realization, and Thoreau (1854) grimly declared that most men live a life of "quiet desperation". Within the psychoanalytic tradition, the theme of suffering that is inherent to being human has been addressed in only three publications: Marmor's (1955) essay on realistic worry, Thompson's (2004) attempt at separating neurotic misery from common unhappiness, and my own (Akhtar, 2009b) delineation of the "burdens of sanity".

Subsequent psychoanalytic contributions

To the best of my knowledge, only eleven psychoanalysts have made direct contributions to the understanding of happiness since Freud. They include: Deutsch (1927), Lewin (1932, 1937, 1941, 1950), Klein (1935, 1946, 1952a), Sachs (1941), Eidelberg (1951), Sternbach (1974), Fine (1977), Kohut (1977), Olinick (1982), Silbermann (1985), and Thompson (2004). Such listing of names is, however, misleading, since the contributions these analysts have made are not comparable in their extent, novelty, or depth. As a result, I would comment upon the work of the four outstanding contributors among these and refer to the views of most others briefly at appropriate places in the remaining part of this chapter. The four major contributors are Deutsch, Lewin, Klein, and Kohut.

Helene Deutsch

In a paper titled "On satisfaction, happiness, and ecstasy", Deutsch (1927) proposed that happiness results from a harmonious co-operation of all the components of the ego and, indeed, of the whole personality. (Presented at the 10th Congress of the International Psychoanalytic Association at Innsbruck, Austria in 1927, Deutsch's paper remained untranslated into English until 1989. It appeared that year in the *International Journal of Psychoanalysis*, with an accompanying commentary by Paul Roazen.) While emphasizing the dissolution of intrapsychic splits and a feeling of oneness within the self as the origin of happiness, Deutsch included merger between self and non-self as an important variable in the genesis of the affect.

> Every aesthetic pleasure, whether it arises from contemplation of a landscape or an art object, from reading a poem or listening to music, is always marked by a sense of identity between the ego and the outside world arising from empathy between the ego and the impressions flooding in from the latter. The happiness-creating factor is to be sought in that identity. [p. 717]

Deutsch felt that moments of happiness were inevitably short-lived, since the ego has, sooner or later, to confront "the rest of the unconquered world" (p. 720) and return to its defeated and divided (between the actual and the wishful) state. None the less, moments of self-object merger did give rise to intense bliss. Deutsch described two patients who achieved such transient but "super-normal pleasure" (p. 717) and "ecstasy" (p. 718) in states of self-dissolution during sexual intercourse and religious meditation. (I suspected that the second patient described in it was Deutsch herself. However, when I read the editorial commentary by Paul Roazen (1989), I noticed that he believes that *both* the "cases" reported are based upon autobiographical material.) Deutsch's conclusion about happiness was that

> It is an endogenous, narcissistically determined ego-feeling; it materializes when the boundaries of the ego have been expanded by the establishment of unity between ego and the world as a result of object cathexis, sublimation, or the attainment of unity in the ego itself. [p. 721]

In a subsequent contribution, Deutsch (1933) distinguished genuine happiness from "chronic hypomania". The former was fleeting, although based upon deep object relations and sublimation, the latter more drawn-out and resulted from a denial and depreciation of object loss. According to Deutsch, if we look closely at individuals who seem perpetually "happy", we note:

> the hollowness of their success in comparison with the energy expended, how the love relationships lack warmth in spite of their passion, how sterile the performance is in spite of continuous productivity. This results from the monopolization of psychic energy in service of the goal we have described: the silencing of the narcissistic wound, of aggression, and of guilt reactions. [*ibid.*, p. 215]

Of importance in Deutsch's contribution are (a) the premise of a universal striving for inner oneness and psychological unity (elsewhere, I (Akhtar, 2006) have noted that our literature's emphasis upon the "search for oneness with the other" overlooks the "search for oneness within oneself". Observing that, as human beings, we are always divided and split into parts, I have proposed that the frustration contingent upon this malady mobilizes a striving to find states that help us become one within ourselves. I find such harmony while writing. Others might utilize different modalities, such as jogging, dancing, listening to or playing music, and so on. Regardless of the particular avenue one takes to reach it, such "oneness within oneself" seems to be an important contributor to personal happiness.); (b) a far more accommodating and respectful attitude towards religious feelings than that displayed by Freud (1927c), (c) the possibility that happiness, even if short-lived, can be achieved through both instinctual gratification and sublimation, and (d) the proposal that persistent and exaggerated happiness is defensive against feelings of loss, and the subsequent anger and guilt.

Lewin

Lamenting the relative neglect of the topic by psychoanalysis, Lewin (1932, 1937, 1941, 1950) undertook a comprehensive study of "elation". He concurred with the view that hypomanic affect was usually a defence against depression (Abraham, 1924; Fenichel, 1945) but went further in his approach to it. He described certain specific syndromes characterized by elated mood, including the following.

- *Neurotic hypomanic personalities*, who show immense enterprise, chronic activity that is often followed by sudden loss of interest, hypersexuality, and distractibility. "Their analysis shows a latency period in which strong identifications are built up with a usually dead or absent parent, and a sharp, often conscious recrudescence of incestuous wishes at puberty, followed by a vehement plunge into activities as a distraction" (1950, p. 59).
- *Hypomanic obsessional neurotics*, who show an admixture of obsessionality and cheerfulness. They deploy a "dead-pan" wit to avoid encountering their inner selves in a meaningful manner and to ward off any analytic interventions.

- *Technical elation* refers to the hypomanic mood that is, at times, evoked by entry into psychoanalytic treatment. Lewin noted that, upon beginning analysis, some individuals display an increase in depression since the facts that are uncovered offend their narcissism. Others, however, respond to such occurrence by denial and a flighty and dispersed attention. Lewin (1950) called this state "technical elation" (p. 70) or "technical hypomania" (p. 71).
- *False elation*, which includes "technical hypomania" but is not restricted to it. The incongruous happiness that characterized "false elation" is found not only in association with clearly psychopathological states, but also in children and dreamers who replace unpleasant facts by contradictory fictions. What gives away the false nature of these affects is their lack of signalling function and their incongruity with objective reality.
- *Ecstasy*, which is a profoundly blissful state where the good breast is "condensed psychologically with a superego, a deathless one with which the ego identifies itself, so that it can participate in its immortality. Along with the active devouring fantasies goes the sense of yielding to the deathless figure, relaxing into it, and ultimately joining it in sleep or a sleep-like state" (1950, p. 144–145).

This brings up the dynamic–genetic aspect of Lewin's contribution. He traced the roots of elation to the "oral triad" of the wish to eat, the wish to be eaten, and the wish to sleep, all of which arise in connection with a satisfactory experience at the maternal breast. In manic happiness, the first wish is obvious (e.g., wanting to devour the world of objects and experiences), while the latter two, having become contaminated with oral aggression, become equated with being murdered and with dying. Therefore, these wishes have to be denied through insomnia and over-activity or expressed via rapt absorption in work, which represents a state of giving up the self. In normal happiness, the three wishes are felt to be comfortable and are, therefore, expressed in a harmonious fashion.

Melanie Klein

In a series of publications, Klein distinguished between the subjective experience of "manic defence" (1935) and "actual feelings of happiness" (1946, p. 17). The former arose from the trio of idealization, denial, and omnipotence, which, acting in unison, upheld the cardboard figure of an "all-good" world where everything was possible and where one did not have to depend upon others for love and support. The latter emanated in the context of deep object relations and the capacity for reparative concern and gratitude. Noting that "the fundamental experiences of happiness are inextricably linked with the mother's breast" (1952a, p. 99), Klein traced the origins of happiness to the experiences of need satisfaction during early infantile life, and underscored the dialectical relationship between pleasurable internalizations and ego strength. She stated that

> the good breast, introjected in situations of gratification and happiness, becomes in my view a vital part of the ego and strengthens its capacity for integration. For this internal good breast—forming also the helpful and benign aspect of the early superego—strengthens the infant's capacity to love and trust his objects, and heightens the stimulus for introjections of good objects and situations. [1952b, p. 67]

Klein (1957) emphasized that envy has an adverse impact upon the development of the capacity for gratitude and happiness. Lack of envy, in contrast, makes it possible for one to admire the character or achievements of others. This source of happiness becomes particularly important as one begins to grow old and the pleasures of youth become less available; identification with the offspring and other young people then provides an access to feelings of happiness. All in all, Klein's perspective on happiness emphasizes (a) its origins in early experiences of satisfaction at the maternal breast, (b) its association with solid reality testing, feelings of gratitude, and a well-integrated ego; (c) its capacity to overcome envy and enjoy others' achievements, and (d) its drawing upon identifications not only with the good objects of childhood, but, as one grows old, with those younger than oneself.

Heinz Kohut

As Kohut (1977, 1980, 1982) broadened his self psychology, elevated the self to a superordinate motivational system, and declared that his perspective has "freed itself from the distorted view of psychological man exposed by traditional analysis" (1982, p. 402); his vocabulary also underwent a noticeable change. The word "joy" now began to appear frequently in his writings. Kohut emphasized that "joy" was distinct from "pleasure". Joy was more encompassing than pleasure. Joy resulted from self-realization, self-expression, self-assertion, and creative success. Pleasure resulted from sensual satisfaction. Joy and pleasure existed on different levels. Moreover,

> The experience of joy has a genetic root different from that of the experience of pleasure; each of these modes of affect has its own developmental line and that joy is not sublimated pleasure. Joy relates to experiences of the total self whereas pleasure (despite the frequently occurring participation of the total self, which then provides an admixture of joy) relates to experiences of parts and constituents of the self [1977, p. 45]

Kohut proposed that "joy" resulted from the sense of cohesion and confidence that developed in association with adequate mirroring by parents during childhood. Parental delight in the child's age-specific capabilities and new-found ego freedoms led the child to feel vital, firm, and purposeful. Even the rivalry and competitiveness towards the same sex parent, and sexual curiosity and interest toward the opposite sex parent, shown by the child during the Oedipal phase, added to the experience of joy. According to Kohut, this joy is fed from two sources.

> They are (1) the child's inner awareness of a significant forward move into a psychological realm of new and exciting experiences, and—of even greater importance—(2) his participation in the glow of pride and joy that emanates from the parental self-objects despite—indeed, also because of—their recognition of the content of their child's oedipal desires. [*ibid.*, p. 236]

Kohut extended the developmental line of joy to adulthood, underscoring the fact that a firm and coherent self that is capable of sublimations and healthy participation in the happiness of the next generation makes the transition to middle and old age easier. This is a point also made by Klein (1957), as mentioned above, and such views of both Kohut and Klein have an unmistakable resonance with Erikson's (1950) notion of "generativity", or the capacity to support, nourish, and guide the next generation.

"Positive" and pop psychology

Putting aside the reflexive attitude of scorn that we psychoanalysts have towards popular psychology makes a pathway for us to see if these texts can also teach us something useful. Now, it is hardly possible to review the shelves full of popular books on finding happiness, experiencing joy, and enhancing pleasure in life. As a result, I have chosen to restrict this survey to the views of three most "popular" contributors to the understanding of happiness: Martin Seligman, Tal Ben-Shahar, and Deepak Chopra.

An Ivy League professor of psychology with an endowed chair, Seligman is the founder of the "Positive Psychology" movement. Distancing itself from psychology's customary preoccupation with abnormal states, the "Positive Psychology" movement has a three-dimensional thrust involving (a) the study of positive emotions, (b) the study of positive traits and abilities, and (c) the study of positive institutions (e.g., democracy, strong families). Material derived from population surveys, psychometric studies, and anecdotal observations is pooled together to construct a body of knowledge regarding adaptive and pleasant human attributes, including the feeling of happiness. Seligman's compilation of ideas regarding happiness from these sources, combined with his own insights, can be summarized as follows:

- the potential for happiness is inherent in all human beings;
- there are evolutionary advantages to being happy. A happy state of mind broadens intellect, increases our physical agility, and facilitates problem-solving;
- happiness resulting from behavioural "short-cuts" (e.g., drugs, shopping) is inauthentic. Happiness that arises from exercising our strengths and virtues is authentic;
- happy people remember more good events and forget more bad events. This, in turn, sustains their happiness;
- positive emotions predict greater chances of gainful employment, better intrapersonal relationships, better physical health, and longevity of life;

- race, gender, education, and economic status (with the exception of extreme poverty) have little correlation with happiness;
- the capacity for experiencing gratitude and bestowing forgiveness greatly influences the level of happiness.

Seligman is critical of psychoanalysis, and especially of Freud's (1930a) pessimistic view of man. He faults Freud for not according man's altruistic tendencies a status equal and comparable to his inherent destructiveness. In this, I am in agreement with him (see Chapter One for more details). (Advancing the cause of studying positive human attributes, I have written on the topics of love (1996a), forgiveness (2002), the healing functions of poetry (2000), and the important role that a mentor plays for young adults (2003b). More recently, I have brought together the scattered psychoanalytic writings on such topics as tact, enthusiasm, courage, humour, etc., in an edited volume titled *Good Feelings* (2009a).) What is troubling about Seligman's approach, though, is that he presents the psychoanalytic perspective in an outmoded and caricatured manner. His harshness is particularly directed at the discipline's developmental orientation. Note the following statement from his best-selling book, *Authentic Happiness*:

> I think that the events of childhood are overrated; in fact, I think past history in general is overrated. It has turned out to be difficult to find even small effects of childhood events on adult personality, and there is no evidence at all of large—to say nothing of determining—effects. . . . If, for example, your mother dies before you're 11, you are somewhat more depressive in adulthood—but not a lot more depressive, and only if you're female, and only in about half the studies. Your father's dying has no measurable impact. [2002, p. 67]

Such debunking of the childhood determinants of adult psychology and psychopathology fails to acknowledge that contemporary psychoanalysis itself looks sceptically upon linear correlations between past and present. Hartmann's (1955) concept of "genetic fallacy" and Blum's (1977, 1981) cautionary note regarding reconstruction of early life events are two major examples of this stance, though many more can readily be cited. But this ought not to result in throwing out the proverbial baby with the bathwater. Outright rejection of the impact of childhood trauma upon adult functioning is a heuristic narrow-mindedness of its own kind.

This blemish robs Seligmann's otherwise interesting contributions of credibility and seriousness. From his "positive psychology" perspective though, repudiating the life-long impact of childhood trauma makes a certain kind of sense. The magical hope of starting afresh, doing it all over, and being happy can only be advanced if all parties are convinced that the past is not dynamically affecting the present. Indeed, Seligman's recipe for finding and sustaining happiness is not to worry about the past, break the patterns of habituation to what one finds pleasurable, savour the moments of joy, and be mindful of the experience. Such emphasis on voluntary cognition overlooks the enormous power of intrapsychic resistances, the unconscious need for punishment, and the lure of masochism.

Ben-Shahar (2007) advances Seligman's movement and claims to bridge the gap between "the rigor of academe and the fun of the self-help movement" (p. xi). Ben-Shahar, a highly sought-out teacher, knows how to sell his message. Perhaps the best way to illustrate this is to quote from Ben-Shahar himself:

> I first taught a positive psychology seminar in 2002. Eight students signed up; two dropped out. . . . The following year the class went public, in a manner of speaking. . . . Three hundred eighty students signed up. In their year-end evaluations, more than twenty percent noted that "the course improves the quality of one's life". The next time I offered the course, 855 students enrolled, making it the largest class at the university. [2007, pp. vii–viii]

He defines happiness as "the overall experience of pleasure and meaning" (*ibid.*, p. 33) and declares that material wealth has little connection with happiness. He distances himself from the edginess of Seligman by (a) acknowledging that "internal obstacles" (*ibid.*, p. 7) can prevent people from pursuing happiness, (b) declaring that the idea of constant happiness is unrealistic and that some suffering is part of life, and (c) adapting a softer stance in his criticism of psychoanalysis. (His referring to Donald Winnicott as a "psychologist" (*ibid.*, p. 114) and not as a psychoanalyst, however, betrays the begrudging attitude that underlies his surface accommodation to psychoanalysis.)

More significantly, Ben-Shahar juxtaposes Freud's (1890a, 1915c) emphasis upon the instinctual need for pleasure against Frankl's (2006) assertion that human beings seek meaning in their lives and thrive upon finding it. His theory of happiness draws on both. He emphatically states that "we need to gratify both the will for pleasure and the will for meaning if we are to lead a fulfilling, happy life" (Ben-Shahar, 2007, p. 43). However, he excludes sacrifice from the factors that can produce happiness; that a cultural bias might be operative here goes unnoticed by Ben-Shahar. Instead, he emphasizes that

> unconditional love creates a circle of happiness—in which we are encouraged to pursue those things that are meaningful and pleasurable for us. We experience the freedom to follow our passions—whether in art, banking, teaching, or gardening—regardless of prestige or success. Unconditional love is the foundation of a happy relationship. [*ibid.*, p. 115]

However, the fact that unconditional love is reserved for infants and young children (and fortunate ones at that) is not acknowledged by Ben-Shahar. The game that promises bliss has begun. Indeed, Ben-Shahar soon proceeds with behavioural recipes for obtaining happiness. He recommends that one create rituals, express gratitude, meditate, map out one's life, and form a "happiness board" (*ibid.*, p. 80), that is, a group of friends and family members who keep track of one's commitments and progress in the pursuit of happiness. The lip service paid to complex intrapsychic determinants vanishes and the discourse narrows down to advice (e.g., "make a mental list of things—from little things to big ones—that provide you with pleasure" (*ibid.*, p. 36)), cognitive exercises, and gimmicky phrases (e.g., "the hamburger model" on p. 14; "the lasagne principle" on p. 45). The "rigor of academe" seems to be rapidly descending towards the "fun of the self-help movement" here. (A hilarious form of such "self-help movement" is constituted by Laughter Clubs. Founded by Madan Kataria, a practising internist in India, in 1995, these groups literally centre upon laughing. Capitalizing on the scattered scientific literature on the benefits of laughter for the human mind and body, these groups claim that laughing aloud together spreads happiness and enhances friendships. The movement has spread world-wide, and laughter clubs have appeared in many countries. Dr Kataria has gone on to develop "laughter yoga therapy" and has been the subject of a documentary film by the renowned director, Mira Nair (Jewell, 2010). An Ethiopian "laugh master", Belachew Girma, is seeking to bring peace between Israelis and Palestinians by arranging for them to laugh together (Sudilovsky, 2010).)

The incline towards such popular, self-help type of thinking is sharper in the "teachings" of Deepak Chopra. An Indian-born endocrinologist turned television celebrity and pop psychology guru, Chopra offers a pastiche of holistic medicine, "West-friendly" Eastern wisdom, behavioural advice, and an upbeat and sunny outlook on life. In more than fifty books authored in the span of twenty-three years, he has tackled any and every thing that people consider a source of happiness. A quick glance at the titles of some of his books reveals their manic promise: *Perfect Health* (1991), *Ageless Body, Timeless Mind* (1993a), *Creating Affluence* (1993b), *Boundless Energy* (1995), *Everyday Immortality* (1999), *The Spontaneous Fulfillment of Desire* (2004), *Reinventing the Body, Resurrecting the Soul* (2009a), *The Ultimate Happiness Prescription* (2009b), not to mention *The Seven Spiritual Laws of Success* (1994) and *Golf for Enlightenment* (2003). Chopra's message is that "happiness is natural to life because it is part of the self" (2009b, p. 247), and his rosy world-view declares that:

> 1. Your true being is connected to all that exists. 2. It has no limitations. 3. It has infinite creativity. 4. It is fearless, and willing to step into the unknown. 5. Intention from the level of being is powerful and can orchestrate syncronicity (a perfect meshing of outside circumstances to bring about your intention . . . Shifting your sense of identity to your true being frees you to create a life of abundance, joy, and fulfilment. [2009b, p. 48]

Holding up such promises of omnipotence and bliss, "pop" and "positive" psychology provide a simplified description of the phenomena involved in happiness. Their easy readability by the masses gives them their appeal and, to a certain extent, this is good. Their critique of the pessimism of early psychoanalysis and the discipline's preoccupation with psychopathology is also legitimate. All this notwithstanding, there are serious problems with their approach to complex human matters. Simplicity is readily transformed by these authors into oversimplification. Declarations are mostly based upon secondary sources, many of which go unacknowledged. Despite paying lip service to the contrary, the tone is insistently uplifting and one that offers the promise of lasting and high levels of happiness.

One other viewpoint

In an essay that is aimed at critically assessing Aristotle's (1566) *Nichomachean Ethics* (ca 330 BC) and distilling what the Master actually had in mind about the nature of human happiness, philosopher–psychologist Jonathan Lear (2000) provides a multi-layered understanding of the topic. He notes that Aristotle identified happiness with that which is ultimately good in human action, though leaving it unclear what the latter might be. It seems, though, that most people identify happiness with finding what they lack and/or have lost. In this way, the idea of happiness is inextricably linked with desire and imagination. As a result, people are vulnerable to seductions that promise the gratification of unfulfilled wishes. At the same time, Lear notes that Aristotle's statement that happiness is self-sufficient in itself and lacks nothing implies that truly happy life is beyond desire.

Lear moves on to discern that Aristotle ultimately declared happiness resulting from following a virtuous path in life to be "second rate". True happiness came only from contemplation. Lear acknowledges that

> Aristotle does say that the life of practical virtue is a happy one. But one does not understand that life properly, nor does one live it properly unless one experiences it as pointed towards contemplation. That is, if one does not understand one's life as so oriented, one can not attain the highest form of happiness—at best, there is second rate happiness. But as soon as one does understand one's life in this way, there is also the recognition that, most likely, this second rate happiness is as good as it gets. [pp. 42–43]

Lear goes on to say that while Aristotle upholds the life of contemplation as the ideal of happiness, he also implies that, in its purest form, such existence is reserved for the gods; human beings cannot achieve it on a complete and sustained basis. "In contemplating, we join the activity of the gods; in contemplating, we fall short of their activity" (Lear, 2000, p. 51). Lear concludes his critical study of Aristotle by drawing three conclusions.

> First, most people are not and will never be happy; second, even the elite who lead an ethically virtuous life achieve only second-rate happiness; third, those few who are able to lead a contemplative life will at best be able to contemplate for relatively short periods of their lives. In brief, happiness by and large eludes the human condition. [*ibid.*, p. 55]

Lear's thoughtful and deft deconstruction of Aristotle's perspective on happiness is a delight to read. However, it appears to take the distinction between the "second rate" happiness of virtuous life and the supposedly better form of happiness resulting from contemplation at face value; it downplays the happiness resulting from wish fulfilment even further. But are these differences quantitative or qualitative? Does a life of contemplation (supposedly like "the gods") produce greater, or merely a different kind of, happiness than, say, reliably showing up at one's child's elementary school events? Is the post-coital glow of mutuality somehow "second rate" as compared to, say, a civic-minded meditation on the state of the world's poor? The answers to these questions are not easy to find, but the questions themselves warn us about the risks posed for constructing a theory by idealizing the ego ("contemplation") at the cost of the id ("wish fulfilment") and the superego ("virtuous life").

Doubt also lurks as to whether happiness is same at different points in the human life span. What makes a child happy might be different from what brings a smile to an adult's face. This consideration is important, since it is possible that Aristotle's (and Lear's) gradations of happiness reflect age-specific phenomena with wish fulfilment, living a virtuous life, and primacy of contemplation being nodal points that mark different developmental periods. Moreover, regarding contemplation as the highest form of happiness might itself be the product of the thinking of a middle-aged man; by all accounts, Aristotle was only thirty-four when he wrote *Nichomachean Ethics;* but then, being thirty-four was middle-aged in 334 bc. Finally, Lear does not seem to question the built-in elitism of Aristotle's proposals, which all but bar a high school educated furniture maker from North Carolina from the hallowed halls of true happiness while opening its gates wide to those well tutored in humanities, philosophy, and, why not, psychoanalysis.

Four kinds of happiness

Synthesizing the literature surveyed above yields a view of happiness that is broad, complex, multi-layered, and often contradictory. Different contributors focus upon different aspects of this phenomenon, using different terminology and different vantage points. The degree of pessimism or optimism in their personal characters and life circumstances also seems to have an impact upon their viewpoints on happiness. For example, Freud's (1920g) positing of death instinct is known to have occurred in the setting of his being ill and his facing many losses. Finally, the methodology used by these investigators to arrive at their conclusions is hardly uniform. It ranges from clinical psychoanalysis to philosophical speculation, from empirical research to literary deconstruction, and from child observation to large-scale population studies. As a result, any synthesis of this material must be taken with a grain of salt. In the striving for didactic clarity, the material might become more schematic and organized than the raw data that lie at its origin.

Another difficulty arises from the existence of certain binaries in the conceptualization of happiness that pervade the realm and yet have remained unresolved. These binaries give rise to the following questions: (a) does happiness result from the merger of the self with the object world, *or* does it result from the dissolution of schisms and splits within the self?, (b) is happiness a regressive emotion that capitalizes on reawakening the bliss of early infant–mother unity, *or* it is the product of a progressive advance in ego's dominance over difficult internal and external realities?, (c) is happiness a defence against unhappiness, *or* is it a subjective state in itself?, and (d) does happiness come from the repudiation of the complexity and uncertainty of deep object relations, *or* does it become available only after such ambivalences have been worked through?, and so on.

The answers to such questions lie in the fact that most emotional experience, at its point of origin, carries a certain self-evident "simplicity" about it. Soon, however, the dictates of internal and external reality challenge such one-sidedness, yielding a state of "contradiction". And, with further working through, a third psychic configuration arrives on the scene. Now one can see not only the co-existence of two affective polarities (e.g., love and hate, joy and fear), but also that even in what appears to one pole of experience subtle reverberations of the other are present. This "simplicity–contradiction–paradox" sequence (Akhtar, 1998), while having many other ramifications, is conceptually pertinent to resolving the binaries pertaining to happiness as well. Put simply, this means that both poles of the dialectics implicit in the binaries outlined above are simultaneously present in the experience, though in various degrees of intensities and in varying arrangements of figure-ground relationships. This might appear questionable when it comes to truly intense moments of happiness (e.g., during sexual union or religious ecstasy) that seem based upon regressive merger with idealized part objects. Close examination, however, reveals the situation to be the contrary. All such experiences contain a fine admixture of "merger" and "murder", that is, libidinal fusion and aggressive take-over of the object and a similar, doubly instinctualized surrender of the self. This is what I (1998) have called the "level of paradox". and this is where all genuine happiness resides.

That said, the phenomenon of happiness seems to comprise four types of experiences: (a) pleasure, (b) joy, (c) ecstasy, and (d) contentment. Distinct in many ways, these experiences also have potential overlaps with each other. In the following passages, I describe these four types of experiences in some detail.

Pleasure-based happiness: elation

Freud's (1930a) statement that happiness consists of accumulation of pleasure and avoidance of unpleasure leads one to think that "elation" results from the pleasure of instinctual gratification. Lewin's (1950) tracing the origins of elation to a gratifying experience during the oral phase supports such conclusion. The experience of instinctual gratification is seen to include elevated mood, a sense of well-being, and freedom from irksome moral and psychosomatic tensions. One can readily find illustrations of such experience from the libidinal realm. A hungry man's pleasure at finding food and a worn out man's pleasure at finding a comfortable place to sleep are associated with feelings of happiness that can be called elation. While logically speaking, the same should apply to the discharge of aggressive impulses, it is not customary to associate the words "happiness" or "elation" with the pleasure of sadism, revenge, and retaliation.

Matters seem more complex. To begin with, instinctual pleasure turns out to be something more than mere removal of the unpleasure caused by accumulated tension. To be sure, one can gratify an instinctual desire in a way that does not result in pleasure (e.g., by having a hungry person eat food that is given with anger and contempt). It seems, then, that in order to feel pleasure, one requires something more than instinctual discharge. Elation might be related to instinctual discharge, but the latter is not sufficient to elicit it.

As one examines the issue at hand, it becomes clear that it is the meeting of "ego-needs", alongside with gratification of "id wishes" (see Akhtar, 1999a, for a detailed discussion of the need–wish distinction) that results in pleasure and the associated experience of elation. This realization leads to the inevitable conclusion that satisfaction of this sort can hardly come from outside the context of an empathic and well-attuned relationship. In effect then, the feeling of elation turns out to be the emotional concomitant of finding pleasurable instinctual discharge in the context of a positive and ego-supportive object relationship. In Eidelberg's (1951) words, "happiness can only be experienced if the individual succeeds in finding an object suitable at the same time for the purpose of the satisfaction of object and narcissistic libido" (p. 243). Even this might not be enough, since a truly attuned object relationship cannot evolve without the adequate blending of libido and aggression within the subject, within the object, and within the dyad (Kernberg, 1974; Silbermann, 1985). Elation, a feeling that appeared simple to grasp and describe, turns out to be a complex state indeed.

Assertion-based happiness: joy

Joy refers to the happiness that accompanies the experience of self-confidence and self-assertion. Pleasurable exercise of ego functions and finding efficacy in one's actions also give rise to joy. The experience of joy is not restricted to any age group and can occur at any point in life. However, certain developmental phases are especially suitable for creating certain kinds of joyous experience. The earliest prototype of joy is to be found in the childhood game of "peek-a-boo". That the child experiences a burst of happiness at refinding the mother, after her temporary disappearance, is due to two factors: (a) the rediscovery of mother firms up his fragile self, since its coherence is dependent upon contact with her, and (b) the discovery by the child that he has been able to tolerate the separation and survive it (see also Kleeman, 1967). A little later in life, joy appears in the form of the exhilaration felt at gaining upright locomotion. Here, too, a duality of causative factors is operative. The child feels happy at escaping the "symbiotic orbit" (Mahler, Pine, & Bergman, 1975) *and* at making use of his newly found motor skills. During the latency period, confident exercise of ego functions in the service of mastering external reality and playing creates joy. Then, during late adolescence and young adulthood, the confidence derived from beginning to live on one's own (say, in a college dorm) or from landing one's first full-time job become important joy-producing events. Becoming a parent for the first time, in favourable circumstances, is yet another developmental epoch that is associated with the experience of joy during adulthood.

A similar kind of happiness results, though at a more sublime level, from the robust use of object-related ego functions (Klein, 1976). The delight one feels in pleasing those one loves, and the "ego pleasure" in synthesis and effectiveness belong in this realm. The last-mentioned has found greater exposition in the work of Wolf (1994). According to him, "efficacy experiences" emanate from the "awareness of having an initiating and causal role in bringing about states of needed responsiveness from others" (p. 73). Such experiences strengthen the ego and provide a sense of vitality to the self; their affective counterpart is joy.

Merger-based happiness: ecstasy

The third variety of happiness is "ecstasy". It is defined by *Webster's* as "a state of overwhelming emotion, especially rapturous delight; mystic or prophetic trance; intense exaltation of mind and feeling" (1998, p. 366), and so on. Other attributes included in the definition of "ecstasy" are "being beyond reason and self control; a state of trance or immobility; intense bliss or beatitude" (*ibid.*). From this, it is clear that the experience of "ecstasy" involves emotions of bliss that are so powerful as to overwhelm the ordinary ego functions of reason, motility, and clear consciousness. The dictionary definition implies that there is something truly extraordinary about the experience.

From a psychoanalytic viewpoint, such extraordinary feeling results from the merger of the self and object, provided, of course, that the union is primarily under the influence of libidinal drive (even though a certain amount of aggression is always discernible in the experience). The fierce coming together of the two sexual partners and the transcendent loss of self-boundaries at the moment of orgasm constitutes ecstatic experience *par excellence*. The frenzied exaltation, and even martyrdom, during a political uprising, the "oceanic feeling" (Romain Rolland, cited in Freud, 1930a) of merger with the universe at large, and the rapt absorption of a mendicant in religious worship can all be associated with ecstasy. The common denominator here is the fusion of the self with the object world. Whether this fusion is regarded as regression to infantile states of non-differentiation (Freud, 1930a) or progression to an advanced, more civic-minded, and world-related state depends, in part, on the theoretical perspective of the interpreter.

Fulfilment-based happiness: contentment

Contentment is a quieter type of happiness, which emanates from a feeling of satisfaction. It is accompanied by a diminution in efforts at seeking a change in the intrapsychic situation. Developmentally speaking, the origin of contentment can be traced to the phase of quietude that follows instinctual gratification; it is a "post-pleasure" experience. Inevitably ruptured by the cyclical awakenings of instinctual pressure, contentment, none the less, becomes "structured" over time, giving rise to the ego capacity to be contented. In adult life, the prototypes of contentment are to be found in "post-prandial and post-coital calm" (Olinick, 1982, p. 468). Freud's (1930a) phrase, "happiness of quietness" (p. 77), though used a bit ironically to describe hermits and recluses, is better suited for the experience of contentment.

Such drive-psychology-based understanding of contentment is enriched by adding the perspectives of structural theory. Contentment, from this viewpoint, is the feeling state generated by the closure of the gap between the ego and the ego-ideal, or, perhaps more accurately, between the realistic and wished-for self-representations. Generally speaking, this developmental achievement occurs during middle age; that is the period when, if all has gone well, we arrive at the goals we had set for ourselves and our actual selves begin to approximate the desired view of ourselves.

Three qualifiers must be added here. First, since contentment depends, at least in part, upon the closure of ego–ego-ideal gap, the timing and degree of its achievement shows great variability. Those with less exalted ego-ideals experience contentment with less effort and earlier in life, while those with more elevated ego-ideals have to strive harder and longer before they can feel content. Second, while remaining discontented owing to the unrealistic demands one has put upon oneself (e.g., in the setting of a narcissistic personality) is clinically well-known (Akhtar, 1989, 1992a; Kernberg, 1975, 1984), the syndrome of "premature contentment" has achieved inoptimal attention. The fate of overly indulged and unduly praised children, this syndrome consists of smugness and lack of ambition in the face of minimal achievement. Third, while contentment is a desirable and gratifying state of mind, complete and sustained contentment is an ideal fiction. Permanently affected at their core by the childhood feelings of smallness and inferiority, trapped in the warp of time, unable to escape the vice of mortality, and belonging to one gender alone, they always long for the ideal self-state (regressive or transcendent) and, therefore, remain discontented. Freud's (1930a) monograph *Civilization and Its Discontents* elucidates these matters in depth, including the burdens that "civilized sexuality" places upon man's instinctual life.

Some caveats

The description of happiness provided here, especially the way it has been categorized, needs to be "softened" by entering some caveats. These include the following.

First and foremost, psychology and psychoanalysis are not the only disciplines that offer meaningful perspectives on human happiness. Evolutionary studies, neurophysiology, philosophy, economics, and religion all have made significant contributions to this realm. As a result, the portrayal of happiness here is incomplete at best.

Second, with minor exceptions, the literature covered here does not distinguish the differences in the experience of happiness over the human life span. To talk of happiness in broad terms without paying attention to the fact that a child's happiness, an adolescent's happiness, a young adult's happiness, a middle-aged individual's happiness, and an elderly person's happiness might be different does disservice to the spectrum of the phenomena involved.

Third, happiness is a highly subjective experience and its nature, as well as its sources, vary greatly from individual to individual. A generalized picture, even with the provision of subcategories, runs the risk of missing individual nuances.

Fourth, forms and intensities of happiness might vary from culture to culture. Also variable is the degree to which happiness is overtly expressed and the environmental triggers that release such a response. The British "stiff upper lip" and the Latin American vivaciousness illustrate the former point. The popularity of "get rich quick" schemes in the USA and the hunger for religious blessing in India exemplify the latter point.

Fifth, while the aetiological titles of the four categories of happiness described here (pleasure-based, assertion-based, merger-based, and fulfilment-based) are more solidly anchored in theory, their colloquial counterparts (elation, joy, ecstasy, and contentment) carry less weight. This is owing to the fact that the latter are used loosely in public discourse and, at times, interchangeably in the professional literature.

Sixth, the four categories of happiness described here are not as surgically apart as the didactic need for clarity has made them appear. They overlap with each other. For instance, obtaining instinctual pleasure can stir pride in self-assertion, thus mixing elation with joy. And, fulfilment of desires is associated with pleasure and followed by satiation; contentment and elation thus get mixed with each other. And so on.

Seventh, psychoactive substances (e.g., alcohol, cocaine) can activate subjective experiences akin to any and all of the types of happiness described above. Whether some intoxicants produce a particular kind of happiness more often than other substances (e.g., alcohol causing elation and joy, marijuana causing ecstasy and contentment) needs further investigation.

Finally, all four types of happiness can have normal and abnormal variants. The pleasures associated with sexual perversion, the malicious joy at beating someone up, the premature contentment of the over-indulged child, and the demonic ecstasy of satanic worship are but a few examples of psychopathological forms of happiness.

Technical implications

The concept of happiness, as it has been elucidated here, has a multi-faceted impact upon the conduct of psychoanalytic treatment. This is evident in the analyst's (i) receiving the patient with happiness, (ii) interpreting the patient's defences against feelings of happiness, (iii) diagnosing false happiness and unmasking its defensive and discharge functions, (iv) enjoying the patient's authentic happiness, and (v) managing the countertransference reactions to happiness-related exchanges in the dyad.

Receiving the patient with happiness

The psychoanalyst must be in a "good mood" when he or she opens the office door and welcomes the patient to come inside. A certain peacefulness, freedom from instinctual tensions and realistic worry, and mild anticipatory pleasure towards the work that is about to unfold characterize this "good mood". A smile of recognizing affirmation upon visually encountering the patient also helps. Of the types of happiness described above, "contentment" comes closest to this state of mind, though there is evidence of mild elation and joy here as well. Needless to add that the degree to which such inner states will become overt, while remaining within the confines of the "analytic persona" (Levine, 2007), depends upon the analyst's personal make-up and culturally sanctioned patterns of behaviour. Guntrip's (1975) description of his (second) analyst, Winnicott, opening the door at the beginning of a session while softly humming a tune captures a glimpse of one such "good mood" moment.

A corollary to this is that the analyst must not undertake a session if he or she is unhappy and cannot find serenity. The following episode, described by Michael Parsons (2000), a distinguished British analyst, shows the simple and self-evident nature of this stance.

> At karate training one evening we were practising with our partners a pre-arranged sequence of attack and defence when the instructor, a great karate master, called Hirokazu Kanzawa, broke off the exercise and dismissed the class, well before the training session would normally have ended. At the next session someone asked why he had stopped the class early. "Spirit no good!", came the reply. He said we had been making our attacks without real commitment or sincerity. He understood that we did not want to hurt our friends, but an empty attack was no expression of friendship. If we were true friends to our training partners, he said, we would strike with all the speed and power we had. [p. 9]

Of course, if the analyst is truly upset (for whatever reason) while approaching the start of the hour, it might be better to bring the patient in, judiciously and briefly explain the situation, and reschedule the session. The feelings and fantasies mobilized (in the patient) by such "intervention" can be analysed in the subsequent hour(s).

Interpreting the patient's defences against feelings of happiness

In his paper, "Some character types met with in psychoanalytic work", Freud (1916d) described, in the section titled "Those wrecked by success", patients who are "not able to tolerate their happiness" (p. 316) since pleasure of success is equated in their minds with the actualization of incestuous and parricidal impulses. Guilt consequent upon such desire precludes their enjoyment of the happiness afforded by achievements in external life. Freud's observation, repeated on many subsequent occasions (see especially, 1930a) became a cornerstone of psychoanalytic understanding of defensive recoil from happiness. While clinically valid, this dynamic does not exhaust the motives underlying patients' reflexive withdrawal from the experience of happiness. To begin with, the guilt that fuels such a defensive move might have origins other than those in the Oedipal situation. It might be pre-Oedipal guilt at having damaged the mother in phantasy (Klein, 1935, 1940), survival guilt at having outlived a sibling or parent (Niederland, 1968), separation guilt at psychologically moving away from a needy parent (Modell, 1965), or guilt because of the self-centred blackmail by parents who brag about their suffering in childbirth and/or child-rearing (Asch, 1976).

To complicate matters, patients' intolerance of happiness (evident in their new phobic avoidance of expressing pride, joy, and contentment) might not have anything to do with guilt at all. The anxiety might pertain to becoming separated or too distinct from a depressed parent and, thus, risking self-coherence. Or, the turning away from happiness might be due to the inability to bear gratitude that comes with acknowledging that the world has given one pleasure and satisfaction. Regardless of the dynamics, the analyst's job is to be vigilant regarding sudden shifts in associations away from happiness and noticeable omission of positive affective experiences. For instance, if a patient's announcement of passing a major examination or buying a dream house is unaccompanied by elation or joy, or is quickly followed by pronouncements of suffering, the analyst must point out the defensive repudiation of happiness. Doing so would open up doors to the subterranean concerns that are making it difficult for the patient to enjoy being happy. At such moments, the particular type of analytic listening called "close process monitoring" (Gray, 1973, 1994) is of great help. Such listening hones in on the moment-to-moment shifts of emphasis and nuance in the stream of the patient's associations, paying sharp attention to a pause, an abrupt change of topic, the emergence of an incongruent affect, and an unexplainable avoidance of the logically expectable thought. Observing such occurrences and bringing them to the patient's awareness makes resistance analysis possible.

Diagnosing false happiness and unmasking its defensive and discharge functions

Encountering the distressing emotions of anxiety, sadness, and psychic pain, patients often resort to defensive levity, telling jokes, and even what appears to be spontaneous humour. Such moments pose both a challenge to, and an opportunity for, deep analytic work. Lack of vigilance can lead the analyst to overlook the driven, tense, and avoidant quality of such "false happiness". Lemma (2009) notes that:

> As clinicians, we can probably all think of clinical situations where the patient's humour was used destructively, perhaps to create a sense of complicity between patient and analyst, and this needs to be taken up. It is vital that we guard against humour to serve our own defensive needs in an attempt to ward off the examination of more threatening material with the patient, or to invite the patient's admiration of our witticism, or to use humour to seduce and collude with the patient. [p. 300]

Effervescent wit is, however, not the only form in which "false happiness" appears in the clinical situation. Joyous story-telling that exerts a mesmerizing influence upon the analyst can also be regarded as a variety of false happiness that needs interpretative attention.

Clinical vignette 5

> Anna Maldonado, a Peruvian woman in analysis, began talking about her beloved grandmother's funeral some years ago, almost immediately after I had told her of my unavailability for a few days. The connection was obvious. I waited. Gradually, intricate details of Peruvian funeral rituals began to occupy her associations. Her momentary sadness upon my telling her that I would not be available for three days was now replaced with a vigorous tone. Her affect was now one of elation. I found myself raptly absorbed in the material, feeling enriched by learning all the cultural details. Returning to a self-observing stance a few minutes later, I noted that she not only had defensively warded off her pain, but also had given me a parting gift, as it were. Interpretative interventions along this line deepened the material and facilitated the analysis of her disappointment at my being away and her subsequent anger about it.

Regardless of what form "false happiness" takes (both within the transference or in the reports of extra-transference material), its defensive quality is betrayed by the rigidity, hollowness, and the slight out-of-context feeling that comes with it. That said, it should be recognized that there also occur moments of genuine happiness and humour in the course of the analytic treatment. These need to be handled in their own separate ways (see below).

Enjoying the patient's authentic happiness

When genuine happiness is felt or expressed by a patient, the analyst must be able to resonate with it and even enjoy it. Such pleasure is consonant with the notion of "unobjectionable positive countertransference" (Fox, 1998; Gill, 1994), referring to the professionally appropriate and personally ego-syntonic positive feelings of analysts towards their patients. Of course, the choice to overtly express the happiness that the analyst might feel in reciprocity with that of the patient is governed by matters of tact, empathy, the specifics of the moment, and the overall idiom of relatedness between them.

The occasions that bring out such happiness vary. They might include the patient's recall of happy events of childhood, delightful accounts of children and grandchildren, major accomplishments in external reality (e.g., promotion at work, purchase of a house), and achievement of significant developmental benchmarks (e.g., marriage, parenthood). While these seemingly innocent events can also pull collusive enactments from the analyst, the situation is more complex when it comes to the (a) patient's happiness at intrapsychic advances made as a result of treatment, and (b) emergence of genuine, not defensive, humour in the relational matrix.

As far as the first matter is concerned, it is my belief that the analyst cannot but provide the auxiliary ego support the patient seems to need. Indeed, the model analyst in Loewald's (1960) viewpoint offers himself to the patient as a contemporary object. He is emotionally related, and mindful of the patient's potentials, which he sees as a parent does. Moreover, he offers the patient opportunities to create new integrations on the armature of maturity that he himself provides. Acknowledging, supporting, and even "celebrating" the developmental advances on the patient's part is an integral part of such therapeutic stance.

Then there is the issue of humour. While "false happiness" and manic defence masquerading as wit need interpretative handling, undue reticence in responding to the patient's humour can cause him narcissistic injury and shame. This used to be the customary stance analysts adopted, though many came to express regret about it towards the later part of their careers (Coltart, 1993). Fortunately, there is now burgeoning literature (Chasseguet-Smirgel, 1988; Christe, 1994; Lemma, 2000, 2009; Poland, 1990; Stein, 1985) which takes a softer position on this matter. Note, for instance, the following observation by Christe.

> It is reasonable to assume that a momentary communication in playful humour can not only put us in touch with otherwise warded-off libidinal and/or destructive impulses, but also allows a brief transformation of their hidden forces. A creative thrust is released that can facilitate further ego-integration and broaden perspective and understanding. [1994, p. 487]

A similar sentiment is voiced by Lemma (2009), who states that

> some patients may indeed gain from exchanges with an analyst who can use humour to gently engage them in thinking about something they cannot otherwise bear to face . . . Sharing a joke and laughing might even represent an attempt to relate more playfully, for the first time. Here, the analyst's response is crucial: if the analyst responds soberly the patient might feel shamed or rebuffed in some way. The use of humour by the analyst might, in fact, function as a kind of meta-communication to the patient about their internal state of mind, which may foster a sense of safety, through discomfirming inhibiting expectations and so increases the patient's ability to be self-reflective. [p. 301]

Putting all this together, it seems that the analyst's capacity and willingness to "enjoy" his or her patient's happiness while keeping an eye on the potential meanings of what is taking place. helps rather than hinders the analytic process.

Managing the countertransference reactions to happiness-related exchanges in the clinical dyad

Comfortable with the narratives of anxiety, anguish, and despair, psychoanalysts are often caught off-guard when facing moments of happiness in their clinical work. Such happiness usually resides in the relational matrix and is thus "intersubjective", though one or the other party in the clinical dyad can certainly contribute more to the origins of the sentiment. In either case, the analyst has to be comfortable in experiencing happiness, keeping it contained if clinical tact dictates that, or sharing it with the patient if that seems indicated. Avoiding expressions of happiness from his side (in response to a major advance in the self-observing function of the analyand's ego) or becoming overly exuberant (at minor and external achievements of the patient) are both evidences of a hitherto undetected countertransference difficulty.

Generally speaking, such problems arise from the analyst's characterologically determined optimism–pessimism ratio and his vulnerability to mobilizing manic defence against the depressive and paranoid anxieties of intimacy. Clinging to the caricatured ideal of a "serious" professional and a conscious or unconscious identification with Freud's grim world-view can also contribute to inhibitions in this realm. The separation of creative "audacity" in conservative training programmes might also leave a legacy of stodginess and discomfort with expressions of joy. The analyst's successful working through of such '"inherited" pseudo-unhappiness via post-graduation self-analysis and growth would determine how free of countertransference he or she can remain while encountering happiness (within the self or within the patient) in the clinical situation.

Concluding remarks

In this chapter, I have summarized the views of Freud and subsequent psychoanalysts on the concept of happiness. Stepping out of the "prisonhouse of psychoanalysis" (Goldberg, 1990), I have tried to extract meaningful material from the writings of the contemporary Happiness Movement as well as those of philosophical and microeconomic perspectives. Pooling these diverse sets of observations together, I have suggested that the affects and experiences subsumed under the broad rubric of "happiness" belong to four different, though potentially overlapping, categories. These categories are pleasure, joy, ecstasy, and contentment. I have then delineated ontogenetic roots, metapsychological correlates, and experiential building blocks for each of these categories. Moving on, I have attempted to demonstrate how the subjective experience of happiness (both in its broad sense and in its constituent categories) impacts upon the conduct of psychotherapy and psychoanalysis.

While I have covered a reasonable ground, my discourse does not exhaust the list of important matters in the realm of happiness. Three such matters are the relationship of gender, culture, and money to happiness. As far as the issue of gender is concerned, it is striking to note that the literature (psychoanalytic or otherwise) makes little mention of this variable. The reasons for this are unclear. Is this omission due to lack of knowledge? Or, have concerns over social reprisal made us tongue-tied? One does not know. Seligman (2002), for one, says that "in average emotional tone, women and men don't differ, but this is strangely because women are both happier *and* sadder than men" (p. 59, original emphasis). Maybe the issue is not one of the extent of happiness but of its quality. The difference in men and women might pertain to the *kind* of happiness they experience and the *sources* from which such happiness is derived. The two genders seem akin in their capacity to achieve pleasure-based ("elation") and merger-based ("ecstasy") types of happiness, and different in their capacity to achieve assertion-based ("joy") and fulfilment-based ("contentment") happiness. Privy to greater social freedom of expression, men seem more comfortable with self-assertion and, therefore, might have greater familiarity with the experience of "joy". In contrast, women might experience "contentment" more deeply and earlier in life than men. This might be traced to a formative event in the early female psychosexual development: the shifting of love from mother to father. In Altman's (1977) words, "this renunciation prepares her for renunciation in the future in a way the boy is unable to match" (p. 48). This capacity of renunciation might ease women's achieving contentment in life. Women's psychosomatic continuity of primary identification with the mother also makes the gap between ego and ego-ideal more tolerable, making it more possible for them to feel content. They draw greater narcissistic gratification than men from the achievement of their children (besides from their own work) and this dual stream of gratification adds to their happiness.

The second issue pertains to the role of culture in creating and sustaining happiness. The much cited study by Biswas-Diener and Diener (2002) comparing the life-satisfaction and happiness levels between the slum dwellers of Calcutta (now called Kolkata) with the street people of Fresno, California, for instance, revealed striking differences in favour of India. In an investigation comparing the self-reported happiness levels in Mexico with those in France, too, the balance tilted heavily in favour of Mexico (Brooks, 2008). The results of these studies de-link societal affluence and happiness and, by implication, suggest that other cultural factors might be responsible for life satisfaction and happiness. The observation by the Nobel prize-winning economist, Amartya Sen (1999), that the people of Kerala (a state in India with a population of thirty million people), China, and Sri Lanka have higher quality of life than the much richer populations of Brazil, South Africa, and Namibia supports this idea. While cross-national generalizations must be treated with suspicion, the above-mentioned studies suggest that the overall levels of happiness are higher in societies with greater communal harmony, less loneliness, and higher premium on the values of altruism, sacrifice, faith, and generativity. Societies that are largely driven by market economies and put a premium on personal acquisition and achievement tend to leave people unsatisfied and less happy in general.

This brings us to the age-old question, and that is: "Can money buy happiness?" The temptation to give an affirmative answer arises from the fact that monetary affluence can free time, bestow a greater amount of psychosocial freedom, satisfy the desires for material acquisition, and increase access to pleasurable experiences. Underlying such realities are the childhood fantasies of omnipotence ("I could do anything if I were wealthy"), as well as the idealization of parents who are seen to have power and control over their lives. The fantasy of winning a lottery deftly combines such "reality" and intrapsychic scenarios. Having a lot of money, it seems, will bring happiness. Empirical studies as well as clinical experience, however, prove the contrary. To begin with, most people who win lotteries squander their money and soon return their prior life styles (Brickman, Coates, & Janoff-Bulman, 1978). Even when acquisition of money seems to result in happiness, it is largely owed to "prosocial spending" (Bennett, 2009; Dunn, Aknin,

& Norton, 2008), that is, buying gifts for others and giving donations to worthy causes. This shows that the source of happiness is not having money *per se*, but the expression of love and morality it can facilitate in some individuals; those who spend large amounts of money on themselves and/or material acquisitions remain unquenched and restless. Moreover, the level of self-reported happiness differs little among the rich and the poor in population surveys (Kahneman, Krueger, Schkade, Schwartz, & Stone, 2006; Myers, 2000) and there is evidence that the overall quality of life (including the feelings of happiness) might at times be better in less affluent countries than in those with greater average income (Brooks, 2008; Sen, 1999). For the psychoanalyst, however, what counts is the clinical experience in a one-to-one situation. Here, too, the lack of correlation between financial affluence and a subjective sense of happiness becomes evident. Patients' sense of satisfaction with their lives hardly seems dependent upon whether they are monetarily well off or not (see Akhtar, 2009f, pp. 47–69). Freud's (1895) declaration, made 115 years ago, that money cannot bring happiness, since happiness results from the fulfilment of childhood wishes and money is not an object of them, turns out to be true after all.

CHAPTER THREE

Playfulness

> "The sunlight playing on the waves qualifies for the attribute 'playful' because it faithfully remains within the rules of the game. It does not really interfere with the chemical world of the waves. It insists only on an intermingling of appearances. These patterns change with effortless rapidity and with a repetitiveness which promises pleasing phenomena within a predictable range without ever creating the same configuration twice"
>
> (Erikson, 1950, p. 212)

Allow me to begin this contribution on the notion of playfulness by talking about a revolver. Yes, you read it right: a revolver. The story goes like this. Donald Winnicott was to present a paper to the British Psychoanalytic Society. After being introduced, he walked up to the podium, opened his briefcase, took out his paper and also a revolver, which he carefully placed on the lectern. A hush fell over the audience. Winnicott began reading his paper and, after a few minutes, stopped and said something like this, "In case you are wondering what this revolver is doing here, let me tell you. It is intended for the person who, instead of discussing my ideas, would begin his remarks by declaring that what I am presenting is not psychoanalysis." The audience laughed, a bit awkwardly to be sure. Winnicott then went on with reading his paper.

This anecdote is radiant with a deft admixture of light-heartedness, bold yet restrained expression of an instinctual agenda, and, with a wink to all the parties involved in the interaction, a thinning of the boundary between reality and unreality. It depicts playfulness in all its glory. But let me not get ahead of myself. Instead, let me lay out the plan of this discourse. I begin by elucidating the phenomenon of playfulness and its various drive-based, ego-anchored, and object-relational constituents. Then I trace the developmental origins of the capacity for playfulness. Following this, I move into the realm of psychopathology and discuss the relationship of playfulness to character organization, its potential overlap with "manic defence" (Klein, 1935; Winnicott, 1935), and five specific types of pathological playfulness. I also illustrate the role of playfulness in analytic technique with the help of some clinical vignettes. I conclude by pulling this material together and raising some questions for us to consider.

Normal playfulness

The meaning of the word "play" seems self-evident, yet, upon a closer look, turns out to be surprisingly multi-faceted. "Play" can mean "a recreational activity", "a particular manoeuvre in a game", "brisk, fitful, or light movement" (e.g., the gem presented a dazzling play of colours), "unimpeded motion" (e.g., the piston had a lot of play), "the stage presentation of a story", "to fiddle with something", and so on. Additional connotations of "play" are evident in the contexts of theatre ("playing a role"), music ("playing an instrument"), and sexuality ("foreplay", "playing around", "playing the field", "playboy"), as well as in the sphere of language via exaggeration ("to play up a point"), and humour (through "wordplay"). With the exception of philandering, acts involved in these wide-ranging contexts are harmless, amusing, and enjoyable. They also have an element of freshness and make-believe quality.

The mental operation underlying them is akin to what Target and Fonagy (1996) have termed "pretend mode". This consists of the knowledge that internal experience might not reflect the facts of external reality, and the separation of internal and external reality with the accompanying assumption that an internal state has no actual impact upon the external reality.

These attributes of "play" discerned through its linguistic versatility also feature in psychoanalytic writings on the subject. However, the gaze is deeper here. The founder of psychoanalysis, Sigmund Freud, noted the subtleties of play—largely involving words and visual images—in the creation of dreams (1900a) and jokes (1905c). Addressing child's play, Freud (1908e) wrote the following remarkable passage:

> Might we not say that every child at play behaves like a creative writer, in that he creates a world of his own, or, rather, re-arranges the things of his world in a new way which pleases him? It would be wrong to think he does not take that world seriously; on the contrary, he takes his play very seriously and he expends large amounts of emotion on it. The opposite of play is not what is serious but what is real. In spite of all the emotion with which he cathects his world of play, the child distinguishes it quite well from reality. [pp. 143–144]

An implication of this proposal is that play (and its trait counterpart, playfulness) is not supposed to have consequences in reality. There is a quality of transience as well as fantasy to it. Indeed, Freud (1911b) traced the origin of fantasizing to childhood play and, in a celebrated observation of the *fort-da* game of his eighteen-month-old grandson (1920g), discovered the adaptive purposes of playfulness.

Subsequent contributions to the psychoanalytic understanding of play (Alexander, 1958; Erikson, 1950; Fenichel, 1946; Ferenczi, 1932; Waelder, 1933; Winnicott, 1971) underscored the fact that play serves many purposes. These include mastery of conflict, reworking of trauma, comprehension of external reality, and fine-tuning of ego skills. These contributions have, however, remained focused upon children's play, and give the adult personality attribute of playfulness short shift. The work of Winnicott (1953, 1971) constitutes a major exception. He described the "transitional realm" or the "intermediate area of experience" where reality and unreality are put aside, imagination is born, and paradox reigns supreme. Once developed, this psychic "area" remains available for the rest of life. It is the location of cultural experience. Poetry, fiction, metaphor, games, faith, and religious belief all reside here, and so does playfulness. In being playful, an individual takes a temporary leave of the constraints of reality, knowingly enjoys the pleasure of "absurdity", and, in the process, lets his authentic self emerge.

Emphasizing the ego-replenishing features of such an attitude and paraphrasing Freud (1900a), Erikson (1950) has called play "the royal road to the understanding of the infantile ego at synthesis" (p. 209). He regards play as an ego function and an attempt to synchronize the somatic and the social strands of the self. According to Erikson,

> When man plays he must intermingle with things and people in an uninvolved and light fashion. He must do something which he has chosen to do without being compelled by urgent interests or impelled by strong passion; he must feel entertained and free of any fear or hope of serious consequences. He is on vacation from social and economic reality. [*ibid.*, p. 212]

Erikson underscores how moments of playfulness allow a periodical stepping out from the strictures of reality (including gravity and time) and can be seen in social settings and in love life. Freed from "the compulsions of conscience and impulsions of irrationality" (p. 214), man can feel authentically one with his ego. Through play, he can express his inner agenda in an aim-inhibited and socially acceptable way. The pleasure of discharge brings about ego relaxation. Later reflection (conscious or preconscious) upon what underlies the play deepens the ego's reach and makes self-knowledge possible. A remark about the nature of poetry made by Nobel Prize-winning Irish poet, Seamus Heaney, captures this point with remarkable precision. Heaney (1995) declared that in writing (and reading) poetry, the movement is always from "delight to wisdom" (p. 5) and not the other way round.

The mention of poetry serves as a bridge to cross over from the island of play, about which much has been written, to the nation of playfulness about which psychoanalytic literature is relatively silent. The word does not appear in the index to the *Standard Edition* of Freud's writings and in any of the twenty-seven psychoanalytic glossaries published so far (see Akhtar, 2009b, for a critical review of them). A search of the PEP Web, the computerized compendium of psychoanalytic literature, reveals only seven papers with "playfulness" in their titles over the last one hundred and twenty years (Auerhahn & Laub, 1987; Ehrenberg, 1990; Feiner, 1990, 1992; Moran, 1987; Shengold, 1988; Solnit, 1998). What I have to say about playfulness is derived from Winnicott's (1953, 1960, 1971) contributions, the seven papers mentioned above, and my clinical and social experience.

The first point that needs to be made is that "play" is an act and "playfulness" is an attitude, which is harder to define. Psychoanalytic literature shows various authors fumbling in an effort to describe "playfulness". Moran (1987) explicitly states that he found "the notion of playfulness difficult to define" (p. 15), though three qualities do occur consistently with it. These include (i) light-heartedness, (ii) a pleasure-orientated flexibility in commitment to reality, and (iii) the retention of the knowledge that one is not being "serious". Ostow (1987) notes that while "play" and "playfulness" are free from the restrictions of logic, "the tendency to play and the tendency to be playful are not necessarily correlated" (p. 195). He makes an emphatic distinction between them, stating that a playful attitude is actually the converse of play.

> The fully engaged player disengages himself from reality, enjoys the disengagement, but obtains even greater pleasure by reintroducing a small amount of reality. The playful attitude on the other hand takes full cognizance of reality but, by treating it as if it were a joke, alternates, to some degree, its accompanying pain or stress. [*ibid.*]

The need to bear the burdens that come from accepting reality and the possibility to derive enjoyment from debunking reality bring up scenarios of early development that contribute to the genesis of playfulness.

Developmental origins

The origins of playfulness can be traced to the earliest period of infancy, when the social referencing and pleasure in the discovery of new relational and conceptual patterns make their first appearance (Emde, 1991). The child's obvious delight in exploring the mother's face, hair, necklace, etc., observing his own hand movements, delightedly responding to the cooing noises of the mother and of his own are all early prototypes from which the later, more complex and subtle phenomenon of playfulness would evolve. An important step in this development is mother's introduction of the peek-a-boo game. This facilitates the tolerance of her absence in a judiciously dosed, pleasurable way (Kleeman, 1967) and shows the child that real–unreal confusion (has the mother gone, or is she still there?) can be used for ego-enriching purposes. The rupture of relatedness (via mother's disappearance) is coupled with the joy of reunion (via her reappearance) and mutuality (in the increasingly solid retention of the shared knowledge that she *will* reappear). Initially passive in their interaction, the child gradually adopts a more active role in the game. He anticipates it and, at times, even initiates it.

While all this is well recognized, three psychoanalytic contributions need special mention. Winnicott (1953, 1960, 1971) holds the child's capacity for playfulness to be a major sign of healthy development. Playfulness is a poem written by the true self. Winnicott's (1989) "squiggle game", a technique of working with children in psychotherapy, is anchored in this conviction. Essentially, it consists of the therapist drawing a wave-like line or figure on a paper and inviting the child patient to add to it or to draw something of his own, to which the therapist can add. He and the child then take turns to complete some sort of a picture from their random drawings. The result of this game could be likened to dreams, since it was a representation of the unconscious. While the game is initiated by the therapist, the two partners must remain equally active in playing it. Spontaneity and surprise are necessary elements to such interaction. (Less known is Winnicott's (1941) "spatula game". This consists of putting a shiny spatula within the reach of an infant and observing how he reacts to it. Under normal circumstances, the infant's response consists of three steps: (i) noticing the spatula, reaching for it, and then, in a moment of hesitation, gauging the mother's response, as if seeking her permission to proceed further; (ii) picking the spatula up and mouthing it; and, (iii) dropping it, as if by mistake. If the spatula is offered again, the child is pleased and repeats the same sequence, though with greater intentionality. Absence or unevenness of the sequence suggests some disturbance within the infant or, more likely, within the infant–mother dyad.)

Echoes of Winnicott's (1953) emphasis upon the "gentlemanly agreement" between the parents and child that his attachment to his "transitional object" will not be questioned are also to be found in Stein's (1985) observation on the birth of the capacity for irony. Stein writes,

> We urge the child to eat his breakfast; he responds with a defiant "No!" and may make his point even clearer by dumping his cereal on the floor. The wily mother, or father as the case may be, changes the procedure. She says, with mock severity, "Don't you dare eat that cereal!" The child looks at her mischievously and immediately proceeds to wolf down his breakfast, as if in defiance. The mother portrays a kind of mock horror, perhaps even exclaiming, "You bad child!" Both laugh gleefully, enjoying the process. This is clearly ironic. The command, "Don't you dare eat that cereal!" and the scolding, "You bad child!" are understood by the child, correctly, as meaning the opposite. He is pleased by being treated not as a stupid literal baby, but rather as an intelligent being who is capable of understanding a joke. [p. 50]

Moran (1987) offers confirmatory evidence for such thinking from The Study Group on Developmental Disturbances at the Anna Freud Centre in London. Moran underscores the impact of the parents' biological bond with their children upon their readily identifying with the latter's needs and frustrations and attempting to lessen them by all means, including playfulness.

> Playful parents find many inventive ways to lighten the demands which they make on the child. In the case of infants, playful parents will try to enhance the infant's feeling of competence and mastery. They may, for example, let their baby hold the bottle and attempt to put it into his own mouth, coming to the baby's aid at the appropriate moment. Such parents will protect their child's nascent frustration tolerance by endeavoring to minimize interference with the child's pursuit of pleasure. Playful mothers may contort themselves while changing a nappy or dressing their babies. Such parents will invent playful interactions to mediate a large variety of tasks. [p. 16]

Subtle forms of such interactional patterns persist through latency and adolescence. Games played in the home's garden, joint dare-devilry at amusement parks, family vacations, and even mutually shared home cleaning projects can provide the nidus of parent–child playfulness and lead to the internalization and consolidation of this capacity on the growing child's part. Moving on from a potentially "hard-wired" substrate through an interactional pattern to a communicative trait, playfulness comes to be a part of the subsequent adult's character. However, this assumes that the development has gone well. This, as we know, is not always the case.

Five psychopathological syndromes

The foregoing survey of literature reveals that "playfulness" is variously regarded to be an area of the mind, a potential attitude, an interactive pattern, a manner of communication, and a character trait. While no attempt has been made to correlate playfulness with specific character constellations, three possibilities seem to exist: (i) those who can be playful and retain the ability to put their playfulness aside; (ii) those who cannot be playful, and (iii) those who cannot stop being playful. Individuals in the first category are closest to mental health, though "higher level" (Kernberg, 1970) hysterical personalities might also behave in a similar fashion. Individuals in the second category are obsessional, depressive, paranoid, or schizoid, though their inability to be playful arises from differing levels of psychic conflicts and different types of ego rigidity. The individuals in the third category are chronic pranksters and those with burdensome effusiveness; they are "hypomanic characters" (Akhtar, 1988). The last two categories reflect psychopathology. Green's (2005) reminder is pertinent in this context.

> It is true that the great majority of the meanings attached to play are positive, but we cannot forget that play is also associated with cheating, from which it is inseparable: to play into somebody's hands, to be caught in someone else's play, or to be trapped. I think that all these expressions can be seen as perversions of play. [pp. 15–16]

While Winnicott did not describe psychopathology of *playfulness*, in a posthumously published paper (Winnicott, Shepherd, and

Davis, 1989, pp. 59–63), he did delineate seven types of pathology of *play*. These included: (i) loss of capacity to play associated with mistrust; (ii) stereotypical and rigid play; (iii) flight into daydreaming; (iv) excessive sensualization of play; (v) dominating play; (vi) playing as a compliance to authority; (vii) flight to strenuous physical exercise. My own way of looking at psychopathology involving playfulness is to categorize it into: (i) deficient playfulness; (ii) pseudo-playfulness; (iii) inhibited playfulness; (iv) derailed playfulness; (v) malignant playfulness.

Deficient playfulness

This is witnessed in the rhythmic and twirling behaviours of autistic children. The sensation-dominated use of "autistic objects" (Tustin, 1980) by psychotic children also belongs in this category. These objects, usually small and hard (e.g., keys, little metallic cars), are deployed as scaffolds to stabilize the mind. "They may have no fantasy whatsoever associated with them, or they may be associated with extremely crude fantasies which are very close to bodily sensations" (*ibid.*, p. 27). Their loss is felt as a loss of a body part and, hence, they are immediately replaced. Play with such objects has a ritualistic quality and the child has a rigidly intense preoccupation with them. The appearance of "playfulness" is deceptive under such circumstances. The repetitive activities of autistic children are "relatively mindless in terms of fantasies, illusion, or a mental or behavioral effort to explore, practice, or try on roles having elaborate defensive and adaptive capacities" (Solnit, 1987, p. 211). Playfulness, in contrast, is based upon symbolizing capacity and facilitates the solution of conflicts in an exploratory, make-believe manner.

Pseudo-playfulness

Individuals with a relentless tendency to joke, pun, rhyme, and act impulsively belong in this category. Their sunny meddlesomeness arises from sustained "manic defence" (Klein, 1935; Winnicott, 1935) and is different from genuine playfulness. The possibility of self-knowledge is impeded by manic defence (i.e., the trio of idealization, denial of dependence, and omnipotence) and enhanced by playfulness. Manic defence erases links to psychic reality and especially the depressive anxiety that is inherent in emotional development. Playfulness, in contrast, permits a well-titrated discharge of id derivatives that can be reflected upon to gain insight into the affective and relational state of the self. Moreover, playfulness is a source of joy for all the parties involved in it, whereas manic defence tends to amuse only the subject and that, too, in a frenetic and ego-depleting way.

Inhibited playfulness

An individual's capacity to be playful can become inhibited owing to many reasons. The fear of unintended breakthrough of aggression keeps the paranoid individual unduly vigilant, robbing his communication of levity and spontaneity (Akhtar, 1990). The intense reaction formations of the obsessional have a similar result, though here the situation is compounded by the pervasive use of intellectualization; the latter is opposed to the elements that are critical to playfulness, especially paradox and metaphor. The ego rigidity and social discomfort of the schizoid also makes playfulness difficult. However, some schizoid individuals can relax with a select few in a sort of "enlarge autism among people of similar persuasion" (Kretschner, 1925, p. 162). Often, this requires the help of alcohol.

Similarly, some highly "logical" obsessional adults and anaclitically deprived, sad children can "borrow" the capacity to be playful from others. While unable to be playful on their own, such individuals can respond to an active playmate by showing increased imagination, trying on new roles, and letting fantasy life emerge into consciousness (Solnit, 1987, 1998). This phenomenon might be termed "induced playfulness". Domestic pets can also elicit playfulness from those who are otherwise dour. A striking example of this is to be found in the fact that Freud, who was tone-deaf and hated music, would start humming under his breath and even singing while playing with his favorite dog, Jo-fi (Gay, 1988).

Derailed playfulness

Ordinarily, the attitude of playfulness consists of a light-hearted, enjoyable, and transient relaxation of the reality–unreality boundary alongside a will-titrated diffusion of the ego by id derivatives, especially of the pregenital variety. At times, however, its make-believe quality begins to disappear. The suspension of reality in the service of enjoyable regression is lost and play is replaced by activity with real consequences. The ego–id balance shifts and direct instinctual gratification is sought. Such "derailed playfulness" is evident in children who are playing with each other, teasing, bursting out in laughter, and even wrestling, until suddenly they lose perspective and start fighting for real. They transgress the "rules" of the game and disregard its context. A daydream of camaraderie has now turned into a nightmare of bitter rivalry.

Similar scenarios can arise in the context of sexual perversions. Indeed, it is possible to envision the pregenital pleasures of foreplay, the idealized thrills of perversion, and the breakthrough of actual violence (toward self or others) during love making on a hierarchal continuum of playfulness. Foreplay involves undressing, facing each other naked, and stimulating each other in ways other than genital to genital contact. Shedding one's shame over nakedness and gently overcoming the partner's shame are important tasks here (Kernberg, 1991). Yet another important aspect of foreplay is the emergence into consciousness of pregenital drive derivatives (e.g., sucking, biting, licking, showing, looking, squeezing, and smelling). Fears regarding the real and imaginary blemishes of one's body also have to be put aside. For all this, genuine self-regard and trust in the partner's goodness is needed, and so is a robust capacity for playfulness. In perversion, too, the two partners enter into an unspoken agreement of suspending judgement for a while. Thus, seemingly sadomasochistic activities such as handcuffing, wax-dripping, paddling, whipping, boot-licking, and even "stronger" acts, including bondage and discipline (Stoller, 1973) retain a pretend quality and remain enjoyable. The difference between pregenital indulgences of foreplay and sexual practices considered perverse, however, lies in the degree of ego-autonomy and reality testing that is maintained; Peller (1954) says that an activity ceases to be play when it cannot be stopped at will. Acts in foreplay are optional and under ego control; acts in sexual perversion are mandatory and id-driven. A naked man frolicking in his wife's panties right in front of her eyes, teasing her fondly as she bursts out laughing, before they settle on sexual intercourse or after they have had it, is being playful. A cross-dresser who is totally unable to have any pleasure without public demonstration of a vestimentary transformation of the self and then, too, can achieve orgasm only through masturbation has a problem. The curious masquerade of transvestism remains less psychopathological, however, than the morbid mutilations associated with transsexualism. While it is a matter of degree, the realm is one of "derailed playfulness" to be sure.

Malignant playfulness

A much more malignant corruption of playfulness is seen among serial killers. Often these deeply troubled (and troubling) individuals "play" with the victims before torturing and murdering them. Needless to add, the "game" is bloody and all one-sided. Their tendency to play "hide and seek" with their official nemeses (e.g., policemen, detectives, etc.) is also mutual only in their imagination. The mocking challenges they pose to legal authorities, by leaving provocative clues and fabricating individualized monikers, betray unconscious guilt and a deep-seated wish to be punished. There is also the variable of grandiosity and a defensively evolved sense of invulnerability involved here. However, what strikes me more is the element of a bizarre and, frankly, rather tragic playfulness in all this. Serial killers appear desperately hungry for a playful father–son relationship, something that most of them have lacked in their backgrounds (Hare, McPherson, & Forth, 1988; Innes, 2006; Stone, 2001). By teasing the police, they are initiating a playful interaction with them. A similar dynamic is evident in Osama bin-Laden's choice of September 11 as the date for the attack against the USA. By flaunting the established nationwide emergency contact number, 911, bin-Laden was being sadistically "playful".

Having reviewed the phenomena of normal and pathological playfulness and the developmental considerations pertinent to them, we are now prepared to tackle the role of playfulness in the therapeutic situation.

The role of playfulness in clinical work

Winnicott (1967) made pioneering observations on the role of playfulness in psychotherapy and his brilliant but outrageous protégé,

Masud Khan, applied some of these ideas to the work of adult psychoanalysis (Hopkins, 2000). More recently, Ehrenberg (1990), Mahon (2004) and Coen (2005) have made significant contributions to this realm. Winnicott, for whom the capacity to play was the hallmark of mental health, declared that

> Psychotherapy has to do with two people playing. The corollary of this is that when playing is not possible then the work done by the therapist is directed towards bringing the patient from a state of not being able to play into a state of being able to play. [1967, p. 38]

Such ever-present and subtle role of playfulness in the clinical situation is a far cry from the use of formal "play technique" (Klein, 1923) in the treatment of children, regardless of whether one equates the child's play with the adult's free association or not, and regardless of whether one's interpretative efforts are preceded by educative and ego-preparatory remarks (A. Freud, 1929) or not. Winnicott's concern—and mine—is not "play" as an activity but "playfulness" as an attitude, even though the latter can only be discerned through the units of action in the clinical dyad. At the risk of repeating myself, such an attitude is one of light-heartedness, blurring of the reality–unreality boundary, imaginativeness, and linguistic innovation. According to Ehrenberg (1990), "in playfulness, words do not stand for what they literally mean, and paradox is often a critical element" (p. 76). She adds that "playfulness" with others assumes a sense of mutuality and, in a dialectical fashion, strengthens that mutuality. Both parties involved in a playful interaction derive pleasure from it. Ehrenberg notes that

> Playfulness can include the use of humor and irony, affectionate kinds of teasing, banter and repartee, joint fantasy, and a host of other possibilities. Because it can be effective as a means to communicate on multiple levels simultaneously, and can allow for transcending communicative barriers, it can work to cut through distance, and to expand the range of communication. [*ibid.*]

Moreover, all parties involved in the "playful" interaction instantly and intuitively recognize its nature. A look at the following clinical vignette would attest to this.

Clinical vignette 6

Sy Goldman, a bright corporate attorney in his forties, is in analysis with me. His chronically, even if subtly, frustrating childhood experience with his cold and "proper" mother has left him resentful and inconsolable: "I am a person for whom ninety per cent is not enough," he says. His disdain for his bumbling father has also contributed to an inward sense of weakness and, despite success and accolades, feeling bereft in this world. He hates being a Jew and has concocted all sorts of ways to come across as a Gentile.

We work well together. Time passes. Layer by layer, his distress unfolds. Holding, "affirmative interventions" (Killingmo, 1989) coupled with interpretations proper and reconstructions gradually help him. He begins to feel better. He becomes more confident overall and especially in his identity as a Jew. He joins a synagogue. However, he retains "soft spots" and is vulnerable to regressions. One day, while preparing for a dinner speech at a prestigious club, he says to me, "Mind you, I am not ashamed of being a Jew." I spontaneously respond, "That is something Richard Nixon might have said." Sy instantly knows what I mean, bursts out into laughter, saying, "Fuck you for calling me Nixon ... That's really helpful!"

In this instance, both the patient and I instantly knew what had happened. We shared the insight that this defence interpretation provided. We also experienced a sense of mutuality and pleasure.

Clinical vignette 7

Sarah Korn, a fifty-or-so-year-old estate agent, is given to talking profusely and incessantly in her sessions. She is always socially busy and overbooked. Her mind is cluttered, though without ever eliminating the one preoccupation she claims to be tortured by, which pertains to her "boring" husband. Day after day, week after week, and month after month, I hear accounts of situations where he appeared uninterested, uninteresting, mindless, and "boring". When I question her need to repeat this, Sarah stops for a while, but shows little actual curiosity regarding what might underlie this pattern. Gradually, things change. My patience bears fruit and my interventions take hold. Now the transference re-creation of a self-absorbed mother who had little mental space for the little Sarah comes to our attention. As an adult, Sarah is driven to make sure that I will listen, take her in, and keep her there (i.e., in my mind). The need to repeat betrays the dread of my having forgotten what she had told me. Sarah's manic defence lessens, though the characterological propensity in this direction does not entirely leave her.

One day, she comes in, lies down on the couch, and says, "I have nothing to say today," and I instantly respond, "But my fear is that you will still talk." Sarah bursts out laughing and says, "You know, you are right. I cannot stay quiet for too long . . ." And the session proceeds in a somewhat more meaningful way.

Like the previous clinical vignette, this one demonstrates the mutuality-building (and, of course, arising from previously existing mutuality) impact of a well-timed, light-hearted comment. The enhanced sense of our "being in this together" and sharing the knowledge of where we might beneficially go next permits further interpretative deepening of the clinical material. Undoubtedly, such exchanges can only take place if the clinical situation is experienced as a "felicitous space" (Bachelard, 1969) or "a safe place necessary to allow the flowering of useful thoughts" (Loewald, 1987, p. 177). A development of this sort, in turn, depends on the mutual fit between the analyst and the analysand, the affective state of their moment-to-moment relatedness, and the analyst's having renounced a rigid clinging to "proper" technique. According to Corradi Fiumara (2009),

> It is a question of overcoming rigidity and advancing towards the sort of spontaneity that allows for psychic leaps. It sounds paradoxical to say that immediate reactions function in the domain of rigidity, while creative actions involve the capacity to leap into staying still, into waiting for the good inspiration. [*ibid.*, p. 69]

Not all goes well all the time, however. The analyst's playfulness can fail to find a receptive partner in the patient, resulting in a serious "disruption" (Akhtar, 2007a) of the clinical process, or, if one is fortunate, merely a moment of awkwardness.

Clinical vignette 8

Barbara Wilkins, a thirty-five-year-old librarian, is quite schizoid. She has few friends and is generally mistrustful of people. She is secretive,

> though rationalizes it on the grounds, "who would be interested in me". In her treatment, too, Barbara is reticent and often quiet for long periods of time. A year or so into our halting and staccato collaboration, she comes, lies down on the couch, reports that she had a dream (her first in the course of our work), but immediately adds that she has "completely forgotten it". Seeing her lapse into her usual silence, I say, "Well, in that case, why don't you make one up?" I am upbeat but Barbara does not respond. She remains quiet. Her silence comes across as stony and cold.

Here my playful attempt to pull the patient into the "intermediate area of experience" (Winnicott, 1953) failed miserably. Was it because it was ill-timed and too rushed? Was it because my comment itself was a cheery denial of having felt let down at her "offering" a dream and then taking it back by saying that she forgot it? In other words, did my playfulness reflect a manic defence against hurt and hostility on my part? To what extent did the patient's characterological mistrust of spontaneity contribute to the failure of this intervention? Questions like these must be raised inwardly if genuine progress is to be made in the future work with rigid and withdrawn patients.

Coen's (2005) observations and suggestions come to our rescue in this regard. He reports the rather disastrous consequences of a prematurely playful remark with a very controlled analysand and warns against beginning "treatment by attempting to draw a schizoid patient into play engagement" (p. 827). With characteristic clinical sensitivity, Coen states,

> When a schizoid patient is very serious, concrete, and terrified, shut down, the analyst must respect these terrors and needs for avoidance, protection, control, domination, rejection. The obvious question is when and how to shift into other therapeutic approaches. How long is the analyst's initial welcome, affirmation, validation, tolerance of the schizoid patient's imperative need for control and acceptance to last? The short answer is for the entire length of the treatment. But within the analyst's acceptance of the patient, creative, playful ways must be found to invite the patient to join in sharing a common world. [*ibid.*]

The idea is to enliven the patient's rigid and calcified persona, enhance "mentalization" (Fonagy & Target, 1997), and make what is pathological a bit curious, even humorous, given its anachronistic stance. The analyst's playfulness can become an irreverent challenge to the patient's fantasied omnipotence, fragility, or both. This is especially true in the case of schizoid patients. With less withdrawn patients, especially if they are psychologically minded, the analyst's witty and imaginative prodding can work like an interpretation while yielding pleasure for the analyst and the patient alike.

Clinical vignette 9

> Jack Lieberman, a highly successful businessman in his mid-sixties, is in psychotherapy with me. He has suffered many losses as a child, though his previous treatments did not unearth some of them. Psychologically sophisticated but sentimental, Jack cries readily in movies and upon hearing songs about separation. Vulnerable to loss, he preemptively rejects love. When his wife tells him that she loves him, he habitually responds by saying "No, you don't." Within our work too, the same pattern emerges, though subtly and with less anxious aggressivity. He likes me, recognizes that I am good to him, but finds my interventions "too kind". He attributes them to my being a "good guy" and my possessing some sort of "Eastern wisdom". I note the multiply-determined nature of these observations but regard them as falling within the overall range of what Freud (1912b) called "unobjectionable positive transference". We go on with trying to understand how his traumatic childhood separations from important people have shaped his character.
>
> One day, he asks me why is it that he dreads separation but loves songs and poems about it. I respond, "Come on! You know that there is a difference between a rooster that's run over by a farmer's truck and an elegantly prepared chicken dish." Jack laughs, looks at me admiringly and, more importantly, knowingly with a broad and sunny smile over his face, he asks me, "Did you just make that up?" I say, "Yes," also with a smile.

Once again, we can see how light-heartedness, imaginativeness, and a momentary blurring of professional work and joking results in expansion of ego dominance over the inner world. And this is what playfulness in the therapeutic situation is about: a shared capacity of the partners in the clinical dyad to create new and surprising ways to advance their work, ways that yield pleasure and enjoyment for both parties. Analysis is not fun and games, but it does not have to be ponderous and dull either. The ego freedom that we want our patients to experience in their lives outside of the treatment situations must be fostered within it.

This brings up the tricky issue of responding to playfulness on the patient's part. Psychoanalytic orthodoxy pressures us to not respond in kind, and, indeed, there might be occasions when remaining impassive is best. It is safe to assume that such a stance is based upon the analyst's "diagnosing" the patient's behaviour as "pseudo-playfulness" and largely defensive. However, the imperative to conform to some "ideal" way of analysing must not lead the analyst to become automaton-like. He must have enough freedom to momentarily join in the patient's playfulness and then, as the session proceeds, decide whether that interaction needs to be brought up for scrutiny, shelved for later reference, or regarded as an "unobjectionable" and useful ingredient of the "working alliance" (Greenson, 1965) between him and the patient.

The possibility of "countertransference enactment" is ever present in such moments. Becoming playful (Feiner, 1979; Jacobs, 1986) might occur as a collusion with the patient's conscious or unconscious avoidance of a difficult issue in transference or in his life outside of treatment. At such times, the analytic playfulness can preclude the needed expression of the affect and/or fantasy that is troubling the patient. Consequently, the analyst must monitor the impact of his participation upon the analytic process and realize that his playfulness can be experienced by some patients as seductive, teasing, provocative, or dismissive. What also remains true is that such monitoring on the analyst's part can itself reveal important data about the state of transference, countertransference, and the nuanced intrapsychic agenda linking the two partners in the clinical dyad at any given time.

Concluding remarks

In this chapter, I have attempted to elucidate the concept of playfulness. I have described it as a character trait and/or interactional pattern comprising light-heartedness, spontaneity, pleasure experienced in the context of mutuality, and a transient suspension of the reality–unreality boundary. I have traced the development of playfulness back to the matrix of early parent–child relationship and even to certain "hard-wired" constitutional capacities of the child. I have noted that, like any other mental capacity, playfulness is subject to the encroachment of psychopathology. To highlight this point, I have described five psychopathological syndromes: (i) deficient playfulness, (ii) pseudo-playfulness, (iii) inhibited playfulness, (iv) derailed playfulness, and (v) malignant playfulness. Finally, I have tried to demonstrate the application of these ideas to the therapeutic situation and, with the help of illustrative vignettes, showed the uses, advantages, and risks of playfulness within the clinical dyad.

Despite covering considerable ground, I am aware that many important areas pertaining to playfulness have remained unaddressed in this contribution. The first such area pertains to *gender*. While differences in the patterns and specific activities of play in the two sexes have been documented (Gilligan, 1982), little in psychoanalytic literature sheds light upon the similarities and differences between the two genders *vis-à-vis* playfulness. Is it possible that men are more playful with men and women with women? After all, the dimmed light upon reality can stir up more intense sexual impulses in the context of heterosexual relationships than can be contained within the confines of playfulness. But, if this is so, are there differences between heterosexual and homosexual individuals in regard to playfulness? Could it be that heterosexual men and women are more comfortably playful with their respective sexes, but homosexual men and women with those of the opposite sex? Do we really know this? Furthermore, what might be social and clinical implications of it?

A related area is that of *culture*. All sorts of questions arise as one pays attention to this variable. For instance, are there cultures (e.g., Latin American) that permit more playfulness than others (e.g., Germanic)? Is it a matter of "more" or "less" playfulness, or do different cultures have different forms of playfulness? Can one be playful with one's elders to a comparable extent in different cultures? What about playfulness across the boundaries of race, ethnicity, religion, and social class? And, is the extent of playfulness permissible at the workplace comparable in different cultures? Clearly, more thought is needed here.

Finally, there is the role of the public media. While idiosyncratic factors of individual experience, especially during the formative years of childhood, determine the blossoming or withering away of playfulness in a given individual, the constant bombardment of senses by the media also has a role here. A less than ponderous tone to the newspaper coverage, a frolicsome air on the morning television shows, a rib-tickling monologue on talk shows, and a mandatory sense of levity injected into television commercials go a long way in creating "induced playfulness" in the audience. A public media climate that is unerringly dour might have the opposite impact. Media and the celebrities that populate it uphold a modal, if not ideal, way of behaviour and invite identification with it. Consequently, playful media makes us a little more playful.

All in all, playfulness turns out to be far more complex a phenomenon than it superficially appears. It is a deft mixture of light-hearted spontaneity, bold paradox, and harmless pleasure. The episode involving Winnicott's revolver at the beginning of this contribution contained all these elements and so does the following sharp retort by Gandhi. Upon being asked by an American news reporter as to what he thought about Western civilization, Gandhi said, "I think that will be a good idea!"

PART II
DEATH

CHAPTER FOUR

Mortality

> "Friends die and the mystery envelops us. Something here calls for attention. With tenacious thought it might be grasped and understood. But from the nothingness toward which our lives are tending we are easily distracted. We lay it aside. Values are winnowed by bereavement and pain, by loneliness and guilt, but death is the ultimate flail"
>
> (Wheelis, 1975, p. 88)

We have a complex relationship with death. To call our attitude towards death "ambivalent" is to oversimplify matters. The gamut of our affects and fantasies involving death is far more wide-ranging than can be captured by the plebeian and workman-like adjective. Let us look a little closely at what we have at hand here. To begin with, we feel a certain unease about the topic of death, especially if it involves that of our own. A shudder of fear rocks our hearts as we contemplate our non-existence. We may or may not like ourselves but, by God, we are hardly at ease in saying goodbye to "dear old me". As a result, we pretend that it is not going to happen to us. We play mental games with ourselves and run after the mirage of immortality. We tell ourselves that by staying healthy we can postpone death (perhaps, forever?), overlooking that people get killed in freak accidents all the time and are even randomly murdered because they have been mistaken to be someone else by a drug-ravaged or blithely forgetful hit-man.

Anxiety about the limited nature of our existence delivers us to the cushion of handed-down magic as well. We open the windows to religious belief and dreams of heaven, hell, reincarnation, or the continuation of our "souls" one way or the other. Beguiled and beguiling, we permit ourselves all sorts of illusions and all shades of plea-bargaining in order to save our lives, so to speak. A recent Newsweek-Belief.net survey (Adler, 2005) revealed that over eighty-five per cent of people in the USA believe in life after death (e.g., heaven or hell, reincarnation, or some other form of continuation of the soul's existence). However, such defensive manoeuvres do not exhaust the list of our reactions to the thought of our deaths. We are also puzzled and intrigued. Our epistemic instinct exhorts us and we concoct elaborate hypotheses about near-death and after-death phenomena, though, slyly, we refer to the latter as "after-life" phenomena. We turn our hapless anguish on its head and crack jokes about the "Grim Reaper". We wax poetic about death. We paint scenes of dying, write stories and screenplays, make films about terminal illness, and stage operas involving death. Injecting imagination and pleasure into what seemed morbid and frightening allows us a good night's sleep. The horrid witch of mortality becomes the maudlin muse of our creativity.

This is not a contemporary or passing fad, however. The panorama of dread, mockery, sentimentalization, denial, "change of function" (Hartmann, 1939), and creativity involving death has existed since time immemorial. From Buddha to Freud, from the Sufi poets of Persia and Afghanistan to the twentieth century existentialists of Western Europe, and from the ancient Hindu mystics down to California-style gurus of today, contemplative thought has invariably found the question of death as central to life. Freud's (1920g, p. 38) declaration that "the aim of all life is death" was long preceded by the great Urdu poet, Mirza Asad-Ulla Khan Ghalib's (1797–1869) lyrical pronouncement that "ishrat-e-qatra hai darya mein fanaa ho jaana". Literally translated, this means that the greatest ecstasy for a drop is to fall upon a river and become one with it.

Such a sentiment not only accommodates the inevitability of death, but ascribes to it a certain sense of desirability and even pleasure ("ishrat" literally means delight). Ghalib, however, is not content with portraying death as a joyous culmination of a long journey. He adds that without the awareness of its finiteness, life would not be as enjoyable at all. In his words, "na ho marna to jeenay ka maza kya?"

This is only one perspective, however. An opposite viewpoint also exists, which regards death as the ultimate humiliation and a great narcissistic injury. Death, from this perspective, is something to be feared, despised, and combated. In the first perspective, the fear of death is moral cowardice, which results in immature clinging to illusions. In the second perspective, acceptance of death is melancholic nihilism and a pathetic rationalization of low self-esteem. But let me not get ahead of myself. Instead, allow me to first address the elusive and controversial concept of "death instinct" (Freud, 1920g). Following this, I return to the "death-averse" and "death-accepting" perspectives mentioned above. Then, I try to elucidate how life and death are not are categorically apart as they seem to be on surface. I conclude with pulling this material together and raising some questions for us to consider.

The death instinct

Based upon observations regarding children's turning traumatic experiences into play, certain analysands' returning over and over again to painful past experiences, the behaviour of those who must go repeatedly through similar calamities, and the dreadful preoccupations of war veterans, Freud suggested that there might be a self-destructive "daemonic force" (1920g, p. 35) at work in them. This force worked in opposition to the pleasure principle and was aligned with a fundamental attribute of mind that searched for reduction of all excitation to quiescence. At its deepest, this search for quiescence—the "Nirvana principle"—was aimed at returning the living organism to its previous, inorganic state. Freud (1920g) thus gave voice to his celebrated though controversial concept of the "death instinct". A threat to the self at birth, this force is deflected outward by the influence of libido and ego using the agency of somatic musculature. Freud termed this outwardly deflected part of the death instinct the "aggressive instinct". In *The Ego and the Id* (1923b), Freud added that the death instinct operates silently. In *Civilization and Its Discontents,* he emphasized that "aggressive instinct is the derivative and the main representative of the death instinct" (1930a, p. 122). In "Analysis terminable and interminable" (1937c), Freud again referred to the death instinct and related masochism, negative therapeutic reaction, and unconscious guilt to its derivative, the aggressive drive. And, finally, in *An Outline of Psycho-analysis,* he reiterated his formulation of "two basic instincts" (1940a [1938], p. 148), one to establish unities and the other to undermine connections and destroy things. He emphasized that the "concurrent and mutually opposing action of the two basic instincts gives rise to the whole variegation of the phenomena of life" (*ibid.*, p. 149).

Freud acknowledged borrowing the expression "Nirvana principle" from Barbara Low, a Sanskrit expert. The notion of "death instinct", thus, from the beginning, had an Eastern touch. Gustav Fechner, the renowned physicist whose "constancy principle" led Freud to the "Nirvana principle", was himself involved in Buddhism (Jones, 1957). And, Romain Rolland, from whom Freud (1930a) obtained the related concept of "oceanic feeling", was an avid reader and biographer of the nineteenth-century Indian mystics, Sri Ramakrishna Paramahansa and Swami Vivekananda. The Indian mystic tradition was, thus, a background conceptual source for Freud's death instinct. This may have been part of why the concept appeared alien to Western minds. With the exception of Klein (1933, 1935, and 1952b), her followers, and Eissler (1971), most subsequent analysts laid the postulate of death instinct to rest. In the Kleinian tradition, however, the concept remains, and it is utilized largely to explain mental operations that seek to destroy sublime thought, well-synthesized ego attributes, and the capacity for in-depth object relations. Rosenfeld (1971), for instance, states that

> The death instinct can not be observed in its original form, since it always becomes manifest as a destructive process directed against objects and the self. These processes seem to operate in their most virulent form in severe narcissistic conditions. [p. 169]

Further nuance is given to this idea by Feldman (2000, 2009) who, in discussing the manifestations of the death instinct in the consulting room, declares that

> this drive does not actually seem to be directed towards death, although threats of death or annihilation, and a fascination with omnipotent destruction, may contribute to its power and its addictive hold on the individual, as well as its destructive impact on any analytic work. We are often aware of the conscious gratification the patient obtains from attacking and distorting the meaning and value both of the analyst's thinking and of his work, as well as his own capacities for thought and creativity, although the gratification is often unconscious. . . . In a certain sense, of course, these activities are murderous and suicidal, but I'm suggesting that their primary aim is not totally to destroy life, but to take the life out. [2009, pp. 98–99]

A similar sentiment is to be found in two other recent papers on death instinct. Schmidt-Hellerau (2006) attempts to reformulate the death drive in object relations terms. Instead of a "dis-objectilizing function" (Green, 1999), which obliterates the self and the object, she proposes that, under the influence of death drive, self and object remain intact but are cathected with negative energy. This results in various "categories of blankness" (p. 1083), hypochondria, self-neglect, and states of "dead self" and "dead object". Unlike Schmidt-Hellerau, Kernberg (2009) proposes that the "death drive" is not a primary drive at all. What has been called death drive actually represents "a significant complication of aggression as a major motivational system" (p. 1018). In Kernberg's conceptualization, self-destructive tendencies are not simply aimed at destroying the self, but at destroying significant others as well. Ordinarily, such a tendency manifests through sado-masochism, negative therapeutic reaction, and suicidal tendencies. It is only when a focused, unconscious motivation towards self-destructiveness is evident (for instance, in cases of severe psychopathology) that the designation of "death drive" seems appropriate.

One thing is clear in all this. Regardless of whether the death instinct (or drive) is seen as purely self destructive or only destructive of the self-object relations and their psychic elaborations and mental meanings, it is ultimately seen as something negative, problematic, and harmful to the mind. There is no scope for thinking that "death instinct" might be a loyal and reliable guide to our final destination. In other words, are its psychological repercussions always distress-producing, or can they be the source of reassuring existential lullabies, especially towards the end of life?

A close examination of psychoanalytic literature offers some support for the latter notion. It shows a recurring notion that there is, in humans, a vague, drive-like, internal pull towards the loss of the boundaries, if not the existence, of the psychic self. Concepts that allude to this internal pull include (1) the merger fantasies, often associated with feeding and with sleep (Lewin, 1950); (2) the deep seated wish for loss of human identity by "metamorphosis" (Lichtenstein, 1963); (3) the everlasting wish for "the lost, original union with the mother" (Jacobson, 1964, p. 39); (4) in the context of neonatal life, "the drive to return to an earlier state where all was gratified automatically" (Stone, 1971, p. 236); (5) man's eternal yearning to recapture the "co-anesthetically remembered harmony of dual-unity stage" (Mahler, 1971, p. 186); (6) the "search for oneness" (Kaplan, 1977); (7) neonates "inborn and immediate wish to return to the intrauterine state" (Chasseguet-Smirgel, quoted in Akhtar, 1991b, p. 751) and man's "nostalgia for primary narcissism" (Chasseguet-Smirgel, 1984, p. 29); (8) the "someday" and "if only" fantasies (Akhtar, 1991a); (9) an attempted reconciliation of "everything" and "nothing" fantasies, which occurs "transiently in dreamless sleep and in the ecstasy of orgasm—but the promise of permanence can be realized only after our individual lives are over" (Shengold, 1991, p. 7). To be sure, these concepts have diverse theoretical foundations, involve fantasy content not attributable to instinctual primitivity, and contain an unmistakable libidinal admixture with aggression.

Yet, collectively, these notions do demand contemporary reconceptualizations of the death instinct concept. Such examination might confirm the ubiquitous existence in humans of a deep-seated wish for the loss of self-boundaries, perhaps an echo of an early desire for (and memory of) fusion with the mother. It might be that this preverbal pull subsequently accrues fantasies from various levels of psychosexual development. Death, too, may enter this scenario, though much after infancy and childhood, perhaps truly not even until middle age. From then onward, the deep-seated desire for fusion with mother might become intermingled with a longing for peace via death; thus, a "death instinct" has been set into motion. On the other hand, individuals who are traumatized by early losses through death, or themselves have faced early life-threatening crises, might incorporate the notion of death into this substrate of fusion/oblivion seeking much earlier (Akhtar, 2001; Settlage, 2001). They might give evidence of possessing a "death instinct" even before middle age. Such a formulation of "death instinct" is clearly different from the original one by Freud (1920g). In this reconceptualization, both *death* and *instinct* are words that seem misplaced.

As one begins to reconsider such matters, yet another conundrum surfaces. This pertains to the fact that Freud often used the term "death instinct" in its plural form. On at least eight occasions in *Beyond the Pleasure Principle* (1920g, pp. 47, 49, 53 twice, 57, 60, 61, 63), in a letter to Max Eitingon (20 February 1920, cited in the Editor's Note to Freud's 1920 paper, p. 4), in *The Ego and the Id* (1923b, pp. 46, 54, 59), in his succinct version of the libido theory (Freud, 1923a, p. 258), and in *The Economic Problem of Masochism* (1924c, p. 160), Freud talks of "death instincts" instead of "death instinct". This linguistic usage has received little attention, though it certainly appears curious. What could he have meant by "death instincts"? Are there many of them? I do not know. However, four possible explanations of Freud's use of the plural denomination are:

- *It is an aesthetic and formal accommodation to the designation "life instincts"* (which subsumed sexual and self-preservatory instincts and, therefore, could legitimately be rendered in the plural form), an expression Freud also uses. However, it is difficult to swallow that a writer of his great excellence and rigour would succumb to a phonetic gimmick of such variety.
- *It is an anomaly produced by the English translation of Freud's original work in German.* This idea falls flat on its face when one finds that the rendition of "death instinct" in its plural form is as frequent in the original work as in its translated form (Peter Hoffer, personal communication, January 2010).

- *It is a manifestation of the defence that has come to be known as "denial by exaggeration"* (Fenichel, 1945; Sperling, 1963). This mechanism rests upon making a threatening id derivative or superego command into a gross caricature. By overstating the issue at hand, an air of mockery or maudlin sentimentality is injected, which helps to minimize the threat to the ego posed by the situation. Extrapolating this idea to the issue under consideration makes one wonder if referring to "death instincts" helped Freud to ward off the anxiety produced by his dark discovery of the "death instinct".
- *It is an indicator that there might be more than one type of "death instinct"*. Varieties of death instinct might exist along the lines of intensity (mild *vs.* strong), energic regulation (bound *vs.* unbound), libidinal admixture (eroticized *vs.* non-eroticized), age-specificity (developmentally appropriate *vs.* anachronistic), and even its aim (malignant *vs.* benign).

The last-mentioned possibility is especially intriguing, since it can help to explain the divergent perspectives on death itself: death as a threat to life *vs.* death as a welcome relief from life. Here, again, the West–East cultural difference comes into play, but matters are perhaps larger than that. The view of death as fundamentally unacceptable might be a manifestation of "malignant" death instinct. The view of death as acceptable and, after a certain age, even desirable, might be the product of "benign" death instinct. The "malignant" variety of death instinct might be responsible for attacks on linking, black holes in the mind, autoimmune disorders, and intense sadomasochism. The "benign" variety of death instinct might be responsible for positive emptiness, dreamless sleep, fallow states of mind, and the psychic pause that often precedes a creative act. If the distinction along these lines holds, then the phenomenological scene involving the two death instincts would appear quite different. It would be evident that the "malignant" variety marches to the drumbeat of impending self-implosion, while the "benign" variety sings soothing lullabies for eternal rest. Clearly, further thinking and newer terminology are needed here. The contradictory views of the "death instinct", as an inner menace or a reliable and even reassuring aspect to man's final destination, especially need to be reconciled. This bifurcation of perspectives is our next stop.

Freud's todesangst

Freud's declarations that "the fear of death has no meaning to a child" (1900a, p. 254) and that the unconscious "does not believe in its own death; it behaves as if it were immortal" (1915b, p. 296) have become shibboleths of mainstream psychoanalytic theorizing—whatever little of that does exist—upon the issue of death. Fitting like hand and glove into the Western (and, especially, North American) unease about the finite nature of man's existence, the idea that there is no such thing as one's death in the unconscious became firmly ensconced in our literature, overlooking the doubt cast upon its veracity by the later views of the Master himself.

Two examples of these should suffice. Freud's (1920g) proposal of "death instinct" as one of the two central forces (the other being "life instinct") of human motivation puts death squarely into the unconscious; after all, it is the system unconscious that is the magical powerhouse where instincts dwell and various forms of psychic energy meld into each other. (Besides the bound and free energies and representations of the two great instinctual drives (the life and death instincts), the "dynamic unconscious" also contains material accrued by "primal repression", material pushed down by the forces of "repression", and primal fantasies representing phylogenetic schemata. This calls the prevalent notion that the unconscious is unstructured into question.) Indeed, it was the dreaded implosion of the self by the operation of death instinct that led to its forceful externalization and creation of the destructive drive. In this conceptualization, death is clearly present in the unconscious and so is the fear of it. Klein's (1948) later elaboration of those notions is a testimony to such assertion. She states,

> If we assume the existence of a death instinct, we must also assume that in the deepest layers of the mind there is a response to this instinct in the form of fear of annihilation of life . . . The layers arising from the inner working of the death instinct is the first cause of anxiety. [p. 29]

This brings up the second concept of Freud (1923b), which contradicts his own assertion made over two decades before that there is no death in the unconscious. Here, I am referring to his notion of *todesangst,* translated as fear of death (p. 58). Freud notes that the mechanism of fear of death is that "the ego relinquishes its narcissistic libidinal cathexis in a very large measure—that is, that it gives up itself, just as it gives up some external object in other cases in which it feels anxiety" (p. 58).

The shift in Freud's thinking from the absence of death in the unconscious to the central position he accorded to the death instinct is striking. Although Freud had been exposed during childhood to major losses (e.g., the departure of his beloved nursemaid, the repeated pregnancies of his mother) and death (of his younger brother, Julius, when Freud was nearly four years old), the events that perhaps contributed strongly to the shift in his thinking happened soon after he turned sixty. He was suffering from cancer. His sons were involved in war. He lost his daughter, Sophie, suddenly, in 1920, and his beloved grandson, Heinerle, in 1923. Devastated by these losses, Freud said that "fundamentally, everything has lost its meaning for me" (letter to Kata and Lajos Levy, 11 January, 1923, quoted in Eissler, 1978, p. 229).

Given such background, it is hardly surprising that Freud would talk about the temptation for the ego to give up its own structure and its ties to objects. While he related such an inward pull to melancholia, later analysts (Guntrip, 1969; Lichtenstein, 1963) went a step further and declared that the ego's wish to renounce the world might not be pathological, but a sort of "built-in" mechanism that stakes its claim on the psyche from the earliest periods of life. Despite the implication that the fear of death arises *de novo,* other psychoanalysts preferred to view it as a derivative of other sources of anxiety. In this predilection, they were lulled into this sort of thinking by Freud who, as we well recognize, could contradict himself with ease. In 1926, he stated that "the fear of death should be regarded an analogous to the fear of castration" (1926d, p. 130). This notion was further propagated by Bromberg and Schilder (1933), and McClelland (1964). The latter noted that the visualization by men of death as an old man with a scythe supports the equation of fear of death and fear of castration.

However, as reported in greater detail by Stolorow (1973), castration anxiety was not the only dysphoric concern that became associated with fear of death. The latter was regarded to be a derivative of the fear of separation or complete and final object loss (Anthony, 1940; Bromberg & Schilder, 1933; Natterson & Knudson,

1965; Norton, 1963) as well. Yet another perspective that evolved considered fear of death to be a derivative of fear of being punished and, therefore, a form of dreaded assault upon the ego by the superego (Chadwick, 1929; Zilboorg, 1938). Freud (1923b) himself emphasized that

> To the ego, living means the same as being loved—being loved by the superego, which here again appears as the representative of the id. The superego fulfils the same function of protecting and saving that was fulfilled in earlier days by the father and later by Providence or Destiny. But when the ego finds itself in an excessive real danger which it believes itself unable to overcome by its own strength, it is bound to draw the same conclusion. It sees itself deserted by all protecting forces and lets self die. Here, moreover, is once again the same situation as that which underlay the first great anxiety-state of birth and the infantile anxiety of longing—the anxiety due to separation from the protecting mother. [p. 58]

A little over forty years later, Wahl (1965) more clearly spelled out the connection between "infantile thanatophobia" and guilt-producing death wishes against parents during childhood.

> These destructive hating thoughts are doubly frightening since the child not only fears the loss of his parents through the operation of his death wishes, but also, since he reasons by the law of Talion (to think a thing is to do a thing; to do a thing is to endure an equal and similar punishment to the self), he becomes fearful of his own death. [p. 140]

Other underlying sources of fear of death have also been described. These include infantile fears of darkness (Chadwick, 1929) and suffocation (Harnik, 1930). Even the fear of ego loss by overwhelming sexual excitement has been seen to contribute to the fear of death. Fenichel (1945) states that

> "Dying" has become an expression for the sensations of an overwhelming panic, that is, for the distorted conception which these patients have formed of orgasm. Every type of excitement tends toward ultimate relaxation. In cases in which the achievement of such relaxation is regarded as the terrible sensation of loss of one's ego, it may be identified with "death" and on occasions when other persons would hope for sexual excitement, death may be feared. [p. 209]

Moving on to recent writings on the subject, one notices that, in accordance with the trend in contemporary psychoanalysis at large, the contributions are far less reductionistic. Death instinct, death anxiety, and fantasies involving death are now located in the broader context of ego-psychology, self-coherence, and object relations. Fayek (1980, 1981), for instance, notes that the main problem posed by the "death instinct" concept lies in the difficulty of distinguishing its psychic representations and symbolic forms. This difficulty is compounded by the fact that we are looking for symbols of something that has never been experienced. Fayek, however, speculates that the patient's vocabulary around the themes of termination might offer a glimpse into the metaphorical operation and/or representation of death. He adds that

> . . . death is the experience of the other or an experience with the other but never with the self. Therefore, the symbolization of death has to be looked for within narcissism and especially within the emergency of secondary narcissism from its primary form. [1980, p. 456]

Fayek (1981) emphasizes that the idea of death as a narcissistic wound results from the refusal to consider death as one's own; it is seen as coming from outside the ego's omnipotence. It does not "belong" to one, as it were. "Death is an absence that is present" (*ibid.*, p. 319).

Another significant contribution to the psychoanalytic study of feelings and fantasies about death has been made by Blacher (1983), who interviewed a number of patients resuscitated after cardiac arrest. They gave evidence of fantasies of rebirth (i.e., coming back as a newborn infant), and resurrection (i.e., coming back as oneself after having died). According to Blacher, their religious background contributed to these ideas but was not sufficient as an explanation, since not all were religious and there were idiosyncratic emendations to the "rebirth" and "resurrection" fantasies that could be traced to individual childhood experiences. The fantasies provided psychological support and helped to diminish anxiety in the face of death. Blacher concluded that, opposite to Freud's (1915b) conviction that no one can contemplate his own death, "these patients can think of death because they contemplate a life after dying—either a return to their regular lives or an immortality" (p. 69). The powerful "holding" impact of internalized culture and, most probably, of a preponderance of good internal objects made this possible.

More recently, in tracing the reworking and refinement of "object constancy" (Hartmann, 1952; Mahler, Pine, & Bergman, 1975) during adult development, I have stated that

> Middle age mobilizes a final mourning of the mute and unexpressed self representations. This is accompanied by broadening of the core self-representation and the compensatory deepening of what one indeed has become. Object constancy is reworked as aggression and envy toward the youth, including one's offspring can no longer be denied, and identifications with one's parents, with all their implicit oedipal ambivalent are buttressed (Kernberg, 1980). Finally, during old age, as one approaches death, a deep and post-ambivalent view of the world that one has lived in and is about to leave needs to be developed in order for this final transition to be smooth. [Akhtar, 1994, p. 445]

Finally, Langs' (1997, 2004) views on death anxiety must be mentioned. According to him, anxiety about death comes in three forms: (a) existential death anxiety, (b) predatory death anxiety, and (c) predator death anxiety. The first refers to the discomfort felt at the personal prospect of dying, the second to the conscious and unconscious dread of being annihilated, and the third to the consequences of destroying others. All three seem to originate from the death instinct, though only the first one constitutes death anxiety in the sense under discussion here. Actually, all the terms used in this realm leave something to be desired. "Fear of death" locates the sources of distress in the outside world and allows little space for intrapsychic aspects to such dread; after all, fear refers to an emotional response associated with anticipation or awareness of plausible danger from the outside world. "Death anxiety" does the opposite, for we know that anxiety refers to danger that is imaginary and internal in origin. Replacing both these terms by "death phobia" solves one problem and creates another. "Phobia" invariably contains an admixture of fear and anxiety. Using this term, therefore, allows for a combination of external and internal factors to be responsible for the dread associated with the anticipation of death. However, the implication in the term "phobia" of it being an exaggerated and ego-compromising phenomenon precludes its use for subtler and subterranean forms of distress pertaining to anticipation of death. This might appear to be phenomenological hair-splitting, but its implications for our view of what is responsible for "death anxiety" is far from trivial.

Another thing to notice is that while these more recent contributions underscore the object relational context of "death anxiety", they hardly mask that this phenomenon has been viewed in the psychoanalytic literature from two fundamentally different perspectives.

One regards it to be a *primary* phenomenon and a subjective reverberation of the death instinct (Freud, 1920g; Klein, 1948) which threatens life from within not only at the outset of life, but throughout the course of the life span. The other viewpoint holds that death anxiety is *secondary* and a repetition of the mortal terror lived through in the early bio-traumatic situations of birth (Rank, 1924) and prolonged separation from the mother during early infancy (Freud, 1923b; Stern, 1977). Additionally, it could be derived from castration anxiety, guilt, and other childhood fears that have become exaggerated due to traumatic experiences. An implicit question here is whether "death anxiety" is a regressive disguise for concerns pertaining to object loss and/or castration, or are the latter developmentally "upward displacements" of the more primal fear of death? Regardless of which of the two perspectives one contributes to, the end result is that the idea of death and its expectations are seen as distressing and capable of stirring up all sorts of unpleasant emotions. It is, therefore, not surprising that all sorts of defensive manoeuvres are deployed against "death anxiety". These include (i) *denial*, which makes one feel immune to the passage of time and one's approaching mortality; (ii) *seeking refuge in religion* and its assurances that one's soul would continue to exist and might even unite with loved ones who have already passed away; (iii) *extracting vicarious reassurance* by reading about train and automobile collisions, and other natural disasters which can yield "egocentric self-delight expressed in the exclamation: 'it is not I who was executed last night; it is not I who was killed in this automobile accident, or train wreck, or earthquake'" (Zilboorg, 1943, p. 469); and (iv) *counterphobic actions* (e.g., dangerous sports) to prove that we are fearless and not afraid of death.

Ghalib's Ishrat-e-qatra

Contrary to that anxiety-producing portrayal of death, there is the viewpoint that death is integral to the life experience, an inherent and, even, enriching component of it. While I, for reasons of familiarity, have chosen the great Urdu poet of the mid-nineteenth century, Mirza Asad-Ullah Khan Ghalib, a similar line of thought can be readily found in sources as diverse as advaitic Hindu mysticism (Vallabheneni, 2005) and mid-twentieth century European existentialism (Heidegger, 1949; Kierkegaard, 1957; Sartre, 1956), Zen Buddhism and Messianic Christianity, and Orthodox Judaism, and Sufi poetry of Persia and the work of certain philosophically inclined psychoanalysts (Corradi Fiumara, 2009; May, 1950; Wheelis, 1966). In some of these perspectives, death is not viewed as an enemy of life. Life and death are not separate but bound together by God's will. "The Lord gives and the Lord has taken away; blessed be name of the Lord" (Job 1:21). Essentially, this perspective holds that death is *a part of life* and not *apart from life*. Far from providing a container for morbid preoccupation, the proponents of this viewpoint regard death as offering a liberating union (reunion?) with the cosmos at large or, at least, a great sense of freedom through renunciation of the individual self. Such freedom can make it possible for the individual to create and re-create his self, breaking the armour of characterological rigidity. In Corradi Fiumara's words,

> The labour of spontaneity does not tread well-worn psychic paths; it develops, instead, through an inner attitude springing from the knowing acceptance of our interlocking experiences of death and birth. As the only form of life capable of living in the awareness of time, and of somehow knowing about death, those who do not attain a sufficient spontaneity have to pretend not to know, and then pretend that they are not pretending, and so forth—in a damaging spiral. [2009, p. 118]

Ghalib thinks alike. However, before proceeding further, it might not be a bad idea to insert a few introductory remarks about him since he remains unfamiliar to vast swathes of Western readers. Born in Agra, the city of the Taj Mahal, in 1797, Ghalib was a classical Urdu and Persian poet who saw the great Mughul Empire collapse and be displaced by the British Empire. According to the Oxford University scholar, Ralph Russell (2000), Ghalib is "one of the greatest poets South Asia ever produced" (p. 8) whose poetry transcended the customary romanticism and earthly preoccupations of the literature of his time. Russell goes on to say that

> . . . in many fundamental respects Ghalib stood alone: his lack of strong sentimental attachment to the old political order, his interest in British achievements and his own lively intelligence and inquiring mind all went to form a distinctive philosophy of life. He is acutely aware of unceasing change. At every moment, something new is coming into being and something is decaying. Reality is infinitely rich, and one who is alive to this can already see things that have not yet come into existence. [p. 103]

Ghalib's statements on various themes (e.g., religion, drinking, love) were not simple exercises in the conventions of the poetry of his time, but expressions of his own unique beliefs and practices. Like many creative geniuses, he was full of contradictions. He largely lived on state patronage, but was also proud of his reputation as a rake. He was capable of writing profoundly religious poetry even though he was quite critical of Islamic scriptures, and, at least on one occasion, playfully wished that he had renounced Islam and become a Hindu (Dalrymple, 2008, p. 41). He was a *bon vivant*, loved to drink, and had many affairs. Yet, there was a melancholic streak about him that perhaps resulted from his exposure to the death of many loved ones. He lost his father at a young age and his only brother during his forties. More importantly, he fathered seven children who were either stillborn or died during early infancy. Ghalib himself, however, lived a long life, acquiring great prestige and popularity towards his old age. His fame spread all over the country and he accumulated a large number of disciples, including many among the ruling British community in India; Sir Thomas Metcalfe (1795–1853), the Agent of the Governor General of India, an amateur Urdu poet himself, frequently sought Ghalib's literary counsel. Ghalib died in Delhi in 1869. He is considered to be the most influential and widely recognized writer of the Urdu language and his poetry is recited and sung not only in India and Pakistan, but also in the South Asian Diaspora around the world. Many movies have been made about his life and many plays have been written about him. The School of Oriental and African Studies at Cambridge University has a section of studies devoted to Ghalib's work.

Returning to the theme of death and Ghalib's discourse on it, we note that death, for him, is the healing hand that cures all the ills of life. Consider, for a moment, his following two couplets (taken from different ghazals) and you might begin to appreciate the point I am trying to make.

> "Ghum-e-hasti ka Asad kis se ho juz marg ilaaj
> Shamma hur rung mein jalti hai sahar hone tak"

Literally translated (and with the resulting loss of prosodic beauty), this couplet means that just in the way the beginning sunlight at the time of dawn relieves the candle from the continued necessity to burn, the arrival of death cures all problems of life. Before going into psychoanalytic speculations about what Ghalib might have in mind here, let me cite another sample from his poetry.

> "Partaw-e-khur se hai, shabnam ko fanaa ki taeem
> Main bhi hoon, ek inaayat ki nazar hone tak."

This one, in literal translation, means that just as the warm rays of sun teach the dew drops the art of vanishing, one kind glance of the Creator will readily draw me back to Him; I exist only until that graceful moment arrives.

Of note in these two examples (and I could have given many others) are the following elements:

- death is recognized to be a natural and expectable event without which life remains incomplete;
- the attitude towards death, which is coming towards us all, is neither ostrich-like denial nor masochistic celebration. It is total acceptance and peaceful waiting;
- an admixture of relief and sacred joy is also seen to be associated with the experience of death.

The metaphors utilized by Ghalib (e.g., "drop–river merger", "sunshine–dew drop connection", "the candle's having to burn until morning") subtly but unmistakably pronounce death to be a merger with something larger than oneself, a return and fusion with the cosmos at large. This is implied to be a pleasant, even ecstatic occurrence. Within the western intellectual tradition, counterparts to Ghalib's vantage point are to be found in accounts of near-death experiences (Greyson, 1984; Stevenson & Greyson, 1979) and certain mainstream psychoanalytic writings. Pollock (1975), for instance, underscored the adaptive aspects of the idea of immortality and traced the origin of the concept of heaven to a regressive symbiotic reunion with the archaic mother as a defence against object loss. His use of qualifiers like "regressive" and "archaic" betrayed the inability to shake loose from traditional psychoanalytic theorizing but his acknowledgement of the potential of pleasure in such experiences was forward-looking. Take a look also at the following excerpt from an essay on aging and death by Madow (1997).

> Most writers describe death as the ultimate loss and it can clearly be seen thus, it is also the final gain of the fusion with mother. On the way, there is an increasing tropism to a more, albeit dependent, sometimes demanding, relationship with caregivers . . . As we age, we physically diminish in size. Our brains shrink and our EEG's become more like a childs tracing. We lose Purkinje cells, affecting our coordination. We lose Betz cells, impairing our motor skills. . . . As we become more incapacitated, we lose our ability to walk and talk, incontinence returns, and we require diapers. We become edentulous and our diet consists of soft foods. We become more sensitive to temperature changes as is the infant. . . . We move psychologically towards a symbiotic state, passing in reverse through modified forms of rapprochement and practicing subphases culminating in an observable and well-circumscribed event—death. [pp. 164, 165, 166]

This seems more in accordance with Ghalib than with Freud. In all fairness, however, it must be acknowledged that Freud took both positions: death is something to be feared, despised, and regarded as an enemy of life (1923b, 1926d), and death is something to be accepted, patiently waited for, and even joyously welcomed for offering us relief from the internal and external conflicts that inherently characterize life (1920g, 1937c). As a result, what appears to be a tension between Ghalib and Freud turns out to be one between the contradictory views of Freud himself. This opens up the possibility that there might be such a thing as an acceptable, or even "good", death. However, before delving into this area, let me briefly address the emotional reactions that generally follow our encounter with the death of loved ones.

A brief digression into the nature of grief

The mere mention of the word "grief" floods the mind with visions of tears and funerals and sounds of wailing and sobbing. Images of crying men and women, rituals of cremation, or of a body being lowered into a freshly dug grave, and tear-soaked words of condolence are among our immediate associations to the word. That it should be so is understandable, for loss of a loved one by death is the most potent trigger of the emotional reaction called grief.

Under ordinary circumstances, this comprises a sequence of gradually unfolding psychic events (Kubler-Ross, 1970; Parkes, 1964, 1972). Shock and *disbelief* ("But I met him just last week and he appeared fine!") are the immediate responses. These are soon replaced by *emotional pain* and a desperate sense of *longing*. Depending upon the gravity of the loss, there might be *physiological disturbances* accompanying this stage. Pacing, sighing, clutching one's chest, pulling at hair, rubbing hands, loss of appetite, and disturbed sleep are often evident. As time passes, the turmoil seems to settle. The lost person is talked about in exalted ways and all his or her blemishes are glossed over; a lost object is an *idealized* object, mused Freud (1917) in his seminal paper "Mourning and melancholia". A mentality of *bargaining* also sets in: "Had I only done this or that, this loss might not have happened". Fleeting moments of *self-blame* appear, although sustained feelings of guilt are not typical of ordinary grief. More often one encounters irritability and even *anger* at the occurrence of the loss in the first place. Sooner or later, this, too, passes. A sense of profound *aloneness* and *sadness* now takes over. The bereaved finds himself or herself *fluctuating* between heartache, pining for the departed one, dull indifference, and the dawn of resigned acceptance of the changed life situation. Gradually, the rays of *hope* appear on the psychic horizon and the potential space for a substitute begins to open up. The night, it seems, is turning into day.

Lest this description appear too schematic or stylized, let me hasten to add a few caveats. *First,* grief comes in waves. It waxes and wanes. Just when recovery seems at hand, one is hit by a fresh upsurge of sorrow. Grief is hardly a linear process. The phases described here are useful largely for didactic purposes; human experience is always more complex than a catalogue of symptoms. *Second,* no mourning is ever complete and, by implication, no lost object of our affection is ever totally given up. It is only moved to a different place in one's heart. The pain diminishes, to be sure, and emotions are not so readily mobilized. The wound turns into a scar, but the story remains. A *third* caveat pertains to the fact that mourning is a process that takes its own time; it takes, for instance, about two years to recover reasonably from the loss of a truly loved one or from the break-up of a serious romantic relationship. The process, like the healing of a bodily wound, cannot be rushed. However, it can be delayed if certain complicating factors happen to be on the scene. Mourning over death, for instance, is prolonged if the death was unexpected, occurred in violent circumstances, was the result of suicide, and if the death left many unsettled accounts, so to speak, between the deceased and the bereaved. Moreover, the greater the impact upon the day-to-day reality of the bereaved, the harder it is to resolve the grief. The sudden death of a wage-earning head of a household is, thus, more difficult to mourn than the passing away of an elderly grandmother who had long been suffering from terminal cancer.

Mourning over the death of a child is profoundly difficult, if not utterly unfathomable. Not only is the occurrence contrary to the natural order of things (e.g., grandparents die first, then parents, then children, and so on), it is tantamount to a murder of dreams and hope for the future. Parents are left with the burden of "survivor's guilt" and find grieving to be a life-long nightmare. The pain is greater when the offspring lost happens to be an adolescent. Having brought the child to the threshold of adulthood and then to lose him or her is truly devastating. The fact that parents are often at cross-purposes with their teenage children further complicates mourning such a loss.

When grief does get stuck or complicated, the manifestations of ordinary mourning get prolonged over time. The tendency to become teary, feel that the deceased is not really dead, or both, normally experienced for a few days or weeks, now extends over months and years. The language changes associated with the acceptance of death (e.g., "Uncle Elvin *is* fond of sweets" changing into "Uncle Elvin *was* fond of sweets") get delayed and the dreams typical of early mourning (e.g., seeing the dead person alive, rescuing him or her from a life-threatening situation) continue long past the first few months.

More significantly, new symptoms appear. The most important among these is a peculiar attitude about the physical possessions of the deceased. Under ordinary circumstances, things left behind by someone dead are (unknowingly) divided into three categories: things that are thrown away (e.g., a toothbrush, socks), things that are given away to the poor (e.g., old clothes, shoes), and things that are kept and passed on as family heirlooms (e.g., jewellery, diplomas, private journals, unfinished manuscripts). Moreover, this disbursement is neither too quick nor too delayed; it usually takes a few weeks to a few months (Akhtar, 2003c). In complicated grief, however, one notices a disregard for time in this context. One either gets rid of the deceased's things immediately (in a magical attempt at denying the significance of what has just happened) or hangs on to them forever, finding oneself haplessly unable to discard these items.

Another development is that things that ought to have been thrown away (e.g., dentures, old underwear, a glass eye, a half empty bottle of cold cream) are kept, held on to in a very strange way. They can neither be used nor thrown away. They cannot even be seen. Looking at them stirs up extremely painful emotions of anxiety, pain, and sadness. These things no longer remain mere physical artefacts; they become what Volkan (1981) has called "linking objects", that is, things that connect the bereaved with the deceased in unspoken and mysterious ways. They are treated in magical ways. The deceased's grave, too, becomes a nidus of complex feelings on the part of the bereaved (see Chapter Six for details). An "obituary addiction" (Volkan, 1981) also develops, whereby an individual with unresolved grief feels compelled to check out the obituary section of the newspaper every day. Not finding the name of a loved one who has died long ago provides an unconscious reassurance; it is almost as if that person is still alive. One thing this description leaves unaddressed is the cause or, to be accurate, the causes, of a grief remaining unresolved. Certainly the depth of attachment one has with the deceased and the external and internal jagged edges left over by his or her departure contribute to the difficulty in mourning. What, however, goes contrary to common sense is that unresolved aggression, if not actual hostility, towards the deceased plays a significant role in "freezing" the process of grief. The dynamics of this are as follows. When there are unspoken hostile and destructive affects and fantasies directed at someone who dies, letting him or her go becomes tantamount to "killing" him or her; this results from the condensation and telescoping of the repressed anger with the reality-dictated necessity of the aggression implicit in moving away from an object. While known to most physicians, one simple fact can hardly be overemphasized: normal grief does not require medical intervention. It is, by definition, a normal process. The attitude that all human suffering is not illness must be maintained; some pains are integral to life. This does not mean that individuals in this state of normal grief might not end up at a physician's door. When this happens, curiosity should be directed at the lack of social and familial support that has led to "medicalizing" a normal process. Parallel to such investigation, the clinical approach should consist of empathic remarks, imparting of information regarding the nature of normal grief, and a relatively hands-off policy, coupled with reassurance of availability should matters become more difficult. If, however, there is growing evidence that the grief is becoming complicated (prolonged emotional distress, unchanged language, difficulty disposing of the deceased's physical possessions, and so on), then active therapeutic interventions do become necessary.

Listening to those with unresolved mourning anguish must be respectful and empathic; loss, after all, is not a pleasant affair. The therapist should allow ample psychological space for the bereaved to elaborate their story. It is advisable to not meddle too much with sharp, intellectual comments. What the suffering of grief needs most is "witnessing" (Poland, 1996). Listening patiently and making occasional, brief, and affirmative remarks that demonstrate that one understands the pain of the patient is generally sufficient. The therapist may help the patient to talk in greater detail and encourage the bringing in of the deceased's photographs for the therapist and the patient to look at together. This would facilitate the emergence of hitherto repressed memories and release pent up emotions.

Such credulous listening and affirmative stance should not, however, eclipse a certain amount of therapeutic scepticism. In listening to someone with pathological grief, one must keep one's "third ear" open for the verbal and non-verbal cues of a hostile attitude in the patient towards the deceased (Reik, 1948). Such hints and allusions should be gathered silently at first. In other words, the tragic motif of grief must be allowed to run its course before one begins to point out that the patient has actually been somewhat ambivalent about the deceased. It is only with the conscious recognition and acceptance of negative feelings towards the dead person that the patient can fully come to grips with his true psychic reality. This step is necessary for the proper resolution of grief. A less known technical ingredient of "re-grief therapy" (Volkan, 1971; Volkan, Cilluffo, & Sarvay, 1975) is the use of linking objects described above. The therapist not only encourages the bereaved to talk more and more openly about his or her feelings of loss but also encourages him or her to bring "linking objects" to the office. Encountering them, touching them, holding them, and reminiscing about them (and, through these, about one's complex feeling towards the lost person) helps to thaw the frozen grief. That inanimate objects should help to revive and resolve emotional reactions about someone who himself or herself has now become inanimate is an amazing paradox that, in the midst of tears, can bring a smile of gratitude to our faces (see also Searles, 1960). That said, let me get back to the loose thread that I have left behind and that pertains to the issue of an acceptable and even "good" death.

The "good-enough death"

Reflecting the majority opinion among the "Western psychoanalysts", Eissler (1955) found the occurrence of death to be always ill-timed and, therefore, inherently frustrating. Eissler believes that

> Death always comes both too early and too late—too early because the ego has rarely realized all its potentialities, and too late because individual life has been a detour leading finally to what it had been at the beginning: nothingness. [p. 142]

In contrast, Weissman (1972), allows for the possibility of what he calls "appropriate death". He defines this as

> one in which there is reduction of conflict, compatibility with the ego-ideal, continuity of significant relationships, and consummation of prevailing wishes. In short, an appropriate death is one which a person might choose for himself had he an option. It is not nearly conclusive; it is consummatory. [p. 23]

The divergence between Freud and Ghalib, between Freud and Freud himself, and between Eissler and Weissman leaves something needing to be resolved. Perhaps, the solution lies in the fact that the psychoanalytic literature on emotional reactions to the thought of one's death has made inoptimal distinction between a premature, unexpected, and violent death and a timely, expectable, and natural death. Blurring the two types of death might, at least in part, explain the fear–acceptance schism in the literature on the topic. Most probably it is the former (the imagination of which can only arise out of unmitigated destructiveness within us) that causes "death anxiety", and it is the latter (death arriving like gently falling snow after a long and emotionally rich life) that causes "death acceptance". It is in this frame of mind that we can speak not only of an "appropriate" but also even of a "good", or, at least, "good-enough" death. Here, the renowned thanatologist and the founding father of North American suicidology, Edwin Shneidman (2008) comes to our intellectual rescue. He states that

> When we speak of a good death, we imply that it is appropriate not only for the decedent, but also for the principal survivors—a death they can "live with." The death is somehow consistent with the decedent's living image. [p. 18]

Shneidman emphasizes that while death might be regarded as a violation of narcissism, the nature of death does not have to rupture the image of the person who dies. Such a death would be

> appropriate to the individual's time of life, to his style of life, to his situation in life, to his mission (aspirations, goals, wishes) in life; and it is appropriate to the significant others in his life. Obviously, what is appropriate differs from person to person: one man's nemesis is another man's passion. Appropriateness has many dimensions, relating, at the least, to the state of one's health, competence, energy, prowess, zeal, hope, pain, and investment in his postself. [p. 19]

Extending Winnicott's (1960) expression "good-enough mother", Shneidman proposes the concept of "good-enough death". He lists the following criteria for it: (i) *natural* rather than accidental suicidal or homicidal, (ii) *mature*, that is, after age seventy, (iii) *expected* and not sudden, (iv) *honourable*, with a decent legacy left behind, (v) *intestate*, with a pre-arranged funeral and a will to complete the administrative chores left behind, (vi) *accepted*, (vii) *civilized*, that is, in the presence of loved ones and pleasant circumstances, (viii) *generative*, in so far as one has helped the younger generation and facilitated their growth, (ix) *rueful*, that is, capable of experiencing sadness without collapse, and (x) *peaceable*, with amicability and love. This long list can perhaps be summarized and brought under three basic categories.

- Actual circumstances: dying without severe pain and humiliating physical limitations; dying in familiar settings and with loved ones around.
- Life accomplishments: a considerably reduced gap between the ego and ego-ideal; confidence that one has given more love than hurt to those around oneself; a sense of having been loved and having enjoyed one's work; generativity towards the offspring and other younger members of society.
- Attitude towards one's death: acceptance; adequate preparation, including having written a will, and provided the family some input about one's funeral and disposition of one's important possessions.

This picture reveals that the difference between an anxiety-producing death and a "good enough" death ultimately has less to do with death than with how much and what kind of life has preceded it. The worry about dying, in the end, might reveal itself to be a concern about living. I have elsewhere noted that "the despair of dying without having joyously lived is far greater than expecting death after having lived well" (Akhtar, 2001, p. 105).

Technical implications

Having surveyed the literature on the death instinct concept, normal and abnormal grief reactions, and emotional attitudes about one's own mortality leads us to the next logical step, and that is to ask what relevance all this has for our day-to-day clinical work. Since the manifestations of the death drive in the clinical situation (Feldman, 2000, 2009; Kernberg, 2009; Rosenfeld, 1971) and the technical strategies dealing with pathological grief reactions (Volkan, 1981) have already been touched upon, I will focus the following discourse upon the ways in which the reality of one's approaching mortality (sooner or later)—Langs' (2004) "existential death anxiety"—has an impact upon the conduct of intensive psychotherapy and psychoanalysis. These are (1) discerning the patient's concern with death; (2) exploring the patient's feelings and attitudes about his or her mortality; (3) helping the patient gain a more active role in his post-death destiny, and (4) managing countertransference reactions to these difficult topics. These technical measures are commented upon in more detail below.

Discerning the patient's concern with death

In all intensive treatments, the topic of death sooner or later comes up. It might appear in the form of the patient's talking about the death of their parents, grandparents, or other loved ones, or it might appear via associations to war, famine, and political assassinations. More commonly, though, it comes in the form of murderous fantasies directed against envied and hated others; such scenarios can involve childhood figures, current relationships, or transference re-creations of either in the clinical situation. Thoughts of suicide and one's own approaching death (especially in older patients) are other ways in which death finds its way into the clinical discourse. None of these items is devoid of multiple determinants and all are subject to customary analytic interventions of empathy, clarification, interpretations, reconstruction, and working through.

A novel perspective that I wish to add here is that the analyst might allow himself or herself to regard these diverse ways of the patient's talking about death as potentially pertaining to his actual mortality. The temptation to think that only orphaned adults (see Chapter Seven), terminally ill patients, and elderly analysands reflect upon their own death must be put aside. All human beings think about their death: young or old, consciously or unconsciously. Having such a perspective would permit the analyst to see that the patient is making an effort to bring this topic up for consideration. When a patient in termination phase, for instance, talks about death, the reference might not only be metaphorical. The patient may be saying to the analyst: "Look, I am leaving the treatment for good and we have not talked about an extremely important topic yet. Can we please do it now?" This is not to say that the usual scepticism about the manifest content of the patient's material should be dispensed with. It is only a plea to sometimes—courageously—take the talk of death on its manifest level. This is not a recommendation for the analyst to introduce the topic of the patient's mortality, only to discern its ubiquitous, though derivative, presence in the patient's associations. The customary inclination is to view the funeral-like atmosphere during the termination phase as metaphorical. This can yield useful interventions as is evident in the following example.

Clinical vignette 10

> Joyce Knight began the last session of her nearly ten-year-long analysis by saying that, on her way to my office, she felt as if she were coming to a funeral. She described her experience of there being to the afternoon an air of finality, solemnity, and feeling lost. As I remained silent, Joyce went on to recount her experiences at a couple of funerals she had attended. She sobbed. I, too, felt sad, but said nothing. Gradually, her associations shifted to her getting a doctorate soon and then to graduation dinners, commencement ceremonies, etc. She began to be animated. Soon, however, she caught herself and observed that this talk of happy endings (graduations) was defensive against her sadness (funerals). Significantly, she added that while this might be the case, the two sides most probably represented her mixed feelings regarding parting

from me: "happy and sad, sad and happy". I responded by saying, "Yes, it does seem like that." And, after a momentary pause, added, "But you know, all well-timed funerals are graduations of a sort, and all graduations contain funeral-like elements." Joyce nodded in agreement. The sense of our being together in each other's apartness was evident as the end of the session approached.

While generally satisfied with the way the clinical process moved in this session held years ago, I now wonder what would have happened had I taken her early reference to funerals on its face value. To be sure, doing so would have been better if it was not the very last session and a few more sessions were available for further exploration. None the less, the alternative approach that I am now proposing might have yielded different clinical material and permitted an exploration of Joyce's feelings and fantasies about her death; my more "traditional" approach allowed this potential material to remain behind a psychic eclipse.

Exploring the patient's feelings and attitudes about his or her own mortality

Once the topic of patient's mortality has been discerned, the next step is to help the patient get in deeper contact with feelings and fantasies surrounding it. Lest such a recommendation appear "unanalytic", I hasten to add that the topic of death is not *introduced* by the analyst; it is merely detected and unmasked, since its derivatives are invariably present in the patient's material. Moreover, pursuing a line of interpretation that deals with a specific topic is by no means incompatible with "proper" psychoanalytic technique. The fact is the psychoanalyst needs an admixture of spontaneity and deliberateness in his work (Parsons, 2000). This is true both of listening, where an "evenly suspended attention" (Freud, 1912e) is complemented by selective and highly focused attention from time to time (Brenner, 2000) and of intervening where a "free-floating responsiveness" (Sandler & Sandler, 1998) co-exists with "strategic" (Levy, 1987) lines of clarifications and interpretations. The exploration of the patient's feelings about his "impending" (remember: it is *always* impending) death becomes a legitimate activity for the clinical dyad to undertake. Any extraordinary affect (e.g., excessive fear, undue longing), attitude (e.g., denial of death via counterphobic flirtations with danger), or fantasy (e.g., death as a lover) should be brought up for associative elaboration, introspection, and gaining a deeper understanding of its origins and purposes. In other words, the indirect and disguised appearance of death in patients' associations must be "translated upwards" into the language of consciousness and mutual understanding. This, of course, is not needed when patients talk overtly of desires to die and even to kill themselves.

The therapist listening to a patient talk about suicide must maintain an attitude of equanimity, non-judgemental seriousness, and patience. He has to remember that "fantasy is not tantamount to the act and that a major therapeutic task is to assist in the construction of a boundary between feeling and fantasy on the one hand and impulsive action on the other" (Lewin & Schulz, 1992, p. 238). The capacity of the therapist to listen peacefully to patients verbalizing suicidal ideation strengthens the boundary between thought and action. It is important to remember that the patient needs to extrude (and, thus, "share") the forces that threaten his existence from within. With the dreaded agenda out in the open, there is a diminution of shame and sense of aloneness. Dynamic exploration then becomes possible. Crucial is the therapist's ability to

> empathize with the patient's suicide temptations, with his longing for peace, with his excitement of self-directed aggression, with his pleasure in taking revenge against significant others, with his wish to escape from guilt, and with the exhilarating sense of power involved in suicidal urges. Only that kind of empathy on the part of the therapist may permit the patient to explore these issues openly in treatment. [Kernberg, 1984, p. 263]

When matters begin to get out of hand, however, the therapist should resort to limit-setting and take "responsible action, with or without the patient's approval" (Kernberg, Selzer, Koenigsberg, Carr, & Appelbaum, 1990, p. 155). Limit-setting is not opposed to "holding"; in fact, firmness of therapeutic stance might be seen as an assertive form of "holding". The developmental prototype of the two is the support–expectation paradigm inherent in all good parenting. The parent offers help to the child but also expects appropriate behaviour from him or her.

Clinical vignette 11

> Sarah Green, a forty-five-year-old librarian, made an appointment to see me upon her sister's insistence. She appeared overwhelmed with pain at the break-up of a romantic relationship. Having lived alone most of her life, she found this belated attachment profoundly significant. The man she was involved with was married. He abruptly left her, saying that he could no longer continue cheating on his wife. She was destroyed. Heartbroken, she came to see me.
>
> We began the first hour of consultation in a customary history-taking way. However, within twenty minutes of the session, she announced that she had decided to blow her head off with a gun that she had bought earlier that day. Alarmed by the earnestness of her tone, I suggested that we take immediate steps to get the gun removed from her apartment, obtain some collateral information regarding the extent of her depression, and consider beginning our work on an in-patient basis. The patient reacted sharply to my suggestion and, refusing to let me contact her sister, who could remove the gun, got up to leave the office. At this point, I said to her: "Look, everybody gets about ten candles worth of life and inside you eight have already gone out. The wind is blowing and to protect the remaining two candles, you came here and put them in my heart. Now, since you have enlisted me for this purpose, it is my duty to keep these two candles protected from the wind. When the storm settles, I will return them to you so that you can light the other eight candles back with their help." The patient broke down in tears and, after some thinking, gave me permission to contact her sister, who subsequently removed the gun from the patient's apartment and encouraged the patient to stay at her house for the next few days.

As this example shows, the behavioural limit-setting is to be combined, as much as possible, with some degree of interpretation of the potential meanings of the patient's impulses and actions. Otherwise, the patient can receive an impression that all the therapist is interested in is his behaviour and not the subjective distress that underlies it. Worse, the patient comes to believe that threatening suicide has inordinate power over the therapist and can be used for sadistic purposes in the transference (Kernberg, Salzer, Koenigsberg, Carr, & Appelbaum, 1990). Continuing to interpret while setting limits demonstrates to the patient that the therapist's analysing function has not been compromised under the influence of the former's regression.

While management of overtly suicidal patients has received considerable attention (for a synopsis, including detailed guidelines, see Akhtar, 2009f, pp. 119–142), the subtler ways in which patients attempt to hasten their exit from this world has mostly remained unaddressed in the literature on psychotherapy and psychoanalysis. This, however, does not mean that there are no technical dilemmas in this realm. Indeed, there are. For instance, how actively should an analyst intervene with a patient who does little exercise, is overweight, and smokes cigarettes? Also, should the analyst ask if, during the course of a five–ten-year analysis, the analysand has ever had a physical examination? What really are the pros and cons of such interventions? Does the analyst's expressed interest in such matters constitute a countertransference enactment or does it simply show a concern for the patient as well as for the analytic process itself? Doesn't ignoring the patient's self-destructive behaviours, however subtle they might be, permit a pocket of masochism to remain unanalysed? Clearly, more thought is needed here.

Helping the patient gain a more active role in his post-death destiny

As the exploration of the patient's feelings and attitudes about his or her death proceeds, three special aspects come to attention. Sometimes, they are explicitly voiced by the patient. At other times, it is their curious absence in the patient's associations that alerts the analyst to their existence. These matters pertain to the patient's (a) fantasies and actual decisions about the disposal (e.g., via burial or cremation) of his or her body, (b) anticipation of parting from cherished possessions and the planning required for their appropriate dispersal, and (c) participation (or the lack of it) in his or her posthumous survival as the "post-self" (Shneidman, 2008).

Each of these realms requires exploration and interpretative resolution of defences if the patient seems resistant to such work. Helping the patient talk about their funeral and burial or cremation often yields rich information about their internal object relations with both ancestors and the coming generations. For instance, one patient felt that he should be buried because it made him feel similar to his parents, who had been buried, *and* because he desired his children to visit his grave after he was gone. Elaborations of these themes led to rich information about his internal life both within the transference and as it existed outside the confines of the analytic treatment.

The same is true of exploring the patient's feelings about the material possessions and money he or she is to leave behind. Discussion of this topic gives access to separation experiences that might not have entered the therapeutic dialogue so far. It also brings to the surface the complex sentiments and fantasies implicit in the dispersal of one's property. While such real and imaginary scenarios are beneficially explored with all patients, the fact that they are richer in middle-aged and elderly patients can hardly be denied. In their treatment, the omission of enquiry regarding such matters (including if they have a properly written will), betrays a collusive avoidance of omnipotent defences on the analyst's part.

Finally, there is the matter of the "post-self". The term, coined by the renowned thanatologist, Edwin Shneidman (2008), asserts that

> the individual who is going to die can, in the present moment, actively entertain notions (fantasies, thoughts, yearnings, dreams) about what the world will be like when he's absent from it. . . . One can, in the present, savor his imaginings of what will transpire after he's gone, and these thoughts and images can influence important aspects of his behavior: the provision of life insurance for his potential survivors, his psychological investment in work that will not only survive him but continue to be identified with him, his preference for having children over remaining childless . . . in short, his concern with his continued "existence" in the minds of others. [p. 29]

Shneidman describes the various ways in which an individual can—while living—exert control on how he survives in others' minds. He also observes that there is a broad range of intensity of investment people show in such endeavours. The main point, I believe, is neither to idealize the laborious assembly of credentials for a glorious obituary in the future, nor to devalue the desire to leave little trace behind after one's death except some fond memories in one's children's hearts. The point is to help the patient explore that the realm of "post-self" does exist and one can, consciously or unconsciously, have an impact upon it and be affected by it.

Managing the countertransference

The first point to note here is that a culturally transmitted blind spot pertaining to death often precludes psychoanalysts' noticing that patients are talking and/or are expressing a wish to talk about their death. (A parallel to this can be found in the cultural abhorrence of anal matters which has led to a clinical and "heuristic repression of the anal phase" (Akhtar, 2009b, p. 14). As a result, patients often undergo analysis for years and do not seem to talk about their faeces, flatus, anus, and anal sensations. This is deceptive. The fact is that the patients do talk about such matters; the analyst fails to discern them since he or she has a culturally transmitted blind-spot about these topics.) Analysts are more comfortable in hearing about death wishes directed at them than in patients' interest in their own deaths, especially when such discourse is not clinically "noisy" and dangerous in reality. When they do listen to the patients' talk of their death, they readily pathologize such interest and trace its origins to guilt and masochism. What escapes them is the ubiquitous human desire to understand death and the need for help in shedding the illusion of immortality. Therefore, I urge that we cultivate the conceptual freedom to think that an analysis is deficient if it reaches termination without a whisper about what awaits the patient as the final chapter of his or her life.

To arrive at such a stance, analysts would need to (a) shift their view of death as being *apart* from life to its being *a part* of life; (b) recognize that man must make peace with the inevitable fact of mortality in order to live fully and truthfully; (c) understand that fear and denial of death are mostly pathological and a calm acceptance of death is mostly healthy; (d) work through the feelings about their own death for, as Freud (1910d) has bluntly reminded us that "no psychoanalyst goes further than his own complexes and internal resistances permit" (p. 145). These four intrapsychic adjustments require a major departure from the customary Western denial of death's significance to the ongoing psychic life of an individual. They also necessitate much self-analytic work, a significant part of which might not have taken place during the analyst's own analysis. It is only when the analyst makes an earnest effort to move in this existential direction that he can help the patient grasp the sham-nature of his "death anxiety". In the absence of such an attitude in the analyst, the patient might finish the treatment with a tightly protected corner of his mind intact where infantile omnipotence prevails in the guise of the denial of mortality. While the patients under consideration here are implicitly in good physical health, this is not to deny that there are clinical populations (e.g., elderly, terminally ill, hospice-bound) with whom psychological work necessitates dealing with death in a far more "experience-near" manner. While denial might prevail here, too, psychotherapists working with such populations often find the patients to be far more accepting of the finality of the situation than their families.

Concluding remarks

Juxtaposing two different vantage points on death, I have attempted to highlight the tension that exists between attitudes emanating from denial of death and those arising from acceptance of death. Their separation has largely been in the service of didactics, and so has been their respective attribution to the Western and Eastern hemispheres of the world. The fact is that denial and acceptance of one's mortality constitutes one of those dialectics that seem ubiquitous in the human psyche; other such dialectics involve the tension between symbiosis and individuation, activity and passivity, homosexuality and heterosexuality, and religious belief and atheism (Akhtar, 2008b). Besides being universally prevalent, these dialectics are characterized by the fact that each pole in them serves profoundly significant dynamic, structural, and existential functions. *Vis-à-vis* death, too, one can discern psychic benefits of either pole of this dialectic (denial, making it easier to go on living, and acceptance, making the experience of life richer and more textured).

While all this seems to make sense, we are, none the less, left with more questions than answers in this realm. Prominent among them are the following.

- Can one draw a "developmental line" (A. Freud, 1963) pertaining to feelings and fantasies about one's death, a line that would hold steady in an "average expectable environment" (Hartmann, 1939)?

- To extend this idea further, is it "healthy" for the young to ignore death and for the old to contemplate it?
- What role does the exposure to family members' deaths (especially during childhood) play in the attitude towards one's own death?
- How does physical illness affect one's feelings about death? Is a terminally ill individual's denial of his soon-to-be encountered mortality a "manic defence" (Klein, 1935; Winnicott, 1935) or a sign of robust mental health?
- How do attitudes towards death differ in the times of war and peace (see Zilboorg, 1943 in this connection)?
- How has the increased life expectancy of man impacted upon the so-called death anxiety?
- Is suicide ever a rational and mentally healthy choice?
- Can psychoanalysts learn something useful from the field of "near-death studies" (Greyson, 1984; Greyson, Holden, & James, 2009; Moody, 1975).
- What is the place of the belief in heaven and hell, reincarnation, and the soul's post-death continuation in psychoanalytic theory? And, in a related way, can a true believer in such phenomena be successfully analysed? Or, to put it more sharply, can such a person be analysed by an analyst who is a non-believer?
- Can an analysis (especially of an older patient) ever be complete without an exploration of his or her attitudes about their death?

The list can be extended, to be sure. However, the point I am trying to make is that, as psychoanalysts, we have paid inoptimal attention to the psychological significance of the fact that all human beings die and that knowing this fact has enormous psychological ramifications. By ignoring, bypassing, or downplaying this fact (and its undeniable, even if unconscious, dynamic impact), we have imbued life, living, physical health, analysis, and analysing with a wishful hypomania. Wheelis's (1966) wise, if ironical, reminder applies to all of us.

> A fire becomes, not less, but more truly a fire as it burns faster. It's the being consumed that pushes back the darkness, illumines whatever there is of good in our days and nights. If it weren't brief, it

> wouldn't be precious. Let me say it flatly: we are lucky that we die, and anyone who pushes away the awareness of death lives but half a life. Pity him! [p. 68]

The good news is that there is still time to wake up from our slumber of repudiation and look at death squarely, deeply, and thoughtfully. By doing so, we may indeed learn something significant about life itself, something significant about humanity at large, and something significant about our own minds and those of our patients. And that is what our enterprise is all about. Isn't it?

CHAPTER FIVE

Graves

> "The idea of the earth as mother and of burial as a re-entry into the womb for rebirth appears to have recommended itself to at least some of the communities of mankind at an extremely early age"
>
> (Campbell, 1991, p. 66)

Located between the large-hearted stoicism of cremation and the wishful denial of mummification, graves represent compromise formation *par excellence*. Simultaneously, they serve as stark reminders of man's mortality and shrill memoranda of life's continuation after death. A commonly used euphemism for graves—"the ultimate resting place"—gives the trick away. Remove the word "ultimate" and you will become aware of the implications that one can get up refreshed from such a place and be all set to resume the day's work. Moreover, the prefix "ultimate" can easily be interpreted as other than "final": it can signify "superiority" and "excellence". Just note how amusement parks and ice cream parlours cheerily announce the "ultimate" roller coaster and the "ultimate" flavour, respectively.

Let not such contemporary "hype" mislead you, however. The practice of burying the dead and making graves is many centuries old, if not prehistoric (Bahn, 1996; Parker-Pearson, 2001; Sloan, 2002). Over this time, graves have lost some features and gained a few others. Prominent among the former is the practice of burying favourite and useful possessions of the deceased alongside his or her dead body with the idea that these might come in handy in the "other world". Prominent among the latter is the emergence, during the 1800s, of more nuanced and personalized epitaphs; these capture the essence of the deceased's life or, at times, carry a message for those left behind. There is an unmistakably relational and "live" quality to such tombstones. The manicured gardens that have become the customary backdrop of cemeteries also seek to undo the fact of "deadness" by seducing the visitor to pay equal, if not greater, attention to the reassuring and fully "alive" beauty of its plants, flowers, and trees. With this in mind, it is safe to conclude that graves have the potential of both facilitating and hindering the process of mourning on the bereaved's part, and this is one of the many issues pertaining to graves that I shall address in this contribution.

Visiting graves

The first visit to the deceased's grave by his or her relatives and close friends takes place at the time of burial or, to use a somewhat sanitized expression, internment. After the pertinent prayers or words of consolation spoken by the clergy or undertaker, the coffin is lowered into the hole—usually six feet deep—dug into the ground for the purpose of burial. (I have been impressed by how religious everyone seems to become at such occasions. Even the funeral of psychoanalysts who prided themselves on being atheists and agnostics make repeated references to God, heaven, afterlife, and so on. To be sure, this can be attributed to the preference of those left behind. None the less, it is curious that few analysts, if any, "prohibit" such references to religious beliefs in their wills.) After this, those present are encouraged to drop a handful of earth or flowers into the grave as a symbolic participation in, and communalization of, the burial ceremony. Then everyone leaves and hired labourers—"grave diggers"—fill the hole up with the pre-dug-out dirt. This simple grave would later acquire a concrete or stone structure of varying degrees of elaborateness and a tombstone with an individualized inscription.

While different religions, ethnicities, and cultural subgroups put their own stamps on the above-mentioned sequence, four nodal points of it appear to be ubiquitous in significance:

- The moment when the coffin is first lowered into the ground is especially potent in triggering emotions. It is the beginning of the final "letting go" of the deceased. Illusions of reversing what has happened crack and one is overwhelmed with helplessness. The resulting pain can be defended against by aversion of glance from the coffin, murmuring to others, and by distracting oneself by focusing upon this or that minor detail of what is going on. Such manoeuvres can render the anguish manageable but might interfere in mentally recording the event in its veracity and affective significance. One often learns about the pronounced deployment of these mechanisms in individuals who later develop prolonged and pathological grief reactions.
- Moving from the passivity of watching the coffin being lowered into the grave to the activity of putting a fistful of earth in it affords one a modicum of control. Helplessness is diminished and a bit of narcissism gets restored. Being one among many engaged in the same act makes one part of a group and this provides the much needed ego support. At the same time, the active role in burying the dead can activate murderous impulses and guilt.
- Taking the first steps away from the gravesite and leaving the cemetery after the burial constitute the next emotional juncture. Returning home without the deceased—even though now dead for at least a day or two—forcefully underscores the point of his or her absence. One is enveloped by a peculiar emptiness, shaken, heavy with sadness, and a little ashamed.
- The final stop in this journey of pain is the construction of a "real" grave and the placement of a tombstone. Intended partly to memorialize the dead and partly to prevent him from coming out of the grave, as it were, the tombstone can become a nidus of complex emotions and conflicts between the family

and friends left behind (see more on this in the section titled "Epitaphs"). The ceremony itself provides an opportunity to further work through the grief with a judicious dose of "manic defence" in the form of family reunion and often a large meal following the event.

These are early experiences with the grave, however. As time passes, most people evolve a preconscious and unspoken schedule of visiting their close relatives' graves; religious holidays and death anniversaries figure prominently in this emotional calendar. Others behave differently. They bypass the funeral and internment and even if they attend these initial rites, they never visit the grave again. They might even "forget" where a loved one is buried. (I can hardly forget the late night conversation in a San Diego hotel with a renowned psychoanalyst who told me that his father is buried "somewhere in New Jersey.") While exceptions can certainly exist, often such behaviour implies warded-off grief. Repudiation of mourning may be so tenacious that the individual remains content with "rational" and logistical explanations for his not visiting the grave. At times, however, some insight is retained. An internist colleague of mine, Stephen Rosenfeld, narrated an account of the latter sort.

> I have never been back to my parents' graves. This is not to say that I do not think about them. In fact, they are very much a part of my inner emotional life. And yet, I do not visit the cemetery which, by the way, is not very far away from where I live. I suppose the reason for my not going is that I want to remember them in their living and loving glory. You know, my father gave an extremely eloquent and moving eulogy at my mother's funeral. He was truly larger than life in those moments. Powerful, restrained, and deeply human. *That* is the image of him that I carry within myself.
>
> Now, as far as my mother's concerned, the story is more complex. Her mother had been institutionalized and she had been raised by an aunt. However, as a child she was told that her mother had died. It was decades later that she found out the truth. Having mourned her "dead" mother, my mother now felt little interest in finding out more. We, her children, also negated the existence of our grandmother. This family legacy, I think, contributed to my own reaction to my mother's death and subsequently to her grave. Unbeknown

> to me, I loyally repeated what she had done: she had not visited her mother living in a state hospital and I did not visit her grave. I suppose you psychoanalysts might call it transgenerational transmission or something like that.
>
> Let me tell you one more thing. Recently, a friend's father passed away and I went to this very elaborate Catholic funeral. I was moved and, in the midst of the proceedings, found myself wistfully thinking that maybe I should visit my parents' graves. It never happened but I think a time might come when I will go.

In contrast to my internist friend's subterranean pain, the affects associated with regular ongoing visits to cemeteries have an air of solemnity, resolve, and subdued righteousness about them (Akhtar & Smolar, 1998). Taking care of the grave, cleaning the shrubbery around it, and putting flowers, etc., on it imbues the visit with positive feelings of continuity, belonging, and ongoing dialogue. (This discussion of visiting the graves of loved ones should not make one overlook that graves of renowned individuals often form a favourite stop for tourists. While pyramids and the Taj Mahal remain topmost on their list, the burial sites of important twentieth century figures also attract frequent visitors. Prominent among these are: Mustafa Kemal Attaturk (Ankara, Turkey), Winston Churchill (London), Charles Darwin (London), Thomas Edison (West Orange, NJ), Mohammad Ali Jinnah (Karachi, Pakistan), John F. Kennedy (Arlington, VA), Martin Luther King, Jr (Atlanta, GA), Karl Marx (London), Pablo Neruda (Isla Nigra, Chile), Elvis Presley (Memphis, TN), Yitzhak Rabin (Mount Herzl, Israel), Oscar Wilde (Paris), and Mao Zedong (Beijing). Note here that Sigmund Freud, Albert Einstein, and Gandhi were cremated, and only Gandhi has a widely visited memorial.)

Maeve O'Brien, an Irish anthropologist who lives in my neighbourhood, described the potential "joy" of visiting the family graves in astute and heartwarming detail.

> A typical Irish response to the question "How are you?" from people of my generation (60 plus) is "Well, I am still above the ground." From our family of twelve children there are only three left "above the ground". Each year when I go home to visit my two brothers, Daemon and Michael, we make the pilgrimage to those of the family now clustered together in the grave yard.

It begins with "the Mammy". She is the one who led us by the hand into what was our weekly ritual after Sunday Mass—a visit with the family gone before us. We used to catch the tram, seven or eight of us, whomever she could gather up, walking maybe half a mile to the family plot. Mammy would tell us a story about each one, often more than we wanted to know, impatient as we were to get back home to play.

Now we arrive in style by car clutching our offerings of flowers. First we cast our eyes around for errant weeds, overturned urns of dead flowers, a scrap of paper. It is all part of tidying up. Any visible signs of neglect are considered "disgraceful". This process is accompanied by a running commentary, "There you are Mammy, all tidy now," or "Here Mammy, your flowers." A moment of quiet reflection might follow, perhaps a prayer silently uttered, then my brothers will start in with "Do you remember the time . . .?" One story leads to another, sometimes leading to tears, more often to our doubling over with laughter. Granny and Grandfather are there too and our older sister Nancy who died at age 22 and is only a shadow of a memory. Frances, the oldest sister is there, and our father who died when we were quite young. There is comfort in seeing that they are together, and in remembering and talking to them and each other. It eases the loss and reduces the fear of our own passing. They will be there waiting for us on the other side.

This year I slipped a pebble from Mammy's grave into my pocket. I had the idea that I would like to be buried holding it my hand . . . a connection with her because my grave will be far away from hers in my adopted country. For now I keep it in a little wooden box, fingering it from time to time. Its hardness feels enduring, like her love for me and mine for her.

We move on to Daemon's wife Margaret, and the month-old baby buried beside her, then to Christie who died just last year, and the wife , stolen away by cancer 15 years before. There are mutterings about how their children never come to tend to the grave. It is different now. Not many of the young ones come. They live further away both geographically and psychologically from the rituals that link life to death.

We were accustomed to the intimate callings of birth and death in our small community. Word spread quickly from door to door, with the postman, or over the back fence as the wash was hung out to dry. In our house a knock might come at any hour of night or day because our mother assisted the local mid-wife at births and the parish priest at deaths. She kept the "last hours set" in a brown box tied with string. It contained a crucifix, a pair of candle sticks, two new candles and the oil for anointing. I can still see it in my child's eye, both the mystery and the ordinariness of that brown cardboard box. On the shelf, beside the box, were the freshly laundered, snowy white bed linens and towels ready for the sacred laying out once the last breath had been drawn. I remember when Granny died. I sat at the top of the stairs listening to Mammy and my older sisters as they murmured to each other, all the while going about the business of cleaning her, dressing her, doing her hair for the final journey. There was no stranger's touch, no taking her away to a funeral home. She stayed with us until it was time to go to the church for the last solemn good-bye.

My brother Michael lives in our old family home. When I visit, I sleep in the room where first Granny, then Mammy, next our oldest sister Frances, and just a couple of years ago, Michael's wife Maeve, died, each one surrounded by family. On the dressing table, in front of the mirror, are the crucifix and the candle sticks from the "last hours set". They provide a sense of comfort and continuity and will be used when the time comes, to prepare the way for my brother Michael as he gets ready to leave this life.

An important point to note about this narrative is how the company of close relatives transforms the subterranean pain of mourning into tolerable amounts of sadness. Conversation and reminiscences become a psychic salve and the whole experience becomes a sober waltz of mutuality. The following clinical vignette illustrates the difference that the company of a loved one can make while visiting a grave.

Clinical vignette 12

Charles LeRoy, a successful attorney in his mid-fifties, was in analysis with me. Having lost his mother to ovarian cancer at age six, Charles had grown up with a sense of not belonging to anyone. This was fuelled by the fact that his father had moved out of town, leaving Charles, as a little boy, to be raised by his maternal grandparents in their rambling, large house in a small town in West Virginia. They did their best and made sure that Charles got a good education, but the sense of not having anyone to call "mum" or "dad" devastated Charles.

He grew up to be a superficially sociable but a heavy drinking and inwardly lonely workaholic. His remarkable tolerance of hardship and his perseverance resulted in social success. He made a lot of money and, from all outward appearances, lived an enviable life. But he was unable to relax and never truly felt "at home" anywhere.

He married a woman far beneath his social and intellectual status in a valiant, if fatally misguided, rescue effort. The marriage ended in divorce a few years later, leaving Charles bereft and at the mercy of fleeting infatuations and mindless one-night stands. He continued to advance in his work, though, and with the passage of time made quite a name for himself.

An outstanding feature of his life was his profound attachment to his mother's grave. From childhood onwards, he had visited the grave numerous times. His memories of these visits were, however, peculiarly bland. He stood looking at the grave and with a nagging sense that he ought to feel sad, perhaps cry, but, in reality, he hardly felt any stirring of emotion. Yet he went, dutifully, to the grave every so often. Even after he moved out of state, he found his way to the cemetery every other year or so.

Around the age of sixty, Charles met Dianne, a woman whom he truly loved and who was a good intellectual and social match for him. Soon they were married. A few months later, he visited his mother's grave with her and the experience was dramatically different. In his own words: "As Dianne and I arrived at the grave, I broke down and started sobbing like a child. Tears were running down my cheeks and I felt the sharp and stabbing pain of loss. Dianne embraced me tightly in her arms and I cried bitterly for well over ten to fifteen minutes. My whole body was shaking. I realized, a little while later, that I was mourning the loss of my mother in a way that had emotional depth and something searingly truthful about it."

This vignette demonstrates how the hitherto "frozen grief" (Volkan, 1981) melted in the reassuring presence of a loved and loving life partner. It was as if the tragedy of loss could be permitted a full-fledged and affectively charged entry into the mind only when the auxiliary ego support of a current love object was in place. Dianne's holding Charles clearly went beyond the literal dimensions of the act. Her embrace became the "holding environment" (Winnicott, 1960) in which the grief could rise to the surface and become bearable.

In a later session, Charles talked about how, once he composed himself, he and Dianne together read the little poem that his father had written for the gravestone. The poem professed the great love he felt for his wife, which was curious in light of the fact that, after her death, he had taken little interest in their son, Charles. This recollection permitted a deeper analysis of Charles's Oedipal experience; the enterprise of interpretation found an ally in the epitaph.

Epitaphs

The word "epitaph" was introduced into the English language in the fourteenth century and is derived from the Latin *epitaphium* ("eulogy") and Ancient Greek *epitaphos* (with "epi" meaning above, and "taphos" meaning tomb). The practice of carving inscriptions on gravestones is ancient and reflects the ubiquitous desire to perpetuate the memory of the dead. The macroscopic similarity between epitaphs written thousands of years ago and those written today betrays the essential kinship of human nature. At the same time, history reveals that modal epitaphs have changed somewhat with time. Early Egyptians, for instance, made little attempt to individualize epitaphs or to reflect the feelings of the survivors. Greeks, in contrast, produced epitaphs of great emotional depth and literary interest. Roman epitaphs contained little beyond a record of facts, though a remarkable feature of them was the terrible denunciation they often pronounced upon those who violated the sepulchre. Long after the Roman form was discarded, Latin continued to be used as the preferred language for epitaphs. Then, in the thirteenth century, French began to be used in writing epitaphs. It was around this time that the practice of the deceased addressing the reader in the first person made its appearance. The next century saw the increasing use of English language epitaphs, a practice that has become widespread as English has, *de facto*, become most of the world's *lingua franca*. For a fascinating account of epitaphs over centuries, see Guthke (2009) and Newstock (2009). Besides the details of the entry, which can be austere or abundant, and the choice of specific language, epitaphs necessarily reflect the religious doctrines, the literary styles, and the extent of individuated *vs.* communal selfhood that was/is typical for the era and the region.

For the purposes of psychodynamic study, epitaphs can be classified according to a number of variables. Of course, many of these variables overlap and criss-cross each other. None the less, such factors help to sift the psychologically meaningful epitaphs from the generic, routine, and banal. Below are some important variables to keep in mind.

- *How detailed is the inscription?* Most epitaphs are restricted to the deceased's name and the years of birth and death. Little of psychological significance can be extracted from this, though the clear indication of the identity of the deceased might remain important for the kin, and, if he or she happens to be renowned, for a wider circle of individuals.
- *In what medium is the message expressed?* Most epitaphs are in prose, consisting of a phrase, or at best, a brief sentence. Others use poetry. While cultural inclinations toward the poetic medium might play a role here, the use of verse is often more revealing of emotions surrounding the death, especially if it is written specifically for that occasion.
- *Who is the author of the epitaph?* The answer to this question varies greatly. Phrases borrowed from religious texts and literary sources might capture the essence of the dead person or of the sentiments of the bereaved, but come across as generic. More significant are epitaphs containing specific observations made by those left behind (e.g., George Washington Carver's "He could have added fortune to fame, but caring for neither, he found happiness and honor in being helpful to the world"). Nothing can, however, top the psychodynamic value of an epitaph chosen or written by the individual himself before dying. Such epitaphs can reveal what the deceased considered the essence of his life (e.g., Karl Marx's "The philosophers have only interpreted the world in various ways; the point is to change it"), the regrets and unfulfilled hopes carried to the grave (e.g, the Argentinian playboy Santiago Vizan Gulizia's negation-filled declaration, "I don't regret anything, thanks"), and admonitions and advice for the bereaved (e.g., from a Nova Scotia graveyard, "Death is a debt to Nature due / Which we have paid and so must you").
- *Does the epitaph reflect acceptance or denial of death?* Gravestone inscriptions can be used to express a peaceful acceptance of the

reality and finality of death. The form of such acknowledgment can range from sombre (e.g., John Quincy Adams' "This is the last of Earth! I am content") to humorous (e.g., Mel Blanc's "That's All Folks!"). On the other hand, one can adopt a stance that combines stoicism with cynicism (e.g., W. B. Yeats' self-written epitaph, "Cast a cold eye / On life, on death. / Horseman, pass by!"). In contrast are the epitaphs that assert that further life awaits one after death (e.g., Frank Sinatra's epitaph, stating, "The best is yet to come"). This can be viewed as a last-ditch manic defence or simply a reflection of one's lifelong religious convictions; in the latter case individual psychopathology plays little role.

- *What is the degree of relatedness with others in the inscribed message?* While often narcissistically tinged (e.g., Bette Davis's "She did it the hard way"), most self-authored epitaphs retain a communicative value *vis-à-vis* individuals who were important to the deceased. The message left behind might be mocking (e.g., "I told you I was sick", from a tombstone in a Georgia cemetery), defiantly schizoid (e.g., "I was somebody who is no business of yours", on the grave of someone in Vermont determined to be anonymous), sardonic (e.g., Primo Levi's "174517", i.e., his inmate number at Auschwitz); tender and loving, (e.g., the Italian actor, Walter Chiari's "O friends, don't cry—it's just unused sleep"), or quite idiosyncratic (e.g., Buckminster Fuller's "Call Me Trimtab"). (A *trimtab* is the smallest part of a rudder of a ship or aeroplane and controls the direction of the craft. By using it as a designation for himself, Fuller was probably alluding to how much power a single individual can have in the world.)

While the above-mentioned variables affect one's understanding of the epitaph and the amount of useful psychodynamic knowledge one can extract from it, something else needs to be kept in mind here. This pertains to the fact that so far the word "epitaph" has been used only in a literal sense. Used in a broader and abstract sense, an epitaph can also be constituted by one's personal will, and/or a detailed letter to the spouse and children written soon before one's death. Even one's life's work can serve as a self-engineered monument by which one wants to be remembered. Note with what delicious irony Allen Wheelis (1975) elucidates the narcissistic dimension of this type of agenda.

> I do not use myself up in living. A part of myself I save, like a miser, hoping to transmute it into something that will go on living for me in the future. With the quick I have little to do; the eminent dead are my models, the yet unborn my legatees. I am a time-binder, obsessed with mortality, spend my life creating an effigy to outlast me. In the graveyard, ceaselessly I carve at my epitaph, trying to make of it something so beautiful, so compact of meaning, that people will come from afar to read.
>
> It need not be in vain, this elaboration of self—great treasures have been so fashioned. What gets served up to the future may be a tasty dish indeed, but what shall we say of the chef, oblivious of the hungry ones around him, garnishing himself for the gourmets of the future? Rather than miss a day of painting, Cezanne did not attend his mother's funeral. Rilke could not spare from his poetry the time for his daughter's wedding. The world cannot do without such people, but pity those whose lot it is to live with them. [p. 53]

The focus in this passage is upon individual narcissism, and it is true that narcissism powerfully affects self-written epitaphs of actual or figurative nature. One's grave is, after all, totally one's own. Moreover, it is the stage on which the last scene of life's drama is played and the epitaph makes for an "exit line" (Gabbard, 1982) *par excellence*. A pithy epitaph gives those visiting the grave much to think about and assimilate about themselves, their relationship with the one buried in the grave, and the nature of life and death at large.

A sociopolitical digression

During a brief academic stint in the Yugoslavian capital of Belgrade (the bloody fragmentation of the erstwhile Yugoslavia would now necessitate Belgrade to be identified as the capital of Serbia) in the early 1990s, I expressed a wish to visit Marshall Tito's grave. Having grown up in post-Independence India, I had idolized the leaders of non-aligned nations—Jawaharlal Nehru, Srimavo

Bandaranaike, Sukarno, Gamal Abdel-Nasser, Jomo Kenyatta, and Tito. So, when the opportunity to pay homage to a childhood hero presented itself, I was readily drawn to it.

My hosts, however, treated my wish to visit Tito's grave with polite indifference. Tito, it turned out, was a Croat and had been labelled a megalomaniac who had done Yugoslavia no good. He was declared *persona non grata* by Serbians, who now controlled the country. My hosts were Serbs. They despised Tito, and, while offering me great hospitality in all other matters, made sure I did not visit the old man's grave.

In retrospect, their attitude appears remarkably benign. Just compare it with what their leader, Slobodan Milosevic, did a few years later. Interestingly, the grave of a famous person figured prominently in his genocidal campaign against Albanians, Kosovars, and Bosnian Muslims. Aiming to stir up hatred, Milosevic dug up the 700-year-old grave of the Serbian king Lazar, who was killed by Ottoman Turks. Milosevic carried his exhumed remains in a coffin on a cross-country excursion. He arranged for the coffin to be buried at each stop of his sojourn, only to be resurrected the next morning. This political ploy was aimed at purifying these towns and reminding their Serbian population that they had been humiliated by the Turks.

It was directed at labelling the Muslim population of southern parts of Yugoslavia as descendants of these invaders. That 700 years had since passed did not seem to matter. Through grotesque dramatization of the centuries-old Serbian defeat, a collapse of time was achieved. A scar was transformed back into a wound, and a modern hatred was manufactured out of a diabolical use of history. The result was an outpouring of Serbian rage and massacre of ethnic minorities. Over 100,000 people were killed. At the refugee camp of Srebrenica alone, 8,000 Muslim men and boys were shot to death in a matter of days. The irony that a grave played a role in creating more graves was too subtle to find notice in the midst of such mayhem. (While the focus here is upon the graves of celebrated individuals, a more disturbing political scenario involves mass graves. Containing the bodies of numerous men, women, and children, such burial pits give testimony to man's ruthlessness and cruelty. Those buried in mass graves often remain unidentified. At times, however, the remains of someone famous is also discovered.

The most recent example is the near certain finding of Frederico Garcia Lorca's remains in Grenada, Spain.)

The fact, however, is that Tito's and Lazar's graves are not the only ones that have figured in inter-ethnic conflicts. Vandalism directed at Jewish cemeteries is an everyday staple of the resurgent anti-Semitism in Europe. In India, the targets of destruction during the infamous anti-Muslim riots in the state of Gujarat included the grave of the revered, and arguably the first, Urdu poet, Wali Gujrati (1667–1707). (In contrast to such desecration are the ritualistic celebrations at gravesites for perpetuating literary and cultural heritage. One interesting illustration of this is to be found in the person of Walter Skold, the founder of the Dead Poets Society of America. He drives around in his "Poemobile" visiting the graves of dead poets and calling attention to their works. According to a recent newspaper item (*The Philadelphia Inquirer*, 2 November 2009), Skold recently finished visiting the graves of 150 poets in twenty-three states. Among the giants of literary world whose graves he visited are Ralph Waldo Emerson, Robert Frost, Henry Wadsworth Longfellow, and Walt Whitman.) One wonders what Gujrati could have done to deserve the wrath of Hindu mobs. What do dead people have to do with communal violence? Why do their resting places get involved in ethnic conflict?

Such questions lead us to how group emotions utilize ethnic symbols for sustaining coherence or unleashing violence. During periods of societal calm, ethno-religious and national symbols (flags, places of worship, and historical monuments) provide a group with a sense of pride and solidarity with its lineage and ideals. During periods of turbulence, however, such pride can turn into ethnic grandiosity. More ominous is the accompanying contempt for another group's emblems and icons.

The destruction of the World Trade Center towers in the USA, the Bamiyan Valley Buddhas in Afghanistan, and Babri Masjid in India are manifestations of an angry group's desire to attack symbols of its enemy. (Babri Masjid was a 1528 AD mosque in northern India, built by a Muslim ruler, Mohiuddhin Babar (reined 1530–1530 AD, and 1555–1556 AD). With the rise of Hindu fundamentalism during the early 1990s, it came to be held that the structure had replaced the birthplace of the Hindu God, Rama. Right-wing political parties stirred up an emotional delirium that ultimately led, on

6 December 1992, to the destruction of the Babri Masjid by a frenzied Hindu mob. Prominent members of conservative political parties aided and abetted the destruction. India watched this horrible event in utter disbelief. Its Muslim citizens were humiliated to the bone. The liberal Hindus of the country felt remorseful and outraged at what the right-wing zealots had done.) The toppling of Saddam Hussein's statue that loomed over the city of Baghdad also can be seen as belonging in this category. After all, all such symbols embody proud memories and historical linkages of the despised group. Demolishing a church or temple, disfiguring a grave, and destroying a community's monument are all attempts at cultural genocide. To violate a group's icons is to attack its honour.

What drives people to do such dastardly deeds? In my view, self-centred, charismatic leaders induce emotional regression in their followers in periods of economic uncertainty. Through fierce and one-sided rhetoric, they cause the group to put reason aside and become sentimental. They declare another group to be the cause of the economic strife that actually everyone is up against. They then remind their group of past humiliation at the hands of the other group and imply that similar injuries are being inflicted upon them. Finally, they inflate group pride by recounting past glories. The three strategies transform a cauldron of emotions into an inferno (for more details, see Akhtar, 2007c).

Human lives are not the only objects laid on the pyre. Material things and structures as well as myths and rituals are destroyed. And, when the orgy of bloodletting looks for more outlets, the graveyard becomes the next stop.

Back to the clinical realm

Visits to the burial site acquire much greater significance in situations of parental loss during childhood and young adulthood. This substitutes for the continued dialogue that the more fortunate young adults have with their parents in the form of face-to-face encounters, phone calls, correspondence, exchange of gifts, and visiting home around holiday times. In other words, the emotional revisiting of primary objects continues throughout adult life. The establishment of romantic intimacy and marriage during young adulthood (Erikson, 1959; Escoll, 1991), the assumption of the parental role with the arrival of children (Colarusso, 1990), the earnest scrutiny of one's identity and the overcoming of emergent sexual competitiveness and unconscious envy of offspring during middle age (Erikson, 1959; Kernberg, 1980), and the final consolidation of a post-ambivalent world-view during old age (Akhtar, 1994; Cath, 1997) are all contingent upon the working through of our relations with the parents of childhood. Those who have lost their parents long before consolidating full adulthood are dependent upon "anniversary reactions" (Hilgard, 1953), the use of the deceased's physical possessions, and visits to the parental graves for accomplishing this developmental task.

This phenomenon, though ubiquitous, has received scant psychoanalytic attention. The fact is that interesting developmental and technical issues exist in this area. The following clinical vignettes illustrate this point. These contain selected aspects of the analyses of two men whose visits to their fathers' graves had a powerful and development-facilitating impact. Both men's desire to visit a parent's grave arose in connection with a major adult-life milestone, namely, marriage. Neither man had visited his father's grave for years. Both undertook the trip to seek their "father's blessing" (Blos, 1985) on the threshold of their weddings. At a deeper level, this subsumed a desire for help in disengagement from their mothers, a proud display of masculinity, a wish to be forgiven for their hostile Oedipal competitiveness (more prominent in the second case), and a need to buttress their heterosexual identifications

Clinical vignette 13

Dr Robert Martin, a forty-year-old physician, sought help for his concern that his recent engagement was a mistake. He had always been "half in and half out" of romantic relationships and thought that his reluctance to marry might reflect more generalized constraints. As he talked about his professional inhibitions, his limited capacity for intimacy with his siblings and friends, and his restricted emotions regarding his father's death during his childhood, I recommended psychoanalysis.

Dr Martin's parents were also physicians. His father had a sudden myocardial infarction when the patient was three years old. A progressive deterioration in his father's strength followed until his death four years later. Dr Martin's mother remained a widow, living with numerous mementos of her brief marital life. She worked full time and raised Robert and his two older brothers with help from her mother.

Dr Martin's analysis was marked by a rapidly emerging longing for his father, which he found surprising. Prior to analysis, he had experienced his father's death unemotionally and resolutely. However, as the analytic process unfolded, Dr Martin conjured up fresh memories of his father and began to experience associated painful affects. He yearned for more attention from me and gradually recognized his underlying wish that he had received something more substantial from his father.

As his wedding approached, he broached the subject of his father's grave, informing me that he had not visited it since he was an intern. He asked me if this was significant. I said that not only was he asking me to help him understand his inhibition, he was asking me to help him overcome it. Memories of the "piercing look of pain that came over [his] mother's face" when the family visited the cemetery now emerged. Dr Martin voiced a fantasy of receiving his father's blessing while visiting the grave before the wedding.

A fantasy about paternal resurrection also seemed to be in the air before Dr Martin left to get married. He announced on a Monday that he had miscalculated his departure and would have to miss the rest of the week's sessions. He was also not sure whether he could come at all the week after his return from his honeymoon because of an anticipated new work schedule. When I pointed out this unusual degree of scheduling confusion and wondered about it, he responded by saying, "Maybe I am transforming the end into one where [father] comes back after the break ... one where I as the son have an open exchange and assessment of our relationship before the end ... I wish you would say something explicit like 'I want you to be here' or 'It would really be worth coming for this or that reason.'" I noted that he wanted to hear something explicit about my love for him as the break approached, that his confusion over our next visit contained his wish that I forestall the end—all of special relevance—and he prepared to visit his father's grave. I added that he might have had similar wishes of hearing his father's proclamation of love for him as his father lay dying, as well as fantasies of his father's returning for future meetings.

Later that day, he informed me that he would come the next day. In the next session, he said that he would also keep his appointments for the week after his honeymoon. He talked more about his father, reflected on his analysis, and said, "I have much more of a sense of sorrow and grieving than I ever did . . . I'm not sure I'll be in town for more than two years . . . I hope there is time to work this all out..." This fear of running out of time was not an infrequent theme. It underlay his fear, stated in the initial consultation, that he would die at a young age like his father, as well as his feelings at the end of sessions that he "has to pack it all in" before the time was up.

When he returned to his hometown before the wedding, Dr Martin borrowed his mother's car to visit the grave, which limited the time he was able to spend there—it reminded him of his annoyance with her intrusiveness when he was seventeen. I pointed out that he, too, seemed to have difficulty freeing himself from their bond; after all, he had other options for transportation. He agreed, and added that his mother shared with him, somewhat reluctantly, a scrapbook devoted to his father. The book contained pictures, poetry his father had written, notes added by his mother, and the eulogy delivered at his father's funeral. "I became tearful reading the book, but she wouldn't give me space . . . I wanted the tears to myself, and I felt pissed at her, so I closed [the book] in the house and went to the grave with [it] so I could thumb through my father's life . . . she said she preferred I didn't take it, that it needed to be guarded and she'd had control of it, but she relented."

The time at the grave was "sad, cathartic, and the tears were more accessible. . . . It was neat to feel something for my father. I credit psychoanalysis for that." Dr Martin wished that his father could be present at his wedding. He had a fantasy of exhuming the body and wondered if it was rotted or intact. He read quotations about his father from the scrapbook that he had heard his whole life: "of infinite grace and devoted benevolence, he lightened the way". He remembered many moments of closeness with his father. When he returned to his mother's home, he continued to seek to reconnect with his father by looking for a treasured picture of father and sons.

When Dr Martin returned from his honeymoon, he conspicuously avoided the topic of sex. It was as if he could not dare tell his father that he was now a truly grown-up man. In fact, he felt that the honeymoon was a failure: he should have had an erotic explosion, not the familiar and comfortable experience he did have. He also reported experiencing more frequent palpitations from a chronic but benign arrhythmia, and that this reminded him of his father. At this moment, he handed me the programme from his father's memorial service. His father's picture was on the back of it. Dr Martin spoke more about what

> his father must have felt as he approached his death. His deepening empathy with his father seemed to serve as a defence against his anxiety upon finding himself in the potentially competitive role of a married man. However, it also reflected genuine progress in his mourning, with enrichment of his inner view of his father and his identification with him.

It is clear that Dr Martin was invoking, as it were, his (deceased) father's help to disengage from an intrusive mother. He was also furthering the work of his mourning while simultaneously buttressing his identification with his father. While illustrating roughly similar issues, the next clinical vignette contains an additional feature. Here a son's visit to his father's grave also serves as a vehicle for seeking forgiveness for his hostile Oedipal competitiveness.

Clinical vignette 14

> Dr Keith Marcus, a thirty-eight-year-old, twice-divorced research scientist, sought help because he was considering marriage again and was worried whether this union would last. Dr Marcus's previous marriages had been with women of subtle sexual ill repute, and he was involved with "a good woman" for the first time. Dr Marcus also wondered whether he was too close to his mother.
>
> Dr Marcus's father, a factory supervisor, was allegedly uninvolved with his children and died suddenly of a myocardial infarction when Dr Marcus was twenty-five years old. He had little recall of the funeral. The only thing he could remember was that upon returning from the cemetery, he had fallen into a deep sleep for a few hours (I sensed elements of denial of the father's death as well as an identification with him in this long nap). Dr Marcus's mother was a housewife who was "always dissatisfied" and whom he felt hopelessly unable to please. His only sibling was an older, mildly sociopathic brother. Dr Marcus himself had grown up as a conscientious individual who, throughout high school, college, and subsequent academic career, had socialized little and remained devoted to his work.
>
> Dr Marcus began analysis in a characteristically industrious manner. Even after he relaxed, the associative material remained focused upon his mother, his previous wives, and his current woman friend. He repeated expressed anxieties about fusion with, and abandonment by, mother (and other women). With interpretative resolution of

externalizing resistances, Dr Marcus's own ambivalence toward these figures became available for exploration. Empathic, affirmative interventions coupled with my sustained emotional availability diminished separation and merger anxieties. With buttressed self-constancy and enhanced capacity for optimal distance, Dr Marcus broached the topic of rescuing women from men who "bothered" them. Father now appeared on the scene.

Over subsequent weeks, Dr Marcus elaborated the profile of a father who seemed disappointed in him and appeared to be "bothering" the mother all the time. Dr Marcus said that his father was a "grown-up boy" and began experiencing the issues directly in transference. Did I have a wife? Did I "bother" her? Did I visit prostitutes? Gradually, the "madonna–whore" split of the maternal imago became fleshed out and so did a childhood rescue theme. Subsequent months also revealed the linkage of this theme to his repeated choice of women in need. Competitive impulses towards me (father) and various anxious retreats from them (feeling weak, wanting to be a woman) now began to fill the sessions.

With further analysis, however, a more benevolent image of father emerged. Dr Marcus recalled his father's teaching him baseball, golf, bowling, etc. He realized with sadness that it was he who had distanced himself from his father. He cried. To his own surprise, he recalled that his father had given him, when he was a teenager, a book on sexual matters and suggested that they talk about it. He never spoke to his father about it. He revealed, with pride, that he still used his father's golf clubs. He sobbed and said he missed his father very much. I spontaneously asked him where his father was buried (as if to put the two in touch for a final goodbye!). He replied that his father's grave was in their hometown, a few hundred miles away. I asked him when was the last time he had visited the grave. He revealed that he had not been there since the day of the funeral some thirteen years ago, though he had thought about going there from time to time.

Over subsequent sessions, he talked about the various times he had considered a visit and then put it off. We began to see that it was his hitherto repressed hostility towards his father that had got in his way. Dr Marcus now began actively to plan a visit to his father's grave. However, as he talked, again he got caught up with who should accompany him. If he went with his mother, would he be mocking his father ("See, I got your woman! I won!")? If he went with his woman friend, the same anxiety would be there ("See, I got a prettier woman than you had!"). If he went alone, would he be deceptive? I pointed out that the common element in all this was his continued inner competitiveness. He saw it and decided to base his external behaviour in this regard on realistic considerations. He visited the grave with both his mother and his woman friend. While there, he felt love and gratitude towards his father, pride about his own accomplishments, and deep sadness over the father's death. He cried. Finally, he was at peace with his father. Soon afterwards, he decided to marry his woman friend.

It is noteworthy that the memory of his visiting his father's grave appeared on two subsequent occasions in Dr Marcus's analysis. The first was a few months after his wedding when he bought a house. In describing the house to me, the only thing he left out was its price. Upon my pointing this out, Dr. Marcus said that he was afraid that I would mock him, since I certainly owned a more expensive house. Soon, however, he revealed a second worry: that I would be crushed by hearing that the house he had bought was more expensive than mine. At this time, I reminded him of the various competitive scenarios he had envisioned before going to his father's grave.

Then, near termination, Dr Marcus "discovered" Peter Gay's biography of Freud and began reading it avidly. As we settled on a termination date, Dr Marcus finished the book and decided to read the reference notes at the end. The footnotes were not the "real thing", but did allow a further lingering on. Dr Marcus wryly compared the main text to his actual interactions with his father and his reading the footnotes to visiting the grave!

While the ego-enhancing impact of visits to the fathers' graves is evident in both these cases, interesting questions remain. Could these individuals have undertaken such "pilgrimages" without the help of analysis? Would the expectable destabilization of the inner world during middle age have propelled them in any event to visit their fathers' graves? We do not know. We also must acknowledge the gender specificity of our data. Is there a difference, for instance, in the nature, timing, meaning, and effects of a bereaved daughter's visits to her father's grave? Are visits to a mother's grave, either by a son or a daughter, different in any or all of these regards? One might also wonder about the situation of individuals whose parents have either been cremated, have graves that are untraceable, or exist in locales that the bereaved cannot visit for one reason or another.

In the technical realm, too, important issues exist. While it is not possible here to do justice to all such issues, enumerating them might not be out of place. The technical issues this clinical material touches upon include (1) the concept of analytic neutrality, (2) the impact of actual life experience on the analytic process, and (3) the relationship between the mourning process and the analytic process during the course of an analysis. These highly complex matters form the nexus of many controversies in the current psychoanalytic literature. I cannot discuss them here. Instead, I focus upon the clinical observations. I can only say that in working with these two particular patients, a dialectical relationship between the actual and the transference experiences and between the mourning and the analytic processes was discernible. The interpretative softening of affects involving the father facilitated the visit to his grave. This, in turn, advanced both the mourning and the analytic processes. However, the situation also presented a dilemma for the analyst. Should the analyst abide by the dictum of "not directing one's notice to anything in particular" (Freud, 1912e, p. 111), remain "without memory or desire" (Bion, 1967), and wait patiently for the analysand to talk and act as he or she pleases? Or should the analyst adopt a "strategy" (Levy, 1987), avoid the "perils of neutrality" (Renik, 1996), and help the patient focus upon the potential meanings of the visit to the grave, even to the extent of encouraging the patient actually to undertake the visit? The latter route was taken here. Questions were asked that prompted the patients to fantasize about visiting the grave, and, in the process, certainly encouraged the actual visit. This approach was in accordance with that of Freud's *vis-à-vis* Elisabeth von R. "To bring up fresh memories which had not yet reached the surface . . . [he] sent her to visit her sister's grave" (Breuer & Freud, 1895d, p. 149).

Historical precedents aside, many unanswered questions remain here. Was this manner of conducting analysis better, more useful? I would like to think so, but I am aware that others might take exception to this approach. Would the patients of such neutral analysts ever undertake a visit to their fathers' graves? Would they do it somewhat later in the course of their analyses? What would be the advantages and disadvantages of such a "neutral" approach? Clearly, more thought is needed here.

Concluding remarks

In this contribution, I have attempted to elucidate the psychological significance of human graves. I have highlighted the potential role of these "ultimate resting places" in facilitating mourning on the part of those left behind. With the help of recollections provided by friends and by using clinical illustrations, I have underscored the complex function that visiting graves of relatives performs in human mental life. And, by taking the liberty to digress into some sociopolitical matter, I have sought to demonstrate how the desecration and destruction of graves become vehicles of "ethnic cleansing" and religious and racial hatred.

While my discourse has been broad-based, I remain aware that it has failed to touch upon many aspects pertaining to graves. The use of the grave as an important, even organizing, feature in literary classics is one such area. While William Shakespeare's plays (e.g., *Hamlet, Romeo and Juliet*) and Edgar Allan Poe's fiction (e.g., *The Cask of Amontillado, The Premature Burial*) are replete with scenes involving graves, there exist other compelling references to graves in short and long fiction as well as in poetry. These include: Emily Brontë's novel *Wuthering Heights* (1847) and Henry James' story "The beast in the jungle" (1903) in English, Gabriella Mistral's *Sonnets of Death* (1914) in Spanish, Jan Nisar Akhtar's poems *The Broken Heart* (1972) and *The Silent Voice* (1954) in Urdu, Yevgeny Yevtushenko's poem "Pasternak's grave" (1960) in Russian, and Nida Fazli's poem "On father's death" (1980) in Urdu. It has not been possible to undertake a meaningful discussion of these literary gems.

Another aspect that has received inoptimal attention here is constituted by the lifetime fantasies about one's own future grave. The fear of being buried alive, seen by Freud (1919h) as a disguised version of longed-for return to the intrauterine life, is a frequent childhood vehicle for thoughts about one's own grave. Guilt-ridden fantasies of all sorts can also contribute to this fear. In a more realistic way, the thought of one's death arrives only as one enters late middle age and begins to get old. This automatically leads to a consideration of how one wishes one's body to be disposed. Fantasies about burial, one's grave, and its location now become important. The last mentioned concern is especially central to the experience of immigrants (Akhtar, 1999b). The site of a grave is usually chosen because of its proximity to where one's ancestors are buried, but the choice is also affected by where the loved ones left behind can conveniently come to visit. The greater, often insurmountable, distance between these two locations makes it difficult for the immigrant to select a satisfactory site of burial. None the less, it is common for immigrants to wish to be buried in their homelands. The fantasy of return thus remains alive in them. In this connection, it is interesting to note that some eight years before her death, the eminent psychoanalyst Margaret Mahler had arranged to have her ashes transported to Sopron, Hungary, and interned in the Jewish cemetery next to her father's grave (Stepansky, 1988). In view of the fact that her mother had perished in a Nazi concentration camp, Mahler's choice of cremation followed by burial next to her father seems to have actualized both pre-Oedipal (merger with the mother) and Oedipal (identification with the mother and closeness with the father) fantasies in a defiant stroke of genius!

Putting aside such tongue-in-cheek comments, one does come back from this sojourn in cemeteries with the realization that graves serve a greater purpose for the living than they do for the dead. They provide a concrete nidus for working through the mourning process, refuelling internal object relations, sustaining familial continuity, and seeking the blessing of those who have passed away while displaying one's own growth and accomplishments to their proxies in the burial ground. Made of brick, mortar, and stones, graves possess the potential of becoming active players, as it were, in the ongoing psychic life of the survivors.

CHAPTER SIX

Orphans

> "Our patients, who teach us so much of what we get to know, often make it clear that they met disillusionment very early indeed. They have no doubt of this and can reach deeper and deeper sadness connected with the thought"
>
> (Winnicott, 1939, p. 21)

Words matter. They help us express and convey or hide and camouflage our thoughts and inner experiences. For we psychoanalysts, this is an issue of paramount importance. We depend upon "associations"—a river-like, undulating chain of words—to deduce the psychologically elusive layers of striving and fear in our patients. Words are our allies. We listen to them and use them with utmost care. As yet, we remain vulnerable to collusion with the public at large in avoiding the use of words felt as too anxiety-provoking or deemed "politically incorrect". We refer to the external female genitalia as "vagina" instead of the medically correct "vulva", lump all militant uprisings as "terrorism", and recoil from calling anyone "mentally retarded" or "handicapped". Under the guise of updating our vocabulary, we renounce powerful and direct communication. We struggle to think and speak fearlessly, but Freud's (1897) *matrem nudam* is the outer wall of our lexical prison. (Freud, in his Letter to Wilhelm Fleiss, 3 October 1897, cited in Masson, 1985, p. 268) lapses into Latin, *matrem nudam,* while describing, at age forty-one, the childhood memory of having seen his mother naked, attesting to the power of certain words and the strenuous efforts we make to avoid using them.)

These introductory remarks, long-winded though they might seem, are intended to underscore the noticeable absence of the word "orphan" from our literature. Indeed, the word "orphan" does not appear in the index to the *Standard Edition* of *The Complete Psychological Works of Sigmund Freud,* nor is it mentioned in any of the twenty-seven glossaries published over the 120 years history of our profession (Akhtar, 2009b). A quick search of PEP-Web, the computerized compendium of the contents of twenty-nine psychoanalytic journals (as well as the contents of fifty-six major psychoanalytic books and the entire twenty-four volume set of the *Standard Edition*), reveals that although there is much written about those who have suffered parental loss during childhood, only two papers (Carveth, 1992; Gordon & Sherr, 1974) have the word "orphan" in their titles. This can be attributed to fashions of the times and to our well-intentioned desire to avoid hurtful labels. However, one wonders whether there is some anxiety resulting in such linguistic avoidance. An attempt to explore the origin of such unease might begin from examining the word itself.

The word "orphan" has its roots in the Latin *orphanus,* meaning destitute or without parents, and the Greek *orphanos,* meaning bereaved, comfortless, and one who has lost parents during childhood. Somewhat greater latitude in the connotation of the word "orphan" evolved over time (e.g., in its application to animals, unpopular technology, and a single line of a paragraph appearing at the end of the page) but the most prevalent meaning continued to be a child whose parents are dead. Two quibbles arise in this context. Does one have to lose both parents to qualify as an orphan? And, what is the cut-off point, age-wise, after which the death of a parent does not lead to one being considered an orphan?

A quick look at Spanish, Chinese, Hindi, and Arabic, the four languages that are collectively spoken by more than half of the world's population, reveals varying answers. Spanish and Chinese have only one word, *huerfano* and *gu'er*, respectively, for orphan, and restrict its use to children who have lost both parents to death. Hindi, too, has only one word, *anath*, for orphans, but its origins do not refer to the death of parents. The word actually means "not protected by anyone", or "not belonging to anyone". Moreover, the word is used only for those who have lost their fathers; there is no specific word for children who have lost their mothers. In contrast, Arabic shows a remarkable latitude and sophistication. Not only does it have different words for those who have lost a father (*al yateem*), a mother (*al munqateh*), or both parents (*al la lateem*) during childhood, it implicitly suggests a continuum of the trauma's severity. *Al yateem* translates roughly into "one has no identity or no self of his own", *al munqateh* into "one who has been severed and lacerated", and *al la lateem* into "one who is in utter despair". Fascinatingly the Arabic distinction between paternal and maternal loss centres upon conflicts of individuation *vs.* the rupture of a fused self-object representation (see the section on mental pain below).

Linguistic and cultural variations aside, the common custom is to restrict the use of the word "orphan" for those who have lost at least one parent before ceasing legally to be a minor. Thus, the word has inherently painful and helpless connotations. There is also an air of immutability associated with a designation of this sort and the nihilism that this can portend makes one recoil from it. Paradoxically, the aversion is diminished if the broader context of parental loss is even more horrifying. A dramatic illustration of this is constituted by the nearly 4,000 children orphaned as a result of the bombings of Hiroshima and Nagasaki towards the end of the Second World War. They continue to be called the "A-bomb orphans".

At the same time, the background of deprivation and of being raised by people other than parents allows rich avenues for writers' imaginations. Orphans are, therefore, often chosen as protagonists of literary fiction. Gordon and Sherr (1974) provide a comprehensive list of novels and plays where the main character has lost one or both parents. (Prominent among their list are *The Adventures of Augie March* (Bellow, 1953), *Great Expectations* (Dickens, 1860), *Tom Jones* (Fielding, 1749), *The Vicar of Wakefield* (Goldsmith, 1766), *Demian* (Hesse, 1919), and *Of Human Bondage* (Maugham, 1915).)

While familiarity with the fictional characters in their list can enhance empathy for such individuals, it is the step-by-step deconstruction of the intrapsychic vicissitudes of this trauma that truly enlightens the clinician.

The lifelong impact of childhood parental loss

The impact of parental loss during childhood is lifelong. Its myriad manifestations can be broadly grouped under the following categories: (i) continued intrapsychic relationship with the dead parent(s), (ii) mental pain and defences against it, (iii) narcissistic imbalance, (iv) disturbances in the development of aggressive drive, (v) problems in the realm of love and sexuality, (vi) disturbances in the subjective experience of time, and (vii) attitudes towards one's own mortality. In what follows, I will address the phenomenological and psychodynamic aspects of these areas in some detail.

Continued intrapsychic relationship with the dead parent(s)

In "Mourning and melancholia", his seminal contribution to the topic of loss and grief, Freud (1917e) declared that

> Reality testing has shown that the loved object no longer exists, and it proceeds to demand that all libido shall be withdrawn from its attachments to that object. This demand arouses understandable opposition—it is a matter of general observation that people never willingly abandon a libidinal position . . . normally, respect for reality gains the day. Nevertheless, its orders cannot be obeyed at once. They are carried out bit by bit, at great expense of time and cathectic energy, and in the meantime, the existence of the lost object is psychically prolonged. Each single one of the memories and expectations in which the libido is bound to the object is brought up and hyper-cathected, and detachment of the libido is accomplished in respect of it. . . . When the work of mourning is completed, the ego becomes free and uninhibited again. (pp. 244–245).

This stance became the centrepiece of the psychoanalytic perspective on mourning and only recently has come under question

(Masur, 2001; Meyers, 2001). Rather than undergoing decathexis, the lost object is now seen as becoming psychically relocated. It continues to have an existence in the mind, but the relationship between it and the self is altered and carries a lesser degree of affect. Freud, who had originated the decathexis idea, took this latter position elsewhere. In a 1929 letter to a friend whose son had died, Freud spoke of grief in the following terms:

> We know that the acute sorrow we feel after such a loss will run its course, but also that we will remain inconsolable, and will never find a substitute. No matter what may come to take its place, even should it fill that place completely, it yet remains something else. And that is how it should be. It is the only way of perpetuating a love that we do not want to abandon. [cited in Fichtner, 2003, p. 196]

Such an outcome is even more marked in children. Although there are individual variations, generally the cathexis of primary love objects is maintained for years after loss and decathexis occurs slowly and painfully in toddlers (e.g., Bowlby, 1960, 1963, 1969; Furman, 1974; Spitz, 1946, 1950, 1965). With somewhat older children, the opposite seems to be the case; there is an inability to decathect the object representation of the deceased (Nagera, 1970; Pollack, 1961; Wolfenstein, 1966). This is due to a developmental lack of tolerance of mental pain and the deeply disturbing threat of narcissistic imbalance; a parent has, after all, been a "self object" (Kohut, 1977) in addition to being a separately experienced object. Thus, a split in the ego is established. One part knows that the parent is dead. The other part holds on to the internal representation of the parent, intrapsychically "behaving" as if he or she were fully alive. Even when they know that the parent is dead, children often show intense distress and make all sorts of actual and imaginary efforts to bring the dead parent back to life. (The award-winning French film, *Ponette* (Les Films Alain Sarde, 1996) poignantly depicts a four-year old girl's anguish upon losing her mother as well as her desperate measures to bring her back to life.)

Pollock (1961) observed approximately similar phenomena in three adult patients who had lost a parent before the age of six. He noted that:

> Throughout the years there had been a retention of the deceased parent in the form of a fantasy figure who was in heaven; to whom the patient could talk and tell whatever he or she wished; who never verbally or actively responded to the patient; and who was always all-seeing and omnipresent. [p. 350]

Cournos (2001) comes very close to this in describing her lifelong reactions to the loss of her father at age three and her mother at age eleven. She notes that she "could certainly recite the fact that my mother was dead and never returning. This belief existed side by side with the fantasy of remaining in an on-going relationship with her" (p. 141). Echoing Furman (1974), she emphasizes that a child has limited choice in seeking a substitute parental figure and, thus, finds an adaptive value in maintaining a living image of the deceased parent. The findings of the Harvard Childhood Bereavement Study (Silverman & Worden, 1993) confirm this. The investigation was based upon contacting families seen by funeral directors in the Boston, Massachusetts, area where a parent had died leaving behind a child between the ages of six and seventeen. Approximately half of the eligible families agreed to participate in the study; this included 125 children whose average age was twelve. When interviewed, 81% felt that the deceased parent was watching over them and 57% reported speaking to him or her. The parent might appear to "spiritually" accompany the child, and later, the adult, everywhere. Or, the belief in his or her being alive might be betrayed by a dream image.

Clinical vignette 15

> During his late teens, Charles LeRoy (also discussed in Chapter Six), who had lost his mother at age seven, felt a sudden sense of discomfort while watching the scene where the protagonist's mother is hiding in the Valley of Lepers in the movie, *Ben Hur* (1959). Two days later, he woke up from sleep in an emotional turmoil that had elements of shock, regret, and sadness. He had dreamt that he was walking on a street and a construction worker invited him to see what was hidden under the ground. With great effort, the latter unscrewed the manhole and lifted it. When Charles looked inside, his found his mother fully alive. Apparently she had not died at all and had been living underground for several years. Charles was shocked by the discovery and felt deeply regretful that he had not known this before.

Less dramatic evidences of a lifelong internal tie to the deceased parent come in myriad forms. Aimless wandering that is unconsciously intended as a search for the lost love object is another manifestation. "Agoraphilia" (Glauber, 1955), involving an inordinate fascination for outdoors, especially ruins and wilderness, is a specific variation of such aimless wandering. Here "the love of the dead mother and the need to master the fears of her, have become the love and mastery of, or triumph over, the petrified aspects of Mother Nature" (p. 703).

Mental pain and defences against it

While they might not have consciously experienced or registered it as such during childhood, adults orphaned as children remain forever vulnerable to separation anxiety, or, to use Pine's (1979) more evocative term, "separateness anxiety"; this involves discomfort and disorientation over the sense of separateness from others. However, it is the emergence of mental pain, with its characteristic admixture of hurt, disbelief, bitterness, and anger that forms the greatest threat for their ego stability. The dysphoric experience can readily emerge at the slightest of betrayals.

Since the nature of this affect is elusive and literature assessing it is meagre, it might not be out of place to elucidate the concept here at some length. Freud (1926d) introduced the concept in psychoanalytic literature under the rubric of *Seelenshmerz* (literally, soul-pain). He acknowledged that he knew very little about this affect and fumbled in describing it. He referred to a child's crying for his mother and evoked analogies to bodily injury and loss of body parts. He also mentioned a sense of "longing" and "mental helplessness" (pp. 171–172) as being components of mental pain. In the *Project*, he suggested that mental pain resulted from a marked increase in the quantity of stimuli impinging upon the mind. This caused "a breach in the continuity" (1895, p. 307) of the protective shield. Pain was a direct result of such shock trauma. In "Mourning and melancholia", Freud related pain to object loss and said that the complex of melancholia behaved like "an open wound" (1917e, p. 253). It was, however, not until an addendum to *Inhibition, Symptoms and Anxiety* (1926d, pp. 169–172) that Freud linked his economic explanations to his object-related hypothesis regarding the origins of mental pain. He suggested that where there is physical pain, in increase in narcissistic cathexis of the afflicted site occurs, and the same is true of mental pain. In illustrating his ideas through the situation of an infant separated from his mother, Freud implied that the object loss leading to mental pain occurred at a psychic level of ego-object non-differentiation. Weiss (1934) made this explicit by stating that

> Pain arises when an injury—a break, so to speak, in the continuity—occurs within the ego . . . Love objects become, as we know, libidinally bound to the ego, as if they were parts of it. If they are torn away from it, the ego reacts as though it had sustained mutilation. The open wound thus produced in it is just what comes to the expression as mental pain. [p. 12]

Thus was born the notion that mental pain is not an accompaniment of any object loss but only of the object loss that leads to an ego rupture. It is perhaps in this spirit subsequent analysts used words such as "pining" (Klein, 1940, p. 360) and "longing" (Joffee & Sandler, 1965, p. 156) in association with mental pain. They also resorted to somatic analogies and metaphors. Indeed, in mapping out the affective world, Pontalis (1981) placed pain "at the frontiers and juncture of body and psyche, of death and life" (p. 131). In a recent effort at bringing these and other scattered writings (Joseph, 1981; Khan, 1979; Kogan, 1990) on this subject together, I stated,

> Mental pain consists of a wordless sense of self-rupture, longing, and psychic helplessness that is vague and difficult to convey to others. It usually follows the loss of a significant object or its abrupt refusal to meet one's anaclitic needs. This results in the laceration of an unconscious, fused self-object core of the self. Abruptly precipitated discrepancies between the actual and wished-for self-states add to the genesis of mental pain. Issues of hatred, guilt, moral masochism, as well as fantasies of being beaten can also be folded into the experience of mental pain. The feeling is highly disturbing and is warded off by psychic retreat, manic defense, induction of pain into others and changing the form and function of pain. Each of these can have a pathological or healthy outcome depending upon the intrapsychic and social context upon whether they ultimately permit mourning to take place of not. [Akhtar, 2000, p. 220]

Among the defences mentioned above, "manic defence", with its trio of idealization, denial of dependence, and omnipotence (Klein, 1935; Winnicott, 1935), is especially suited for warding off mental pain. *Idealization* tenaciously retains an "all good" view of the world and oneself which, in turn, defends against guilty recognition of having injured others in fact or fantasy. *Denial* is aimed at erasing the awareness of dependence upon others. *Omnipotence* is utilized to control and master objects, but without genuine concern for them. Excessive reliance upon "manic defence" depletes the capacities for mature aloneness, self-reflection, and genuine attachment. Mild, transient, and focal (i.e., only in one or the other area of psychosocial functioning) deployment of manic defence, on the other hand, can safeguard mental stability, and, in a paradoxical fashion, permit gradual acceptance of current and childhood losses.

Narcissistic imbalance

A frequent result of parental loss during childhood is lowering of self-esteem. Not having someone to belong to and nobody to call one's own results in a sense of existential shame. One feels different from others, sensing that something is missing that should have been there in one's environment (and in its internalized representative, one's psychic structure). This feeling of being different is more marked in association with pre-adolescent parental loss and tends to persist throughout the later course of life. Ameliorative impact of substitute care-givers (e.g., grandparents, step-parents) helps, but does not wipe out this inner shame completely.

Such narcissistic imbalance has many consequences. Idealization of parents, parenthood, and parenting is common. Envy of friends and relatives who did not lose parents in childhood is often evident, and so is the tendency to overprotect one's own offspring. Hunger for belonging and narcissistic demonstration of finally having someone to call one's own extends to the marital context, leading, at times, to behaviour patterns that could be annoying to the spouse.

Clinical vignette 16

Sharmila Ghosh, a thirty-five-year-old, attractive school teacher, was in psychotherapy with me. Having married a somewhat older man who was an internist, she had expected to receive a sense of protection and support besides financial security from him. He was known to be a generous man and, to all external appearances, lived an opulent life. Soon after marriage, Sharmila saw the real picture. Her husband chronically spent beyond his means and his indulgent attitude towards others had a driven quality. She and her husband began to argue about household expenses, among other things. This led to marital strife and, later, to her seeking my help.

As our work unfolded, an interesting detail of their interaction emerged. This involved her husband's handing over the telephone to her whenever a family member or a friend called him, or even when he had initiated the call. Somehow, he appeared incapable of carrying out a phone conversation from beginning to end on his own. Initially, I thought that Indian cultural emphasis upon communal togetherness (Roland, 1988) was responsible for this behaviour of his. However, when I learnt that he had lost both his parents during early childhood, I surmised differently. His handing over the phone to her now appeared to be his way of telling others that he did have someone in his life, and that someone did belong to him. When I shared this insight with Sharmila, she instantly understood and experienced a sense of tenderness towards her husband. Her telling this experience to him led to a softening of the tension between them.

Narcissistic imbalance consequent upon early parental loss might not remain restricted to such "minor" psychopathology, however. A tendency to view oneself as an "exception" (Freud, 1916d) might also develop, leading to egregious violations of societal limits and taboos. Arrogance, promiscuity, stealing, embezzlement, and near-incestuous cross-generational sexual activity may all arise out of such an unduly entitled attitude.

Disturbances in the development of aggressive drive

A frequent concomitant of early parental loss is the disturbed development of the aggressive drive. Three kinds of problems can occur. In order of decreasing severity, these include the aggressive drive undergoing atrophy, splitting, and repression. In order to understand the first of these concepts, the atrophy of aggression, one has to revisit Anna Freud's (1972) statement that a coherent aggressive drive can only evolve if there is certainty of a libidinal object being available. In simpler words, one can be meaningfully angry only if there is someone there to be angry with. This is precisely what is lacking in the life of orphans. Ever uncertain of their belonging to anyone, children without parents fail to develop the normal entitlement to be angry. They lack a "healthy capacity for indignation" (Ambassador Nathaniel Howell, personal communication, 4 April, 1996). As adults, they either do not adequately register conflict with others or readily withdraw inwards; instead of confrontation, there is mere resignation. Commonly seen in schizoid (Akhtar, 1987, 2009c) and "as if" (Deutsch, 1942) personalities, such striking absence of reactive aggression is not based upon repression. No displaced and disguised forms of resentment and anger can be found. This distinguishes atrophy of aggression from repression of aggression, since the latter is inevitably accompanied by derivative (e.g., via dreams and parapraxes) or displaced expressions.

The second type of disturbance in the metabolism of aggression involves its splitting off from the libidinal and affectively neutral sections of personality. This results in a personality organization that is essentially "borderline" (Kernberg, 1975) in structure. Self- and object-constancy do not develop if the parental loss has occurred during the first two years of life, or are retrospectively weakened if the parental loss has occurred after that period. In either case, the resulting arrest of the separation–individuation process perpetuates excessive dependency, keeping the individual psychologically in the position of a child. Splitting off of aggression also depletes the central core of the ego of the assertive energy required to negotiate the adolescent passage. Of course, this is not an all-or-nothing matter. Ameliorative presences in the environment may help the orphaned child to muster enough strength to separate from primary objects and form an autonomous identity. Yet, in most instances, some tendency towards splitting remains at the core and leads to the persistence of idealized and hated objects in the inner world.

If, however, the love–hate economy in the external surround is in favour of the former, a more integrated self can emerge. Even under such circumstances, one sees evidence that much of aggression has undergone repression and finds only limited expression in rational ways.

> Aggressive feelings are not confronted, labeled, mutually managed, and brought under modulated ego regulation by the child. Instead, they remain unchanged in the unconscious mind and are subjectively felt to be a potentially dangerous, internal liability. When stimulated by loss or threat of loss in a current important relationship, the repressed aggression threatens to breach the defense of repression and erupt in an uncontrolled aggressive act. Other defenses are then evoked to reinforce repression. [Settlage, 2001, p. 62]

Prominent among such defences are turning against the self (leading to self-neglect, self-sabotage, and self-destructiveness), projection (leading to fear of others), undoing (leading to superstitious and compulsive rituals), and reaction formation (leading to inordinate generosity and pathological altruism). For a thoughtful discourse on the normal and pathological forms of altruism, see Seelig and Rosof (2001). All in all, atrophy, splitting, and repression are mechanisms that form a hierarchy in the inner processing of early aggression in parentally deprived individuals. Keeping this spectrum in mind has implications for the treatment of orphaned adults (see details below).

Problems in the realm of love and sexuality

Developing and sustaining attachments, especially in the realm of romance and marriage, are difficult for those who have lost parents in their childhood. The anxiety inherent in intimate bonds (e.g., abandonment, loss, mobilization of aggression) can tax their egos and lead to a reflexive avoidance of attachment or tenacious clinging to loved ones. Often, there are oscillations between these poles. Alternatively, the closeness–distance conflict (Akhtar, 1992b) is displaced upon family pets, who are overindulged, or upon inanimate objects which are omnipotently controlled; deep discomfort at any change in their location or, conversely, constant re-arrangement of furniture and artwork on the walls betrays the underlying difficulties of attachment.

While there is no one-to-one correlation, the earlier the parental (especially maternal) death, the greater is the vulnerability of developing an "oral fixation", that is, a hungry, yearning, and, mostly, passive orientation towards life with an entitled desire to be fed and taken care of. To escape from such dependent needs and find alternative gratification, intense sexual strivings might develop prematurely. Kernberg (1975) emphasizes that such development powerfully reinforces Oedipal fears by pregenital fears of the mother. Under these circumstances, a positive Oedipus complex is seriously interfered with. Adult sexuality is then characterized by either sexualized dependency or prominent negative Oedipal trends. These manifest in greedy promiscuity and orally derived homosexuality among men, and among women in an intensified penis envy, flight into promiscuity to deny penis envy, or a sexualized search for the gratification of oral needs from an idealized mother, leading to homosexuality.

Disturbances in the subjective experience of time

Individuals who have lost a parent (especially the mother) during early childhood also display subtle—and sometimes, not so subtle—disturbances in the subjective experience of time. Now, we know that the origins of the sense of time are intricately bound with infantile experience of intervals between need and its gratification (Arlow, 1984, 1986; Birksted-Breen, 2009; Meissner, 2007; Orgel, 1965). Furthermore, we know that the mother's gratifying and frustrating responses are accompanied by intense emotions of pleasure and disappointment to that the "mother becomes the conveyor of time and timelessness" (Erikson, 1956, p. 246). In the Kleinian idiom,

> the baby endures and tolerates the separation because he/she can count on a good object that is firmly established inside himself; therefore, being able to identify with some aspects of this object. The ego builds up concomitantly to the initial notions of the present (which is based on the memory from the past) and it develops the ability to wait for the reappearance of the object in the future. The future emerges as a possibility of representing and waiting (instead of despairing), of repairing and affectively finding again the same emotional state of the contact between nipple and mouth. [Bornholdt, 2009, p. 101]

Among other factors that contribute to the consolidation of a sense of passing time are the "forward projection of narcissism"

(Chasseguet-Smirgel, 1984, p. 28) on the older generation and the associated injunction to wait (to marry, to be an adult) that Oedipal children receive from their parents. All in all, it sees that parental availability and "good-enough" parental functioning is essential for the evolution of a proper and realistic time sense in the child.

All this falls apart with the death of a parent. Not only are the subtle structuring functions lost, the child's ego is split between a developmentally pressured and inescapable forward movement in time and a stunned clinging to the object before it was lost. The former might go through post trauma development with variable degrees of authentic participation and accruing of structure. The latter remains fixated upon a nostalgic longing for the now idealized past or a desperate conviction that the tragic loss can and will be totally undone. The former tendency is embodied in an "if-only . . ." fantasy that claims that life would have been conflict-free were it not for the childhood parental loss. To be sure, there is some truth to this idea, but the embellishment resides in feeling that life was devoid of all problems before the parental death and that everything would have turned out well had the tragedy not occurred.

A variant of the "if-only . . ." fantasy is the "someday . . ." fantasy, whereby the orphan relentlessly expects to find and reunite with the parent whom, in a separate section of his mind, he recognizes to be dead. The manner in which such individuals seek a "fantasied reversal of a calamity that has occurred" (Renik, 1990, p. 234) and strive to materialize this "someday" varies greatly (Akhtar, 1996b). Some pursue it actively while others simply wait and turn towards spirituality. Abraham's (1924) observation, though made in a different context, is pertinent in this regard as well.

> Some people are dominated by the belief that there will always be some kind person—a representative of the mother, of course—to take care of them and to give them everything they need. This optimistic belief condemns them to inactivity. [p. 399]

Frequently, the "if only . . ." and "someday" fantasies (Akhtar, 1996b) coexist and form a tandem theme. "If only this had not happened, life would have been all right, but someday this will be revealed and life will (again) become blissful." Such attitudes push the individual out of the present time; he shuttles between past and future, feeling nostalgic at one moment and hopeful at another, but always out of tune with the calendar of actual life.

Attitudes towards one's own mortality

The adult orphan often displays an attitude towards his own mortality that differs from his more fortunate counterparts in life. He is either inordinately afraid of dying or, equally likely, is idealizing of death and fascinated by the idea of his own mortality. Referring to the first constellation, Settlage (2001) declares that his

> clinical experience suggests that the inadequate structuring of object and self constancy is an important factor in the fear of facing one's eventual mortality. Impairment of these structures deprives the individual of the inner sense of being loved and cared about that underlies emotional equanimity and being at peace with oneself. When present, this inner sense makes it easier to accept the reality of one's own death. [p. 64]

I agree with this observation. However, I think that there is both a quantitative and qualitative difference in the fear of death experienced by normal persons and that felt by maternally deprived individuals. In the former, fear of death draws affective tributaries from the deepest remnants of annihilation anxiety, fear of separation from love objects, and castration fantasies (for details, see Chapter Five). In those who have experienced childhood parental loss, all these factors are operative. In addition, there is a repudiated pressure to identify with the dead parent, give up the human aspects of identity, and return to an inanimate status (Lichtenstein, 1963). Having, at times, been treated as inanimate by callously inattentive or enraged substitute care-takers has also blurred their inner boundaries between the animate and inanimate, and resulted in their fear that the latter will take over their entire existence. Finally, the despair at dying without having joyously lived is far more, as one would imagine, than at expecting death after having lived well.

The second outcome of having lost a parent in childhood is a tendency to be over-involved in thoughts about death and dying. Death can become idealized and, unconsciously, personified as a beckoning mother or lover (Wheelis, 1966). One might pursue it actively (via gross or subtle self-destructive acts) or await its arrival with inordinate eagerness. The following poem by an East Coast-based psychotherapist eloquently captures the latter sentiment.

> The train of death has started towards my city.
> Only, it is at some distance right now.
> Or, is it?
> Thinking of death at thirty-seven,
> Waiting on the train station,
> I sense the aching of the tracks for the
> Crushing embrace of oversized wheels. Can smell
> The perspiration of the engine.
> Am awed
> At its dark surefootedness.
> Yet, the cold certainty is familiar.
> For thirty years,
> I have waited on this station.
> The pile of newspapers besides me growing each day
> All the news of the world, cross word puzzles,
> Cartoons, editorials, ads
> My luggage for the journey to come.

The poem is titled "Thinking of death at thirty-seven", the age at which the individual (who prefers to remains anonymous, though has given permission to include this poem) wrote it. What became evident to him much later is that in writing "For thirty years / I have waited on this station", he had revealed that he was seven years old at the time of his mother's death.

Some caveats

The foregoing description of the psychopathological consequences of childhood parental loss needs "softening" by a reminder that the outcome of such calamity is far from uniform. Many variables have to be taken into account, with each having its own pathoplastic impact upon the inner goings on.

- The resemblance to what has been described above of certain features of severe character pathology (Kernberg, 1975; Akhtar,

1991a, 1992a) should not lead one to conclude that childhood parental loss always results in such disorders. The fact is that grown up orphans give evidence of a wide range of personality functioning, ranging from severe to mild psychopathology and even mental health. (Few, if any, psychoanalytic texts describe "mental health" explicitly, though implications about it are scattered throughout the corpus of our literature. Over three decades of absorption in this literature has led me to conclude that the following ten developmental achievements and ego capacities, if mostly intact most of the time, are sufficient to constitute mental health: (i) intact reality testing, (ii) capacity to experience and tolerate ambivalence, (iii) capacity for separateness, genuine attachment, and a mournful reaction upon separation, (iv) muted affects and reasonable degree of impulse control, (v) establishment of incest barrier, (vi) acceptance of generational boundaries, (vii) a well-internalized sense of morality, (viii) capacity to play, (ix) fusion of affection and erotic desire giving rise to a capacity for mature romantic love, and (x) a coherent sense of identity.)

- Like all traumas, being orphaned may, at times, become the basis of personality strengths as well. Character traits of stoicism, ambition, and generativity especially can be intensified. Diminished fear of death, in some adults with childhood parental loss, can result in remarkable acts of courage and sacrifice.
- As a follow-up to the point above, the presence of "God-given" talents (e.g., artistic inclination) and superior intelligence can greatly modify the impact of being orphaned. A healthy and ambitious nucleus of personality can be organized around such extraordinary abilities and lead to great fame and social success. (An admittedly incomplete list of renowned orphans in the course of man's history includes *prophets* (e.g., Muhammad), *great philosophers* (e.g., Aristotle), *kings and conquistadors* (e.g., Julius Caesar), *musicians and singers* (e.g., Louis Armstrong, Johannes Sebastian Bach, and John Lennon), *writers and poets* (e.g., John Keats, Rudyard Kipling, and Leo Tolstoy), *political leaders* (e.g., Bill Clinton, Nelson Mandela, and Malcolm X), and *film personalities* (e.g., Ingrid Bergman and Marilyn Monroe). The positive traits of courage, resilience,

perseverance, imaginativeness, and creativity displayed by these individuals, though multiply determined, might have been fuelled by the trauma of childhood parental loss. A far less celebrated and yet profoundly impressive individual who could be added to this list was Korczak Ziolkowski (1908–1982), the Polish-American orphan from Boston who grew up to undertake the carving of the world's largest statue (in honour of the Native American chief, Crazy Horse) in South Dakota.)

- The impact of a parent's death varies with the child's age at the time of such loss (Bowlby, 1961, 1963; Furman, 1974; Wolfenstein, 1966). The degree of psychic autonomy achieved, the particular developmental conflicts active at the time, and the level of ego maturity together determine how and to what extent the trauma would become adequately "metabolized" and the nature of meanings that would be assigned to the tragedy.
- The death of a mother might have a greater or, at least, different affect upon a growing child than the death of a father. Provided all other variables remain the same, maternal death tends to deprive the child of "a secure base" (Bowlby, 1988) and a source of emotional refuelling and the father's death robs the child of firm investment in external reality and the outer rind of the ego.
- The gender of the child might also play a role in the impact of parental loss. In general, girls tend to be more adversely affected by the loss of the mother than boys. The loss of mother deprives them not only of the primary love object and symbiotic partner, but of a role model and scaffold for the elaboration of core gender identity. The same applies to the boy's losing a father during childhood.
- A major role in determining the outcome of parental loss is also played by the nature of relationship the child had with the parent before his or her death. Unresolved conflicts, especially those laden with aggression, tend to complicate the healing of the wounded psyche by adding a sense of guilt and responsibility for the parent's death (Volkan, 1981).
- The socioeconomic status of the family can also affect what final shape the trauma of childhood parental loss would take.

The availability of ample monetary resources can shield the child from the harshness of external reality while also providing access to better educational resources and institutions.

- The role of ameliorative influences is of paramount importance *vis-à-vis* childhood parental loss. The auxiliary ego support provided by the substitute parents (e.g., step-parents, grandparents) can go a long way in helping the orphaned child mourn, salvage self-esteem, and retain a sense of purpose in life. Extra-familial figures such as housekeepers, nannies, neighbours, schoolteachers, and clergy can also be of considerable help in mitigating the deleterious impact of such trauma. Much more important than all this is the behaviour of the surviving parent. If he or she remains stable, continues the appropriate development-facilitating role, and attempts to compensate for the child's loss while also empathizing with it, the child can show remarkable resilience. A non-clinical anecdote captures this point very well. Recounted by a Pakistani colleague, Naeem Jaafri, the story goes like this:

> I was a little over seven when I lost my mother. It had a devastating impact upon me. But my father, an internist with a large private practice, was kind and loving and helped me a lot. A year or two later, he remarried. My stepmother was also good to me and yet I felt something was not quite right. I felt she never gave me sufficient food to eat. When I told this to my father, he did something remarkable. He told me that I could go and eat whatever and however much I liked at the corner restaurant down the street from his office, free of charge; he would pay the bill on a monthly basis without ever questioning me. I was at first flabbergasted, then thrilled, by this newfound power. I visited the restaurant at all sorts of times, ordering this and that item on the menu. The bills were always paid and no one raised an eyebrow. Within a few months, I got tired of the whole thing and stopped going to the restaurant. The complaint I had against my stepmother also withered away. Matters seemed more manageable and peaceful to me. [personal communication, December 2009]

While it can be argued that my colleague's father should have sat himself and his wife down and chatted about whatever was going on between them, such an expectation from a busy physician in 1950s Lahore is merely a psychoanalyst's dream. The fact is that the father intervened to restore the loss sense of omnipotence in his boy, most likely knowing (at least, on an unconscious level) that the matter had little to do with actual food. In doing so, he did help his child.

What this anecdote, as well as the foregoing caveats, demonstrates is that simply knowing that someone is an orphan is not enough. A larger number of biopsychosocial variables and their complex interplay with each other must be taken into account in order to grasp the deep psychological significance of childhood parental loss. In the words of Anna Freud (1974)

> It is on the one hand the total character and personality of the child and on the other hand the totality of environmental circumstances which determine the outcome of the experience. Here, as in all other areas of the child's life, the interaction between internal and external forces decides between the possibility of normal developmental progress and the incidence of pathological developmental distortion or arrest. [p. vii]

Armed with such nuanced empathy, one can approach the treatment of adult orphans in a meaningful manner.

Guidelines for treating orphaned adults

Based upon my clinical experience with adults who have suffered the loss of one or both parents in childhood, I have delineated six technical guidelines for working with them. I must emphasize, though, that I am not recommending specific strategies, only a background for the "evenly suspended attention" (Freud, 1912e, p. 111) that is customary in our work.

Providing a greater amount of "illusion" and "holding"

Those who have lost a parent in early childhood have been introduced to "reality" in a brutal manner. The illusion of absolute safety, afforded by parental "holding" (Winnicott, 1960), has been prematurely ruptured. Infantile omnipotence, instead of being renounced gradually and in a piecemeal fashion, has had to be given up abruptly. All this results in a longing—however dormant and disguised it may be—for a type of interpersonal relatedness in which one can truly relax and express oneself with little worry about the dyadic partner's needs. All one desires is to be fully accepted, cared for, and treated with exquisite empathy and devotion. Not that there is no aggression, hostility, and revenge fantasies contained in the patient's psyche, but, at the beginning stage of treatment, these are not fully accessible for the patient to experience and explore. That work will emerge, but only after the patient has experienced an illusory "dual unity" (Mahler, Pine, & Bergman, 1975) for a sufficiently long period of time.

The predominant therapeutic task with orphaned adults is, therefore, to create and sustain a proper "holding environment" (Winnicott, 1960). Besides the physical comfort and stability of the office where the two parties meet (for details, see Akhtar, 2009e), this includes a psychological ambience of trust, safety, non-judgemental acceptance, and containment of affects while helping the patient's growth potential to be activated. To be sure, such provision is important in the treatment of all patients, but it acquires greater valence in those with a background of childhood parental loss.

A concrete expression of such therapeutic attitude resides in seeing the patient in a face-to-face position. The availability of visual contact with the actual person of the analyst subliminally gratifies the "real" object hunger of these patients to the extent that it becomes possible to discuss it. Even when a more traditional psychoanalytic treatment is undertaken, an initial period of sitting up for at least a few weeks is helpful; this leads to a certain amount of internalization of the analyst and diminishes the impact of the visual loss upon beginning to lie down on the couch (Akhtar, 1992b, 2007b). During the analytic treatment also, an atmosphere needs to be created whereby the patient feels comfortable to sit up from time to time; such departures from the recumbent position might be interpreted or benignly accepted, depending upon the analyst's empathic sense of what is going on and how to handle it best. Celenza's (2005) recommendation that "every analysis should, at some point, include both modalities [sitting up and lying down] for some period of time" (p. 1656) is important to remember in this context. She notes that both lying down on the couch and sitting up on the chair have their own pros and cons, and each can facilitate dialogue, even self-revelation, though in different ways.

Individuals who have suffered childhood parental loss also need a greater leeway with physically settling in the office and making it their own, so to speak. They often borrow magazines from the waiting room and, indeed, should be readily allowed to do so without making any interpretations. Abrams' (1978) concept of "developmental intervention" is pertinent in this context. This refers to the analyst's supportively "permitting" or underscoring the progressive trend when a hitherto thwarted capacity has emerged as a result of the analyst's "holding" or interpretive activity. From this perspective, an orphaned adult's taking things from the office or the waiting room is seen as the resumption of the healthy sense of entitlement (over parents) that had been ruptured by the parental death. The analyst's upholding this newly acquired ability of the patient facilitates the emergence of experiential building blocks necessary for further development.

Validating the importance and the "unfairness" of the loss

The therapist must offer empathic resonance to the adult orphan's loss and its profound effects upon him. If the patient asks whether it was "fair" that his mother or father died when he was a little child, the therapist should not hesitate to say that it was certainly "unfair". Somewhat later in their work, the therapist might also point out that the question of something being "fair" or "unfair" is itself a concern of childhood; adult life is replete with randomness and unfairness both against and in favour of oneself. Subsequently, the therapist might add that, given the vantage point of a developing child, it *is* unfair to have lost a parent and be left bereft of support and belonging. Such "mirroring" (Kohut, 1977) and "affirmative" (Killingmo, 1989) interventions can have healing effects of their own. Pine's (1998) remark that, at times, the seemingly nonspecific elements of technique acquire high individualized therapeutic effects is relevant in this context.

In working with such patients, one often comes across the fact that significant adults in their background did not help them mourn the death of the parent. In fact, they avoided the topic and acted as if everything had returned to normal very soon after the child's parent had died. The true subjective experience of the orphaned child was not validated. This, in turn, led to the child (and, subsequently, the adult) feeling even more lonely and isolated. The longing for genuine recognition became intensified and, at times, quite blatant.

Clinical vignette: 17

> Charles LeRoy (see Clinical Vignette: 15, above) had lost his mother at the age of seven and was soon abandoned by his father. Raised by ageing grandparents and sundry relatives, Charles had no memory of any adult every talking to him about his mother's death. Everyone treated him kindly, but this in itself was far removed from the shattered inner experience that he was going through. Charles once visited a remote uncle who worked as a superintendent of an old-style orphanage. Upon seeing the place and the collective life of the institutionalized children, Charles felt a sharp pang of longing to be enrolled there. The environment mirrored his true self and held the promise of an authentic identity for him.

Listening to this kind of experience teaches us the importance of genuine mirroring and validation while dealing with orphaned adults. Any attempt to minimize the long-term, indeed lifelong, impact of childhood parental death negates the patients' subjectivity and erodes therapeutic alliance with them. At the same time, it should be underscored that validation is not restricted to verbal remarks. The well-timed raising of an eyebrow, the attuned leaning forward in the chair while talking to the patient, and a confirming nod of the head often carry more weight than the therapist's words. Even a respectful acceptance of the patient's silence can make the patient feel deeply understood. The following observation of Klein (1963) eloquently captures this point.

> However gratifying it is in later life to express thoughts and feelings, to a congenial person, there remains an unsatisfied longing for an understanding without words—ultimately for the earliest relations with the mother. This longing contributes to the sense of loneliness and derives from the depressive feeling of an irretrievable loss. [p. 301]

That this longing is much more intense in individuals who have lost parents (especially the mother) goes without saying.

Discerning the defences against the awareness of the pervasive impact of the loss

Not infrequently, adults who have been orphaned as children enter psychotherapy and psychoanalysis for reasons that are overtly unrelated to their childhood trauma. They know the facts of their loss, but do not realize how deep and pervasive its impact has been over them. The following cases illustrate how a background of pain pervades their lives and, in unconscious ways, contributes to their presenting symptoms.

Clinical vignette 18

> Sol Ackerman, a thirty-five-year-old internist, became symptomatic a few months after the birth of his son. He was madly "in love" with the baby and reacted with intense pain to the slightest inattention of his wife towards the child. This led to friction between them, which was fuelled by Sol's repeatedly calling home from work to check on his infant son's welfare. The marital tension was not the whole problem, though. Sol was aware of some gnawing anguish that was threatening to break through his otherwise composed persona, a pain the true origins of which he could not fathom.
>
> In the second session of his treatment, Sol reported the following dream: "I am flying a small plane, solo. Its engine is having some trouble. I land the plane at the North Pole and come out seeking help. There is snow everywhere. I walk. And then suddenly I come across this woman sitting on a bench. But there is something very peculiar about the woman. She is made entirely of small icicles. She is brittle and cannot move. Just as I am looking at her, my good friend Bob appears on the scene. He and I help the woman to rise up and begin walking. The scene changes. Now I am in Spain, a country I have never visited in reality. I am in a tavern. There is red wine being served. And, there are lively and beautiful women everywhere."
>
> Sol's associations led to the memory of his mother's developing scleroderma when he was four years old and, over the next two years, developing contractures of skin and joints. She died, when Sol was six, in an

immobile and "frozen" state. Amid sobs, Sol began to see how the dream revealed his wish to be helped by his analyst (represented by his friend, Bob) to thaw this frozen grief and move on with his life to more enjoyable activities. The analysis of this dream not only opened up the floodgates to the memories of his childhood loss (and how it had always remained with him) but also to associations that provided links between his maternal loss and his anxious insistence upon his wife remaining constantly available to his baby son.

Such stirring up of childhood loss at the time of becoming a parent is understandable (see also Pollock, 1970). However, events that can trigger the trauma of orphanhood are diverse and, at times, far removed from the realm of parent–child interaction.

Clinical vignette 19

Mary Thompson, a retired librarian in her mid-sixties, sought my help for panic attacks which interfered in her ability to function optimally. She had received ongoing but ultimately unhelpful treatment for the past twenty years. Mary had managed to function, but her anxiety attacks had never gone away. She grew increasing disenchanted, angry, and depressed as she found herself unable to maintain the lifestyle that she had in the past.

Her symptoms appeared twenty years ago when she was bitten by a venomous snake while vacationing with her friends. She was treated by the local doctors with the appropriate anti-venom and flown home. However, upon her return, she suffered a toxic reaction, which affected her body such that it swelled up and she was unable to move. Her medical doctor, unfamiliar with the particular anti-venom administered, put her through a series of tests that caused further incapacitation and left her feeling helpless and furious. Although the situation was eventually rectified, it precipitated the onset of her anxiety-related symptoms.

During the initial sessions of the treatment, Mary revealed the details of a tragic childhood. She lost both parents at three years of age. Her father bludgeoned Mary's mother to death. He then took a shotgun to his head and killed himself as his young daughter (Mary) and his infant son lay in a crib in the next room. The children were soon placed in an orphanage and, over time, adopted by different families. Mary, at age five, was sent from her native state to live with adoptive parents.

Mary grew very fond of her adoptive mother, though she cared little for her adoptive father, who was abusive towards both her and his wife. Mary moved out of the house during her late teens, when her adopted mother died. She then pursued a semi-professional degree and found a job, which earned her a decent income. An avid sportswoman, she became active in the local women's soccer team. She also enjoyed writing poetry and had, over the years, written a fair amount of it. Although Mary had maintained some connection with her brother, spending her summer holidays with him, it was only after she became an adult that she had the freedom and flexibility to develop family ties of her own choosing. This consisted of a female lover with whom she had been living for over forty years.

Although Mary knew of her early parental loss, it was only during our work together that she began to connect that trauma with her current symptoms. Initially, she spoke of these losses through clenched teeth and with tense posture, and responded with anger to my enquiries. I decided to stop asking questions and simply listen as her narrative unfolded. Mary was sceptical of any treatment and angry at the world of doctors. I listened patiently, affording her the space that she needed, yet maintaining a neutral yet empathic stance towards her. I did not offer immediate relief, just the sense that that in time we would understand all this together.

In time, both Mary and I were able to link the onset of her symptoms to her early childhood trauma. The loss of her parents, which left her an orphan, introduced her to a profound sense of helplessness. She recalled hearing her father bludgeoning her mother and then the sound of the shotgun. While she attempted to run out of the house (at age three!) with her baby brother, the sense of being overwhelmed and without any support remained inside her. This feeling of helplessness emerged repeatedly during her stay in the orphanage. Such was the case when she had to abide by idiosyncratic "house rules" and, more importantly, to witness her brother (and the little friends that she had made there) being sent away for adoption. Mary could now begin to understand why the immobility following the snake-bite episode had stirred a deep sense of anxiety in her. As she developed a deeper insight into the nature of her current symptoms and the childhood narrative that lay hidden in them, Mary began to feel less anxious and resumed some of her earlier activities.

While both foregoing cases portray anxiety-related symptoms as the presenting features that gradually led to the discerning of the long-term effects of childhood parental loss, the clinical picture in such situations varies greatly. At times, patients seek help because they have become depressed in the face of a current loss that triggers the earlier, but dormant, trauma. At other times, the clinical picture is one of self-destructive acting out that turns out to be a desperate cry for help.

Clinical vignette 20

> Susan King, an attractive college student in her mid-twenties, was referred to me following a sudden onset of depression precipitated by the death of her maternal grandmother. Despite a trial of anti-depressants by her family physician, Susan's symptoms did not lessen. Instead, she found herself abruptly ending a relationship of five months. Her uncontrollable crying and inability to study finally brought her to my office.
>
> I gathered that Susan had lost her mother in an automobile accident when she was five years old. Following this, her father remarried and Susan was placed in the charge of care-takers who came and went as the family struggled to deal with their departures. Susan later moved away from home to attend college. Following this, she procured a job in the adjoining state where I had my practice.
>
> Later, Susan narrated a more complex history of her childhood and adult life. She had terminated a relationship of five months, describing it as nothing but sexual and one that could not be sustained anyway. Prior to that, she had ended a meaningful relationship with a young man that had lasted five years. Although she described this relationship as being "ideal" in many ways, she nevertheless engaged in destructive behaviours, including sexual promiscuity, that were bound to destroy the bond.
>
> A picture of early childhood neglect also emerged. After her mother died, Susan was placed in a new school. Too ashamed to talk about her loss, she kept silent. She often went to school with a dishevelled appearance, receiving little supervision from her stepmother or the ever-changing cadre of housekeepers. The youngest of five siblings, she was often in the company of teenagers who overlooked her need to be supervised. She soon became a participant in their sexual play and this dominated most of her adolescent life.
>
> As our work deepened, the pattern of self-destructive behaviours became more apparent. On one occasion, she, along with a girlfriend,

> went on a trip and "played a game of roulette with the drug Ecstasy". What this essentially entailed was taking the drug without knowing the vendor, off the street—an extremely dangerous thing to do. Susan had a history of some drinking and doing drugs, but this was certainly out of character for her. At another time, she "crashed" a party in her neighbourhood wearing a short leather skirt, boots, and a sexy top. Again, this was out of character for her, as she attended the church at weekends and was a devout Christian. Besides such dangerous enactments, there was a deepening attachment to me. Susan now began to have enormous difficulty leaving the office. She cried in almost every session as she recalled painful memories of her deceased mother. As a child, she was numb, but clung to her housekeepers, becoming distraught when they left. This part was now present in my office.
>
> Susan could now begin to connect her symptoms to her early childhood loss of her mother. It became clear that her counterphobic risk-taking was an unconscious cry for help; it betrayed a wish that I (as a parent) protect her from all dangers. The hitherto unrecognized and yet dominant role of the number five (e.g., her breakups at five months and five years, her going to the fifth floor of my building even though my office was located on the fifteenth floor) could be seen as a magical attempt to return to age five (when she lost her mother) in order to thaw the frozen grief within her.

Besides the sort of interpretative linkages described in the three vignettes above, the analyst must keep his ears attuned to listening for the subtle ways in which the death of a parent in childhood is denied and the full recovery from it postponed. Here, the disarmament of the "if-only" and "someday" fantasies (Akhtar, 1996b) acquires a central technical role. It is as if what the child could not mourn, the adult is refusing to mourn. That this needs holding, containing, unmasking, and interpreting goes without saying (for details of technique *vis-à-vis* such fantasies, see Akhtar, 1996b).

Additionally, an eye must be kept on the vicissitudes of aggression in such patients. If one suspects a maldevelopment and atrophy of aggression in them, gentle questioning about it and encouragement to be more expressive might be indicated. Also useful might be unmasking the patient's lack of entitlement. With patients whose aggression has become split off from the main sector of the personality, it might help to make "bridging interventions" (Kernberg, 1975) that involve the analyst's display (by gentle verbal reminders or a subtle shift in the tone of voice) that he, at least, has not forgotten the transference configuration that is opposite to the one currently active. Finally, with patients in whom aggression has undergone massive repression, the customary work of defence analysis and transference interpretation is indicated.

Interpreting the defensive uses of one's status as an orphan

Another important task in the treatment of orphaned adults involves discerning the moments when the lament of loss is serving a "screen" (Akhtar, 2009b, p. 253) function and keeping even more troubling intrapsychic matters in abeyance. Often the "predeath" family environment has not been as tranquil as initially portrayed by the patient. In the case of one particular patient, for instance, there had been many shifts of family residence, the death of a beloved aunt, and a painful separation from the biological father *before* the patient lost his mother at age seven. The traumatic effects of the preceding incidents had, however, been glossed over by the patient, who attributed all his difficulties to the death of his mother. Certainly, there is little reason to regard this case as exceptional in clinical practice.

Given the fact that orphanhood has diverse consequences and there is a dialectical relationship between the direct and indirect damage that has occurred as a result, it is hardly surprising that patients can use one as a defence against the other. Take, for instance, the patient's need for validation that he or she has suffered a major loss and this indeed has been a very unfortunate occurrence. This can acquire a sadomasochistic colouration. One who asks over and over again if it was "good" or "fair" that his parent(s) died during childhood is hardly looking for a mirroring confirmation. Such "interrogation" is better responded to by clarifying its affective tone, unmasking the denial (of the therapist's having already stated that it was "unfair") implicit in it, and interpreting the sadistic ("you do not believe me") and masochistic ("see how fate has dealt me a cruel blow") transferences inherent in it. The desperate object hunger, the near-addictive masochism, and the unconscious sadism can only then come to the surface. Endlessly patient listening to repetitive material and going on and on with "affirmative interventions" (Killingmo, 1989) is not technically appropriate under such circumstances. Here, I wish to iterate an earlier comment of mine.

> Listening is good. Listening patiently for a long time is better. But listening forever to material that is all too familiar constitutes a collusion with the patient's sadomasochism and narcissism. Such listening is contrary to the purposes of psychoanalysis. [Akhtar, 2007d, p. 13]

Paying special attention to termination and post-termination phases of the treatment

Although it is not possible to generalize, there is ample foundation for the thought that terminating treatment might be harder for those with a background of childhood parental loss (Furman, 1974). Letting go of the nurturing and development-enhancing relationship provided by psychoanalysis (or intensive psychotherapy) is likely to reawaken the wound of childhood loss. This can be mitigated by the judicious use—in varying and individually tailored combinations—of the following measures:

- arriving at the decision to terminate more slowly than usual and with much greater attention to the patient's vulnerability in this regard;
- having a longer interval between the day one agrees to terminate and the day one decides the actual date of termination;
- setting the date of termination fairly in advance, that is, with at least six months or so still left to work together.
- following Bergman's (2005) recommendations, conducting the last few hours of treatment with the patient sitting up and with the analyst and patient assessing what has been accomplished and what further work might still be there to do on one's own: "During this time, the two partners are speaking to each other more as equals than they did during the analysis itself" (p. 251);
- following Joseph Schachter's (1990, 1992) recommendations, bringing up the possibility of post-termination contacts, though leaving the choice to exercise this option and to initiate it to the patient.

These five guidelines seek to provide auxiliary ego support for the patient for whom separation and loss are especially painful. However, these are only pointers, not rules. Their use has to be tailored to individual situations, keeping the strengths and "soft spots" of each particular patient in mind.

Managing the countertransference experience

Working with adults who have lost one or both parents in childhood can evoke powerful countertransference responses. Pertinent in this context is the following observation by Parens (2010), even though it is made in the context of children grieving over the death of a parent.

> Many empathic adults find it difficult to tolerate a young child's experiencing intense psychic pain. We know in our field that helping such a child deal with his/her feelings, thoughts, and fantasies is extremely painful not only for the remaining sensitive parent, but also for such teachers, and it is even taxing for therapists. Yet, we know that we cannot help a child cope with painful experiences without empathetically allowing the child's affects to resonate within our own psyche, with our own experiences of object loss, an experience unavoidably painful to a greater or lesser degree for each of us. [p. 43]

Similar difficulties can arise in the treatment of adults who have suffered childhood parental loss. Their desperate hunger for the deceased parent, their wistful longing for the analyst to provide the guidance expected from the parent who is no more, their soul-wrenching pain at the inability to turn the clock back, and their recurring reminder about the unfairness of what happened, can together strain the analyst's work ego. The fact that the transferences of these patients have a markedly "real" quality can also compromise his interpretative skills. The difficulty is compounded if the analyst has also suffered a similar childhood loss.

The resulting countertransferences can lead either to a defensive recoil from the patient's anguish or to an over-identification with the consciously avowed "traumatized child" self. The former tendency can lead to viewing the patient's wailing mostly as a defence against other, more "primitive" or more "advanced" conflicts. The latter tendency can lead to over-gratification of the patient and non-activation (hence, non-interpretation) of negative transference constellations. The former stance overlooks the patient's dependent strivings. The latter ignores the patient's resilience and creativity in face of the loss. The former type of countertransference leaning minimizes the patient's need for continuity and availability (e.g., knowing where the analyst is going for vacation, having some contact during long breaks in treatment). The latter type of countertransference leaning minimizes the patient's developmental need for autonomy and to bear a modicum of pain at separations. Clearly, both extremes are to be avoided. A sustained, though benevolent, vigilance towards one's own emotional participation in the therapeutic process goes a long way in assuring a balanced stance.

Concluding remarks

In this chapter, I have surveyed the multi-layered consequences of childhood parental loss. Employing the much avoided, but direct and evocative, designation "orphan", I have elucidated the lifelong struggles and vulnerabilities of individuals whose parents have died early on in their lives. The realms in which long-term consequences of this trauma can be found include those of aggression, narcissism, love and sexuality, subjective experience of time, and attitudes toward one's own mortality. However, a more central issue is the intrapsychic relationship the "orphan" maintains with his or her lost parent. Never fully relinquished, this internal object representation exerts a powerful influence on the individual, an influence that can be pathogenic (e.g., lifelong vulnerability to separation anxiety) or salutary (e.g., enhanced ambition and creativity). Clearly, the balance of outcome depends upon a large number of factors that include the age at which the loss occurred, the nature of relationship with the parent before he or she died, the constitutional talents of the child, the degree of love and reliability offered by the surviving parent and/or substitute parental figure(s), the availability of health-promoting role models, the monetary stability of the family, and the degree to which those around the child were willing and/or able to facilitate his mourning of the loss. This last mentioned factor cannot be overemphasized, since many adults feel uncomfortable in seeing a child sad and distract him from the work of mourning instead of helping him with it.

All this has consequences for the treatment of adults who have lost one or both parents during childhood. A greater degree of "illusion" and "holding", validation of the tragic nature of the loss, clarification and interpretation of defences against mourning, unmasking of the defensive uses of the tragedy and of its consequences, and careful monitoring of the countertransference experience constitute the needed background for conducting psychotherapy and psychoanalysis with such patients.

While I have covered a fairly large territory of concerns, there still remain matters that need to be understood. Four unaddressed areas readily come to mind. *First,* and foremost, since childhood parental loss hardly ever occurs in isolation from other potentially pathogenic influences (e.g., destabilized family, compromised monetary situations, depressed care-takers), it is important that comparative long-term studies be made of "real" *vs.* "psychic" orphans. The latter designation includes children abandoned by parents and raised in haphazard ways by this or that reluctant relative, and children who were misinformed that their mother or father had died only later to find out the actual truth about the situation. Such comparative data might help distinguish the psychopathological impact of parental loss from other complicating factors that are often associated with it but are not specific to it. *Second,* while I have mentioned, in passing, the poignant depiction of orphans in literature, a thorough comparison of the personality characteristics attributed to them is still pending. Such pooling of the available "data" might help in developing a finer and more sophisticated composite profile of the adult orphan's psychic functioning. *Third,* more knowledge is needed regarding whether the old-style orphanages (or some contemporary reincarnation of them) are more ego-supportive of an orphan child, or whether it is better that the child be shielded from orphanhood becoming a part of his identity. Investigations along this line might also yield strategies to help diminish what I call the "shame of the motherless child" and to improve coping skills of the traumatized child. *Finally,* a critical revisiting of the psychoanalytic case reports dealing with orphaned children and adults—since it was last done over three decades ago (Furman, 1974)—is warranted in order to fine-tune therapeutic strategies that best serve this clinical population. The technical guidelines I have offered in this chapter need to be examined, supported, or refuted, and further elaborated upon by others.

As work along the lines suggested above evolves, the answer to the most frequently asked question in this realm ("Does one ever fully get over an early childhood parental loss?") might find further refinement and nuance. Meanwhile, Furman's (1974) observation remains valid: "Some may be better able to cope with this tragedy than others; for all, it becomes a life-long burden" (p. 172). At the same time, how one carries this "burden" and to what extent the subterranean anguish fuels creative efforts also remain important. Braque's (1982–1963) following statement is good to keep in mind in this context: "art is a wound turned to light".

PART III

LIFE AND DEATH

CHAPTER SEVEN

Coda

> "In biological functions, the two basic instincts operate against each other or combine with each other. Thus, the act of eating is a destruction of the object with the final aim of incorporating it and the sexual act is an act of aggression with the purpose of the most intimate union. . . . This concurrent and mutually opposing action of the two basic instincts gives rise to the whole variegation of the phenomena of life"
>
> (Freud, 1940a [1938], p. 149]

We regard life and death as categorically separate. The absolute, final, and immutable nature of death has made us accustomed to this view. Only in our wishful fantasies, dreams, and literature—mournful, gothic, or science fiction—do we overcome the insurmountable barriers between life and death. Otherwise, we stand hapless and ashamed in front of the wall separating the two, our helplessness diminished, to some extent, by religion, which offers us the reassurance of life's continuation after death. The doctrines and imagery it provides link life and death by a bridge of faith. We feel better and can fall asleep more easily at night. However, upon careful scrutiny, it turns out that death is always with us. It is not as apart from life as we had mistakenly assumed. Think about it.

Death before death

Life subsumes focal and mini-deaths on an ongoing basis. Big and small parts of our bodies are continually dying (and being reborn) all the time; illustrations of these include skin, brain cells, red and white blood cells, hair, fingernails, and so on. The imperceptible yet ongoing decay of the human body as it passes through the one-way tunnel of time provides numerous illustrations of how the animate gradually changes into inanimate. Moved by this realization, I have elsewhere (Akhtar, 2005) recorded the following episode:

> One day while I was getting a haircut, my eyes went to the clumps of the previous customer's hair on the floor. And once Tony began cutting my hair, I could see similar samples of my own—now quite gray—hair on the floor. The sight made me ask whether the hair that had been cut from my head still belonged to me. It somehow did not seem to, yet to say that I did not feel any affinity or sense of ownership toward it would also be called a lie. More significantly, I became aware that, due to the decisive intervention of a pair of scissors, what was a part of me moments ago had become an inanimate thing, cold and, frankly, a bit distasteful to behold. Now, let me hasten to add that Tony is a gentle and kind man. His purpose in cutting my hair is to improve my appearance, make me feel comfortable, and sustain my social acceptability. From his perspective, it is all a benign act. The follicular massacre that occurs daily in his shop is merely collateral damage as far as Tony is concerned. I, however, am left a little unnerved. If a part of me can so readily turn into a thing, what assurance is there that the whole of me would not succumb to the seduction of eternal inertia? Thoughts of death begin to surface in my mind. They make me uneasy. Tony and I exchange a few polite remarks. I pay the bill and leave. Looking back, I can see that parts of me are still lying on Tony's floor. [pp. 182–183]

(Upon hearing me read this piece at a party held at Frank Sacco's New York apartment, the charming and ever-so-analytic Joseph

Reppen smilingly asked when I was going to write something about circumcision. John Gilkey, the Michigan-based psychoanalyst, who was also present at the event, quipped, "He just did!" Everyone, including myself, was amused and found these remarks to be thought-provoking and not merely witty. The thinking that underlies them regards "death anxiety" as a developmentally "downward" displacement of castration anxiety. This is certainly possible. However, it is also possible that castration anxiety might contain developmentally "upward" derivatives of the fear of death.)

Besides such tangible icons of the occurrence of "death in life", there are subtle psychological matters of this very type to consider. Being emotionally and interpersonally dead while being physically alive is inherent in concepts like "dead mother" (Green, 1980) and "dead father" (Kalinich & Taylor, 2008), denoting parents who lack or who have abdicated maternal and paternal functions, respectively. On a different, though overlapping, level, the same applies to old friends whom one has not met for, say, four or five decades. Their representations in our internal world become psychically "calcified". We can hardly evoke them (i.e., their facial characteristics, their voices, etc.) with a convincing sense of vitality or vividness. Even the self-representations that were relationally configured in the matrix of such object ties fade way or "die" with the passage of time. The same is more or less true of our unexpressed and unlived wishful childhood self-representations. Where is my cricket-loving, stamp-collecting, and jet-black-haired self now, I would ask myself if I could bear the sadness of it all. And, whatever happens to those innocent aspects of our selves that were ignorant of sexual mysteries and tremblingly enamoured of finding even the littlest piece of the erotic jig-saw puzzle? Like it or not, the fact is that parts of us keep dying all the time. We are, therefore, never all alive; we are always partly dead. Indeed, there are philosophical traditions that advocate living as though one is already dead. In Zen Buddhism,

> . . . there is a term for this experience, namely, the Great Death. In Zen, the Great Death means dying to ordinary, dualistically conditioned consciousness in which I am I, I'm not you, and I'm not not-I. Dying to all ideas of self, to all dualistic clingings, to all

> dependency on the patriarchs, is Zen's awakening: I am I, I'm you, and simultemporally I am not I. [Kramer, 1988, p. 63]

The Zen exhortation is to live a life of detachment, including detachment from one's own self (which is regarded as an ever-changing process rather than a consolidated structure). This results in healthy stoicism and perceptual clarity (Suzuki, Fromm, & de Martino, 1963). As the Zen saying goes, "one who dies before dying never dies again" (Stryk & Ikemoto, 1963, p. 15).

In contrast is the clinically serious matter of "psychic death" *in toto*. Elucidating this notion in the broader context of schizoid withdrawal, I (Akhtar, 2009c) have delineated the steps along the regressive pathway of self-dissipation.

- The schizoid withdrawal is, at its core, an instinctive ego response to stimuli that are experienced as noxious or overwhelming. It resembles the amoeba's retraction of pseudopodia and pulling the protoplasm back.
- A related agenda is to numb the perceptual rind of the ego, dull the "mental pain" (Freud, 1926) and go into a conservative, hibernating mode of existence.
- Avoidance of hope which is felt as being the culprit, leading to betrayal by the object, is also an important motivator here. However, underneath such resolute "self-sufficiency" lies a different scenario and this brings up the next dynamic feature operative in this context.
- Giving up hope (of a fruitful exchange with the object) is hardly ever complete. On the one hand, it results in a traumatic identification (hence, merger) with the depriving object; death of the self stands for identification with the empty and "dead mother" (Green, 1980). On the other hand, the affect of futility itself, through the process of masochistic libidinization, becomes an anchoring point; this psychic position is midway between loss of its object and loss of the self. It is a stop-gap measure before the next and final step in the process.
- This consists of loss of the capacity for "mentalization" (Fonagy & Target, 1997), horrid emptiness, depersonalization, and a state of regressive "dehumanization" (Akhtar, 2003a). Body feels unattached to mind, seems automaton-like and

> foreign. Gaze avoidance appears. Language becomes faulty and belabored. Mental processes turn brittle, superficial, and reactive. Often mutism and shades of catatonia prevail. This is psychic death. [p. 52]

Such catatonic devastation of the self is an extreme that, fortunately, we come across only infrequently in our clinical work. More often we encounter less severe forms of "dead selves"; a woman who has given birth to children but lacks all maternal function, a man—talented and accomplished though he might be—who simply does not find within himself what it is to be someone's—his wife's, to be precise—husband, and so on. Many ruthless narcissists, untiring seekers of immortality (since that is the only way they can come "alive"), slick sociopaths, and serial killers also belong in this realm. Such individuals remind us that only fortunate people live first and die later. Others are not so lucky. They have already died and, therefore, can live in any and all imaginable manners. At worst, their psychic terrain sprouts the cactus of indifference and cruelty. At best, their striking stoicism and tolerance of hardship yields great achievements, especially if the desert of the emotional life contains an oasis of talent. Most individuals who have met "death in life", however, do not belong to such extremes. They lead pallid, unimaginative, and sterile existences and time passes on without ever taking a note of them.

Regardless of whether we have lived happily or miserably, a day does come when all of us die. The end point of life arrives and changes feeling, thinking, and dreaming individuals with hopes and aspirations into cold, still, and dead bodies. The transformation shocks us. Our reaction to this change is almost exactly the opposite of what we feel upon visiting the renowned wax museum of Madame Tussaud. Crafted with attention to the minutest details of their subjects, the museum's human approximations make one forget the distinction between animate and inanimate and, by implication, between life and death. Made of wax and attired in astutely appropriate costumes, the statues give the impression of being alive. We almost expect them to begin walking and talking or, at least, to say hello and shake our hand. It is amazing how this expected transformation of a thing into a human being is a matter of excitement while the transformation of a human being into a thing is deeply disturbing. Our reaction to professional mimes in amusement parks falls in between these extremes. By adapting a statue-like stillness and then unexpectedly showing movement ("coming alive"), these mimics of mortality impress upon us that the line between inanimate and animate is indeed thin. What is alive one moment can be dead the next. In the words of the renowned Urdu poet, Jan Nisar Akhtar (1972, p. 89):

> "Jism-o-jaan ka yeh aarzi rishta
> Kitna miltaa huaa hubaab mein hai"

(Literally translated, this couplet means, "Ah, this temporary bond between the body and the soul / how fragile like a bubble!")
The bubble does break in the end and we are reduced to mere cadavers, which are then disposed of by burial or cremation.

Life after life

Burial has long been the customary way in Judeo-Christian and Islamic cultures, and cremation in the Hindu culture, though it is becoming more popular in contemporary Western societies. Burial creates the illusion that we still have a home on this earth (see Chapter Five for the multi-faceted significance of graves). Cremation, on the other hand, affords us a different type of illusionary omnipotence. We can put our ashes in boxes and distribute one to each of our dear ones. Besides, getting cremated is less expensive than being buried. These two reasons—being able to be at various places simultaneously and saving money—seem to be responsible for the increasing popularity of cremation in the West. Families that are geographically separated as a result of divorce or migration especially prefer this way of disposing of dead bodies. If one is cremated, one can be close to both one's parents and one's children, after death, even if they live in different cities or countries. Each party can have some of the ashes. No need for the bereaved to travel long distances to visit a grave; no torment for the dying to choose where to be buried.

Such private disposal aside, our bodies can, at times, contribute to the society at large in an act of posthumous benevolence. Mary

Roach, the author of *Stiff: The Curious Lives of Human Cadavers* (2003), deals extensively with this matter. A condensed version of her list includes the following.

- Our dead bodies are used by medical students to learn anatomy and by future surgeons to practise their operating skills.
- As cadavers, some of us are used in laboratory experiments testing automobile safety during crashes and accidents.
- Our posthumous generosity lets others have our organs and can give an additional lease to others' lives after our own term has expired.
- In a similar vein, though admittedly on a much less frequent basis, our body parts can be used for medicinal purposes. Placenta, for instance, is still consumed occasionally by women to ward off postpartum depression. Lest you regard this as entirely esoteric, Roach is there to remind you that the popular cooking show *TV Dinners* on British television aired a garlic-fried placenta segment!

The "life in death" scenarios, however, go beyond the literal dimension and include the alluring subject of immortality. Now, this is hardly a simple matter. According to Kundera (1990), immortality comes in three varieties: minor, great, and ridiculous. *Minor immortality* refers to the lasting memory of person in the minds of those who knew him. *Great immortality*, reserved for poets, artists, and statesmen, denotes the revered posthumous presence of someone in the minds of those who never knew him in person but were deeply affected or moved by his work. *Ridiculous immortality* is accorded to one who dies under truly ludicrous circumstances. Kundera cites the instances of the astronomer Tycho Brahe who died of a burst bladder because he felt too ashamed to go to the lavatory during a festive dinner. Closer to home, the first President Bush, had he died while he threw up on the Japanese prime minister during an imperial gathering, would have earned ridiculous immortality.

To Kundera's list, two more types can be added: genetic and clinical. *Genetic immortality* (Colarusso, 1997) refers to the feeling of transcendence over death that one experiences in becoming a grandparent. It is as if, by middle age, one can conceptualize one's own death and, by the time one reaches old age, even that of one's children, but one cannot conceptualize the death of one's grandchildren. It seems that they will go on forever and, with them, one will also go on. *Clinical immortality* (Akhtar, 2007a, p. 168) refers to the post-termination unforgettability consciously or unconsciously sought by some patients from their analysts. This complexly determined phenomenon (with its many defensively altered versions) seems to occur with greater frequency in individuals who were not kept alive on a sustained basis in the minds of their parents.

An even more experience-near evidence of continued "life" in the "dead" is to be found in the "linking objects" (Volkan, 1981) of the pathological mourner. Such an object is

> Actually present in the environment that is psychologically contaminated with various aspects of the dead and the self. . . . The significance of this object does not fade as it does in uncomplicated mourning. Rather, it increasingly commands attention with its aura of mystery, fascination, and terror. [p. 101]

Linking objects can neither be rationally used nor discarded. They are usually hidden away in the house and might remain so for years. Looking at them stirs up pain as well as a vague sense of fear. Pain is caused by the physical object's reminding one of the original loss. Fear results from the mechanism of projective identification that endows the object with menacing and accusatory qualities.

Regardless of whether the evidences of the psychophysical coexistence of life and death appear in the mundane activity of getting a haircut, a visit to Madame Tussaud's, watching a professional mime, or witnessing the ambivalently held physical artefacts of the chronic mourner, they are reminders of the fact that the boundary between life and death is thin and, viewed from the floppy balcony of primary process thinking, often non-existent. Moreover, the confluence of the two does not have to be morbid. Indeed, under man's innovative capabilities, the "death in life" and "life in death" dialectics can yield truly sublime results. Let us not forget here that the Taj Mahal, perhaps the most awe-inspiring and life affirming man-made structure in the world, is a tomb. Taking twenty years (1632–1653) to complete, the grand mausoleum was built by the Mughal Emperor of India, Shah Jahan, in the memory of his beloved wife, Mumtaz Mahal.

Concluding remarks

While none of us is thus celebrated, we do become an everlasting part of this universe in one way or the other upon dying. Our blood assumes the stillness of this earth and our bones fall apart like an orphan's toy. Our flesh rots. Our ashes are dispersed and our bodies are eaten up by underground insects and microbes. Bit by bit, the distinction between what we were as human beings—with love, hate, malice, lust, pride, envy, and joy—and what a piece of earth is, or a worm crawling out of a small pocket of soil is, or a flower opening its petals for the first time to the world is, becomes unclear. The water from our bodies is absorbed by the land if we are buried, and is evaporated into the air if we are cremated. Either way, the water from our bodies adds to the bodies of water in this universe, and from them we rise as clouds and then fall on the ground as raindrops. Sometimes, if we are truly lucky, it is our grandchild or great-grandchild who catches the raindrop that we have become in her little hand and protects us from hitting the ground too hard. In that brief and shining moment of human kindness, the tears of those who cried the day we passed away are transformed into a wet inscription of joy on a little child's palm. Crossing the barrier between life and death and travelling across the psychic landscape of generations, we leave our bodies behind and return to life as a playful and generous metaphor.

REFERENCES

Abraham, K. (1924). The influence of oral eroticism on character formation. In: *Selected Papers of Karl Abraham, M.D.* (pp. 393–406). New York: Brunner/Mazel.

Abrams, S. (1978). The teaching and learning of psychoanalytic developmental psychology. *Journal of the American Psychoanalytic Association, 26*: 387–406.

Adler, J. (2005). In search of the spiritual: move over politics. Americans are looking personal, ecstatic experiences of God and, according to our poll, they don't much care what the neighbors are doing. *Newsweek,* 29 August, 2005.

Akhtar, J. N. (1972). *Khak-e-Dil.* Amroha, India: Idarai-ishaait Urdu/Danishkada.

Akhtar, S. (1987). Schizoid personality disorder: a synthesis of developmental, dynamic, and descriptive features. *American Journal of Pyschotherapy, 41*: 499–518.

Akhtar, S. (1988). Hypomanic personality disorder. *Integrative Psychiatry, 6*: 37–52.

Akhtar, S. (1989). Narcissistic personality disorder. *Psychiatric Clinics of North America, 12*: 505–529.

Akhtar, S. (1990). Paranoid personality disorder: a synthesis of developmental, dynamic, and descriptive features. *American Journal of Psychotherapy, 64*: 5–25.

Akhtar, S. (1991a). Three fantasies related to unresolved separation–individuation: a less recognized aspect of severe character pathology. In: S. Akhtar & H. Parens (Eds.), *Beyond the Symbiotic Orbit: Advances in Separation–Individuation Theory* (pp. 261–284). Hillsdale, NJ: The Analytic Press.

Akhtar, S. (1991b). Panel report: sadomasochism in perversions. *Journal of the American Psychoanalytic Association, 39*: 741–755.

Akhtar, S. (1992a). *Broken Structures: Severe Personality Disorders and Their Treatment*. Northvale, NJ: Jason Aronson.

Akhtar, S. (1992b). Tethers, orbits, and invisible fences: clinical, developmental, sociocultural, and technical aspects of optimal distance. In: S. Kramer & S. Akhtar (Eds.), *When the Body Speaks: Psychological Meanings in Kinetic Clues* (pp. 21–57). Northvale, NJ: Jason Aronson.

Akhtar, S. (1994). Object constancy and adult psychopathology. *International Journal of Psychoanalysis, 75*: 441–455.

Akhtar, S. (1996a). Love and its discontents. In: S. Akhtar & S. Kramer (Eds.), *Intimacy and Infidelity: Separation–Individuation Perspectives* (pp. 145–178). Northvale, NJ: Jason Aronson.

Akhtar, S. (1996b). "Someday . . ." and "if only . . ." fantasies: pathological optimism and inordinate nostalgia as related forms of idealization. *Journal of American Psychoanalytic Association, 44*: 723–753.

Akhtar, S. (1998). From simplicity through contradiction to paradox: the evolving psychic reality of the borderline patient in treatment. *International Journal of Psychoanalysis, 79*: 241–252.

Akhtar, S. (1999a). *Inner Torment: Living Between Conflict and Fragmentation*. Northvale, NJ: Jason Aronson.

Akhtar, S. (1999b). *Immigration and Identity: Turmoil, Treatment, and Transformation*. Northvale, NJ: Jason Aronson.

Akhtar, S. (2000). Mental pain and the cultural ointment of poetry. *International Journal of Psychoanalysis, 81*: 229–243.

Akhtar, S. (2001). From mental pain through manic defense to mourning. In: S. Akhtar (Ed.), *Three Faces of Mourning: Melancholia, Manic Defense, and Moving On* (pp. 95–113). Northvale, NJ: Jason Aronson.

Akhtar, S. (2002). Forgiveness: origins, dynamics, psychopathology, and technical relevance. *Psychoanalytic Quarterly, 71*: 175–212.

Akhtar, S. (2003a). Dehumanization: origins, manifestations, and remedies. In: S. Varvin & V. D. Volkan (Eds.), *Violence or Dialogue?: Psychoanalytic Insights on Terror and Terrorism* (pp. 131–145). London: International Psychoanalytic Association.

Akhtar, S. (2003b). Mentor: a developmental object of young adulthood. In: R. S. Murphy (Ed.), *Mental Health in India 1950–2000: Essays in Honor of Professor N. N. Wig* (pp. 2–8). Bangalore, India: PAHN.

Akhtar, S. (2003c). Things: developmental, psychopathological, and technical aspects of inanimate objects. *Canadian Journal of Psychoanalysis, 11*: 44.

Akhtar, S. (2005). *Objects of Our Desire*. New York: Harmony Press.

Akhtar, S. (2006). Experiencing oneness: pathological pursuit or normal necessity? In: S. Akhtar (Ed.), *Interpersonal Boundaries: Variations and Violations* (pp. 87–97). Lanham, MD: Jason Aronson.

Akhtar, S. (2007a). *Regarding Others: Reviews, Responses, and Reflections*. Charlottesville, VA: Pitchstone Publishing.

Akhtar, S. (2007b). Disruptions in the course of psychotherapy and psychoanalysis. In: B. van Luyn, S. Akhtar & W. J. Livesley (Eds.), *Severe Personality Disorders: Everyday Issues in Clinical Practice* (pp. 93–108). Cambridge: Cambridge University Press.

Akhtar, S. (2007c). From unmentalized xenophobia to messianic sadism: some reflections on the phenomenology of prejudice. In: H. Parens, A. Mahfouz, S. Twemlow & D. Scharff (Eds.), *The Future of Prejudice: Psychoanalysis and the Prevention of Prejudice* (pp. 7–19). Lanham, MD: Jason Aronson.

Akhtar, S. (2007d). The "listening cure": an overview. In: *Listening to Others: Developmental and Clinical Aspects of Empathy and Attunement* (pp. 1–16). Lanham, MD: Jason Aronson.

Akhtar, S. (Ed.) (2008a). *The Crescent and the Couch: Crosscurrents Between Islam and Psychoanalysis*. Lanham, MD: Jason Aronson.

Akhtar, S. (2008b). Introduction. In: M. K. O'Neil & S. Akhtar (Eds.), *On Freud's* "The Future of an Illusion" (pp. 1–8). London: Karnac.

Akhtar, S. (2009a). *Good Feelings: Psychoanalytic Perspectives on Positive Attitudes and Emotions*. London: Karnac.

Akhtar, S. (2009b). *Comprehensive Dictionary of Psychoanalysis*. London: Karnac.

Akhtar, S. (2009c). *The Damaged Core: Origins, Dynamics, Manifestations, and Treatment*. Lanham, MD: Jason Aronson.

Akhtar, S. (2009d). The schizoid wish to die and be reborn. In: *The Damaged Core: Origins, Dynamics, Manifestations, and Treatment* (pp. 67–86). Lanham, MD: Jason Aronson.

Akhtar, S. (2009e). The analyst's office. In: *The Damaged Core: Origins, Dynamics, Manifestations, and Treatment* (pp. 113–133). Lanham, MD: Jason Aronson.

Akhtar, S. (2009f). *Turning Points in Dynamic Psychotherapy: Initial Assessment, Boundaries, Money, Disruptions, and Suicidal Crises*. London: Karnac.

Akhtar, S., & Smolar, A. (1998). Visiting the father's grave. *Psychoanalytic Quarterly, 67*: 474–483.

Alexander, F. (1958). A contribution to the theory of play. *Psychoanalytic Quarterly, 27*: 175–193.

Altman, L. L. (1977). Some vicissitudes of love. *Journal of the American Psychoanalytic Association, 25*: 35–52.

Anthony, S. (1940). *The Child's Discovery of Death: A Study in Psychology*. New York: Harcourt and Brace.

Aristotle (1566). *Nichomachean Ethics*, J. L. Ackrill, J. O. Urmson & D. Ross (Eds.). Oxford, UK: Oxford University Press, 1998.

Arlow, J. A. (1984). Disturbances of the sense of time with special reference to the sense of timelessness. *Psychoanalytic Quarterly, 53*: 13–37.

Arlow, J. A. (1986). Psychoanalysis and time. *Journal of the American Psychoanalytic Association, 34*: 507–528.

Asch, S. (1976). Varieties of negative therapeutic reactions and problems of technique. *Journal of the American Psychoanalytic Association, 24*: 383–407.

Auerhahn, N., & Laub, D. (1987). Play and playfulness in Holocaust survivors. *Psychoanalytic Study of the Child, 42*: 45–58.

Bachelard, G. (1969). *The Poetics of Space*. Boston, MA: Beacon Press.

Bahn, P. (Ed.) (1996). *Tombs, Graves, and Mummies*. New York: Barnes and Noble.

Balsam, R. (1988). On being good: the internalized sibling with examples from late adolescent analyses. *Psychoanalytic Inquiry, 8*: 66–87.

Bellow, S. (1953). *The Adventures of Augie March*. New York: Viking Press.

Ben Hur (1959). Directed by William Wyler. A Metro-Goldwyn-Mayer (MGM) Production.

Bennett, D. (2009). Happiness: a buyer's guide. *The Boston Globe*, C-17, 23 August.

Ben-Shahar, T. (2007). *Happier: Learn the Secrets to Daily Joy and Lasting Fulfillment*. New York: McGraw-Hill.

Bergman, M. (2005). Termination and re-analysis. In: E. Person, A. Cooper, & G. Gabbard (Eds.), *The American Psychiatric Publishing Textbook of Psychoanalysis* (pp. 241–253). Washington, DC: American Psychiatric Press.

Bion, W. R. (1965). *Transformations*. London: Karnac, 1984.

Bion, W. R. (1967). Notes on memory and desire. *Psychoanalytic Forum, 2*: 272–273.

Bion, W. R. (1970). *Attention and Interpretation*. London: Karnac, 1984.

Birksted-Breen, D. (2009). "Reverberation time", dreaming, and the capacity to dream. *International Journal of Psychoanalysis, 90*: 35–51.

Biswas-Diener, R., & Diener, E. (2002). Making the best of a bad situation: satisfaction in the slums of Calcutta. *Social Indicators Research, 38*: 261–278.

Blacher, R. (1983). Death, resurrection, and rebirth: observations in cardiac surgery. *Psychoanalytic Quarterly, 52*: 56–72.

Blos, P. (1985). *Son and Father*. New York: Free Press.

Blum, H. (1977). The prototype of pre-oedipal reconstruction. *Journal of the American Psychoanalytic Association, 25*: 757–785.

Blum, H. (1981). Object inconstancy and paranoid conspiracy. *Journal of American Psychoanalytic Association, 29*: 789–813.

Bornholdt, I. (2009). The impact of the time experience on the psychoanalysis of children and adolescents. In: L. Glocer Fiorini & J. Canestri (Eds.), *The Experience of Time: Psychoanalytic Perspectives* (pp. 97–116). London: Karnac.

Bowlby, J. (1960). Grief and mourning in infancy and early childhood. *Psychoanalytic Study of the Child, 15*: 9–52.

Bowlby, J. (1961). Processes of mourning. *International Journal of Psychoanalysis, 42*: 317–340.

Bowlby, J. (1963). Pathological mourning and childhood mourning. *Journal of the American Psychoanalytic Association, 11*: 500–541.

Bowlby, J. (1969). *Attachment and Loss, Vol. I: Attachment*. New York: Basic Books.

Bowlby, J. (1988). *A Secure Base*. New York: Basic Books.

Brenner, C. (2000). Evenly hovering attention. *Psychoanalytic Quarterly, 69*: 545–549.

Breuer, J., & Freud, S. (1895d). *Studies on Hysteria. Standard Edition, 2*: 1–17.

Brickman, P., Coates, D., & Janoff-Bulman, R. (1978). Lottery winners and accident victims: is happiness relative? *Journal of Personality and Social Psychology, 36*: 917–927.

Bromberg, W., & Schilder, P. (1933). Death and dying. *Psychoanalytic Review, 20*: 133–145.

Brontë, E. (1847). *Wuthering Heights*. New York: Kaplan, 2006.

Brooks, A. C. (2008). *Gross National Happiness: Why Happiness Matters for America—and How We Can Get More of It*. New York: Basic Books.

Campbell, J. (1991). *The Masks of God, Vol. I: Primitive Mythology*. New York: Penguin.

Carveth, D. L. (1992). Dead end kids: projective identification and sacrifice in "Orphans". *International Review of Psychoanalysis, 19*: 217–227.

Casement, P. (1991). *Learning from the Patient*. New York: Guilford Press.

Cath, S. (1997). Loss and restitution in late life. In: *The Seasons of Life: Separation–Individuation Perspectives* (pp. 127–156). Northvale, NJ: Jason Aronson.

Celenza, A. (2005). Vis-à-vis the couch: where is psychoanalysis? *International Journal of Psychoanalysis, 86*: 1645–1660.

Chadwick, M. (1929). Notes upon the fear of death. *International Journal of Psychoanalysis, 9*: 321–334.

Chasseguet-Smirgel, J. (1984). *Creativity and Perversion*. New York: W. W. Norton.

Chasseguet-Smirgel, J. (1988). The triumph of humour. In: H. P. Blum, W. Kramer, A. K. Richards, & A. D. Richards (Eds.), *Fantasy, Myth, and Reality: Essays in Honor of Jacob Arlow* (pp. 197–213). Madison, CT: International Universities Press.

Cheney, D. L., Seyfarth, R. M., & Silk, B. M. (1995). The role of grunts in reconciling opponents and facilitating interactions among adult female baboons. *Animal Behavior, 50*: 249–257.

Chopra, D. (1991). *Perfect Health*. New York: Harmony Books.

Chopra, D. (1993a). *Ageless Body, Timeless Mind*. New York: Three Rivers Press.

Chopra, D. (1993b). *Creating Affluence*. New York: Amber-Allen.

Chopra, D. (1994). *The Seven Spiritual Laws of Success*. New York: Amber-Allen.

Chopra, D. (1995). *Boundless Energy*. New York: Three Rivers Press.

Chopra, D. (1999). *Everyday Immortality*. New York: Gramercy.

Chopra, D. (2003). *Golf for Enlightenment*. New York: Harmony Books.

Chopra, D. (2004). *The Spontaneous Fulfillment of Desire*. New York: Three Rivers Press.

Chopra, D. (2009a). *Reinventing the Body, Resurrecting the Soul*. New York: Harmony Books.

Chopra, D. (2009b). *The Ultimate Happiness Prescription*. New York: Harmony Books.

Christe, G. (1994). Some psychoanalytic aspects of humour. *International Journal of Psychoanalysis, 75*: 479–489.

Coen, S. (2005). How to play with patients who would rather remain remote. *Journal of the American Psychoanalytic Association, 53*: 811–834.

Colarusso, C. A. (1990). The third individuation: the effect of biological parenthood on separation–individuation processes in adulthood. *Psychoanalytic Study of the Child, 45*: 179–194.

Colarusso, C. A. (1997). Separation–individuation processes in middle adulthood: the fourth individuation. In: S. Akhtar & S. Kramer (Eds.), *The Seasons of Life: Separation–Individuation Perspectives* (pp. 73–94). Northvale, NJ: Aronson.

Coltart, N. (1993). *Slouching Towards Bethlehem*. London: Free Association Books.

Corradi Fiumara, G. (2009). *Spontaneity: A Psychoanalytic Inquiry*. London: Routledge.

Cournos, F. (2001). Mourning and adaptation following the death of a parent in childhood. *Journal of the American Academy of Psychoanalysis, 29*: 137–145.

Dalrymple, W. (2008). *The Last Mughal: The Fall of a Dynasty, Delhi, 1857*. New York: Vintage Press.

Deutsch, H. (1927). On satisfaction, happiness, and ecstasy. *International Journal of Psychoanalysis, 70*: 715–723, 1989 (reprint).

Deutsch, H. (1933). The psychology of manic-depressive states with particular reference to chronic hypomania. In: *Neuroses and Character Types* (pp. 203–217). New York: International Universities Press, 1965.

Deutsch, H. (1942). Some forms of emotional disturbance and their relationship to schizophrenia. *Psychoanalytic Quarterly, 11*: 301–321.

de Waal, F. B., & van Roosmalen, A. (1979). Reconciliation and consolation among chimpanzees. *Behavioral Ecology and Sociobiology, 5*: 55–66.

Dickens, C. (1860). *Great Expectations*. New York: W. W. Norton, 1999.

Dunn, E. W., Aknin, L. B., & Norton, M. I. (2008). Spending money on others promotes happiness. *Science, 319*: 1687–1688.

Ehrenberg, D. (1990). Playfulness in the psychoanalytic relationship. *Contemporary Psychoanalysis, 26*: 74–95.

Eidelberg, L. (1951). In pursuit of happiness. *Psychoanalytic Review, 38*: 222–244.

Eissler, K. (1955). *The Psychiatrist and the Dying Patient*. New York: International Universities Press.

Eissler, K. (1971). Death drive, ambivalence, and narcissism. *Psychoanalytic Study of the Child, 26*: 25–78.

Eissler, K. (Ed.) (1978). *Sigmund Freud: His Life in Pictures and Words*. New York: Harcourt, Brace, Jovanovich.

Emde, R. (1991). Positive emotions for psychoanalytic theory: surprises from infancy research and new directions. *Journal of the American Psychoanalytic Association, 39*(Suppl): 5–44.

Erikson, E. H. (1950). *Childhood and Society*. New York: W. W. Norton.

Erikson, E. H. (1956). The problem of ego identity. In: *Identity and the Life Cycle: Selected Papers* (pp. 104–165). New York: International Universities Press, 1959.

Erikson, E. H. (1959). *Identity and the Life Cycle: Selected Papers*. New York: International Universities Press.

Erikson, E. H. (1968). *Identity, Youth, and Crisis*. London: Faber and Faber.

Escoll, P. (1991). Treatment implications of separation–individuation theory in the analysis of young adults. In: S. Akhtar & H. Parens (Eds.), *Beyond the Symbiotic Orbit: Advances in Separation–Individuation Theory. Essays in Honor of Selma Kramer, M.D.* (pp. 369–388). Hillsdale, NJ: Analytic Press.

Fayek, A. (1980). From interpretation to the death instinct. *International Review of Psycho-Analysis, 7*: 447–457.

Fayek, A. (1981). Narcissism and the death instinct. *International Journal of Psycho-Analysis, 62*: 309–322.

Fazli, N. (1980). On father's death. In: *Khoya Hua Sa Kuchh* (pp. 77–78). New Delhi: Aiwaan-e-Ghalib, 1998.

Feiner, A. (1979). Countertransference and the anxiety of influence. In: L. Epstein & A. Feiner (Eds.), *Countertransference* (pp. 105–128). New York: Jason Aronson.

Feiner, A. (1990). Playfulness and the interpersonal ideology. *Contemporary Psychoanalysis, 26*: 95–106.

Feiner, A. (1992). Playfulness as a way. *Contemporary Psychoanalysis, 28*: 407–410.

Feldman, M. (2000). Some views on the manifestation of the death instinct in clinical work. *International Journal of Psychoanalysis, 81*: 53–65.

Feldman, M. (2009). Manifestations on the death instinct in the consulting room. In: B. Joseph (Ed.), *Doubt, Conviction and the Analytic Process: Selected Papers of Michael Feldman* (pp. 96–117). London: Routledge.

Fenichel, O. (1945). *The Psychoanalytic Theory of Neurosis*. New York: W. W. Norton.

Fenichel, O. (1946). On acting. *Psychoanalytic Quarterly, 15*: 144–160.

Ferenczi, S. (1932). Suggestion in (after) analysis. In: *Final Contributions to the Problems and Methods of Psycho-Analysis* (pp. 269–270). New York: Brunner/Mazel, 1980.

Fichtner, G. (Ed.) (2003). *The Freud–Binswanger Correspondence 1908–1938*. London: Open Gate Press.

Fielding, H. (1749). *The History of Tom Jones, A Foundling*. New York: Penguin Classics, 2005.

Fine, R. (1977). Psychoanalysis as a philosophical system. *Journal of Psychohistory, 5*: 1–59.

Fonagy, P., & Target, M. (1997). Attachment and reflective function: their role in self-organization. *Development and Psychopathology, 9*: 679–700.

Fox, R. P. (1998). The "unobjectionable" positive countertransference. *Journal of the American Psychoanalytic Association, 46*: 1067–1087.

Frankl, V. (2006). *Man's Search for Meaning*. Boston, MA: Beacon Press.

Freud, A. (1929). On the theory of the analysis of children. *International Journal of Psycho-Analysis, 10*: 29–38.

Freud, A. (1963). The concept of developmental lines. *Psychoanalytic Study of the Child, 18*: 245–265.

Freud, A. (1972). Comments on aggression. *International Journal of Psychoanalysis, 53*: 163–171.

Freud, A. (1974). Foreword. In: E. Furman (Ed.), *A Child's Parent Dies* (p. vii). New Haven, CT: Yale University Press.

Freud, S. (1890a). Psychical (or mental) treatment. *S.E., 7*: 283–302. London: Hogarth.

Freud, S. (1895). *Project for a Scientific Psychology*. *S.E., 1*: 295–343. London: Hogarth.

Freud, S. (1897). Letter to Wilhelm Fliess, October 3, 1897. In: J. M. Masson (Ed.), *The Complete Letters of Sigmund Freud to Wilhelm Fliess* (p. 268). Cambridge, MA: Harvard University Press.

Freud, S. (1898). Letter #82. In: *The Origins of Psychoanalysis*. New York: Basic Books, 1954.

Freud, S. (1900a). *The Interpretation of Dreams*. *S.E., 4–5*: 1–626. London: Hogarth.

Freud, S. (1905a). On psychotherapy. *S.E., 7*: 257–268. London: Hogarth.

Freud, S. (1905c). *Jokes and Their Relation to the Unconscious*. *S.E., 7*: 1–122. London: Hogarth.

Freud, S. (1908e). Creative writers and daydreaming. *S.E., 9*: 141–153. London: Hogarth.

Freud, S. (1910d). The future prospects of psychoanalytic therapy. *S.E., 11*: 141–151. London: Hogarth.

Freud, S. (1911b). Formulations on the two principles of mental functioning. *S.E., 12*: 213–216. London: Hogarth.

Freud, S. (1912b). The dynamics of transference. *S.E., 12*: 97–108. London: Hogarth.

Freud, S. (1912c). Types of onset of neurosis. *S.E., 12*: 227–237.

Freud, S. (1912e). Recommendations to physicians practising psycho-analysis. *S.E., 12*: 109–120. London: Hogarth.

Freud, S. (1912–1913). *Totem and Taboo. S.E., 13*: 1–162. London: Hogarth.

Freud, S. (1915b). Thoughts for the times on war and death. *S.E., 14*: 273–300. London: Hogarth.

Freud, S. (1915c). Instincts and their vicissitudes. *S.E., 14*: 117–140. London: Hogarth.

Freud, S. (1916d). Some character types met with during psychoanalytic work. *S.E., 14*: 310–333. London: Hogarth.

Freud, S. (1916–1917). *Introductory Lectures on Psycho-analysis Part III. S.E., 16*: 243–463. London: Hogarth.

Freud, S. (1917e). Mourning and melancholia. *S.E., 14*: 237–258. London: Hogarth.

Freud, S. (1919h). The uncanny. *S.E., 17*: 219–252. London: Hogarth.

Freud, S. (1920g). *Beyond the Pleasure Principle. S.E., 18*: 7–64. London: Hogarth.

Freud, S. (1922). Two encyclopaedia articles: the libido theory. *S.E., 18*: 255–259.

Freud, S. (1923a). Two encyclopaedia articles. *S.E., 18*: 235–259. London: Hogarth.

Freud, S. (1923b). *The Ego and the Id. S.E., 19*. London: Hogarth.

Freud, S. (1924c). The economic problem of masochism. *S.E., 19*: 155–170. London: Hogarth.

Freud, S. (1926d). *Inhibitions, Symptoms, and Anxiety. S.E., 20*: 77–175. London: Hogarth.

Freud, S. (1927c). *The Future of an Illusion. S.E., 21*: 5–56.

Freud, S. (1930a). *Civilization and Its Discontents. S.E., 21*: 64–145.

Freud, S. (1933a). *New Introductory Lectures on Psychoanalysis, S.E., 22*: 7–182.

Freud, S. (1933b). Why war? (letter to Albert Einstein). *S.E., 22*: 203–215.

Freud, S. (1937c). Analysis terminable and interminable. *S.E., 23*: 211–253.

Freud, S. (1940a [1938]). *An Outline of Psychoanalysis. S.E., 23*: 144–207.

Furman, E. (Ed.) (1974). *A Child's Parent Dies*. New Haven, CT: Yale University Press.

Gabbard, G. (1982). The exit line: heightened transference–countertransference manifestations at the end of the hour. *Journal of the American Psychoanalytic Association, 30*: 579–598.

Gay, P. (1988). *Freud: A Life for our Time*. New York: W. W. Norton.
Ghalib, A. U. K. (1839). *Diwan-e-Ghalib*. New Delhi: Maktaba Jamia, 1971.
Gill, M. (1994). *Psychoanalysis in Transition: A Personal View*. Hillsdale, NJ: Analytic Press.
Gilligan, C. (1982). *In A Different Voice: Psychological Theory and Women's Development*. Cambridge, MA: Harvard University Press.
Glauber, P. (1955). On the meaning of agoraphilia. *Journal of the American Psychoanalytic Association, 3*: 701–709.
Goldberg, A. (1990). *The Prisonhouse of Psychoanalysis*. New York: Analytic Press.
Goldberg, A. (2007). Pity the poor pluralist. *Psychoanalytic Quarterly, 76*: 1670.
Goldsmith, O. (1766). *The Vicar of Wakefield*. Oxford: Oxford University Press, 2008.
Gordon, K. H., & Sherr, P. C. (1974). Orphans in literature: a bibliography for the study of the adolescent. *Journal of the American Psychoanalytic Association, 22*: 537–541.
Gray, P. (1973). Psychoanalytic technique and the ego's capacity for viewing intrapsychic conflict. *Journal of the American Psychoanalytic Association, 21*: 474–494.
Gray, P. (1994). *The Ego and the Analysis of Defense*. Northvale, NJ: Jason Aronson.
Green, A. (1980). The dead mother. In: A. Weller (Trans.), *Life Narcissism, Death Narcissism*. London: Free Association Books.
Green, A. (1999). *The Work of the Negative*. London: Free Association Books.
Green, A. (2005). *Play and Reflection in Donald Winnicott's Writings*. London: Karnac.
Greenson, R. (1958). Variations in classical psychoanalytic technique. *International Journal of Psychoanalysis, 39*: 200–211.
Greenson, R. (1965). The working alliance and the transference neurosis. *Psychoanalytic Quarterly, 34*: 155–181.
Greyson, B. (1984). *The Near-Death Experience: Problems, Prospects, Perspectives*. Chicago, IL: Charles Thomas.
Greyson, B., Holden, J. M., & James, D. (2009). *The Handbook of Near-Death Experiences: Thirty Years of Investigation*. Santa Barbara, CA: Praeger.
Guntrip, H. (1969). *Schizoid Phenomena, Object Relations and the Self*. New York: International Universities Press.

Guntrip, H. (1975). My experience of analysis with Fairbairn and Winnicott. *International Review of Psychoanalysis, 2*: 145–161.

Guthke, K. (2009). *Epitaph Culture in the West Variations on a Theme in Cultural History*. London: Edwin Mellen Press.

Guttman, S. A., Jones, R. L., & Parrish, S. M. (1980). *The Concordance to the Standard Edition of the Complete Psychological Works of Sigmund Freud*. Boston, MA: G. K. Hall.

Hagman, G. (2000). The analyst's relation to the good. *Journal of the American Academy of Psychoanalysis, 28*: 63–82.

Hamilton, N. G. (1986). Positive projective identification. *International Journal of Psychoanalysis, 67*: 489–503.

Hare, R., McPherson, L., & Forth, A. (1988). Male psychopaths and their criminal careers. *Journal of Consulting and Clinical Psychology, 56*: 710–714.

Harnik, J. (1930). One component of the fear of death in early infancy. *International Journal of Psycho-Analysis, 11*: 485–491.

Hartmann, H. (1939). *Ego Psychology and the Problem of Adaptation*, D. Rapaport (Trans.). New York: International Universities Press, 1958.

Hartmann, H. (1952). The mutual influences of the development of ego and id. *Psychoanalytic Study of the Child, 7*: 9–30.

Hartmann, H. (1955). Notes on the theory of sublimation. *Psychoanalytic Study of the Child, 10*: 9–29.

Hartmann, H. (1960). *Psychoanalysis and Moral Values*. Madison, CT: International Universities Press.

Heaney, S. (1995). *A Redress for Poetry*. New York: Farrar, Strauss, and Giroux.

Heidegger, M. (1949). *Existence and Being*. Chicago, IL: Henry Regnery.

Hesse, H. (1919). *Demien: A Dual Language Book*, S. Appelbaum (Trans.). Mineola, NY: Dover Publications, 2002.

Hilgard, J. (1953). Anniversary reactions in parents precipitated by children. *Psychiatry, 16*: 73–80.

Hoffer, A. (1985). Towards a definition of psychoanalytic neutrality. *Journal of the American Psychoanalytic Association, 33*: 771–795.

Hopkins, L. (2000). Masud Khan's application of Winnicott's "play" techniques to analytic consultation and treatment of adults. *Contemporary Psychoanalysis, 36*: 639–663.

Hrdy, S. B. (1999). *Mother Nature: A History of Mothers, Infants, and Natural Selection*. New York: Pantheon Books.

Innes, B. (2006). *Serial Killers*. New York: Book Sales.

Jacobs, T. (1986). On countertransference enactments. *Journal of the American Psychoanalytic Association, 34*: 289–307.

Jacobson, E. (1964). *The Self and the Object World*. New York: International Universities Press.

James, H. (1903). The beast in the jungle. In: *Short Stories by Henry James*. New York: Signet Classics, 2003.

James, W. (1902). *The Varieties of Religious Experience*. New York: Modern Library, 2002.

Jewell, W. (2010). Science hero: Dr Madan Kataria, http://www.myhero.com/myhero/heroprint.asp?hero=Kataria.

Joffee, W. G., & Sandler, J. (1965). Pain, depression, and individuation. In: J. Sandler (Ed.), *From Safety to Superego* (pp. 154–179). New York: Guilford Press.

Jones, E. (1913). The God complex. In: *Essays in Applied Psychoanalysis, Vol. II* (pp. 244–265). New York: International Universities Press, 1973.

Jones, E. (1957). *The Life and Work of Sigmund Freud, Vol. III*. New York: Basic Books.

Joseph, B. (1981). Towards the experiencing of psychic pain. In: M. Feldman & E. B. Spillius (Eds.), *Psychic Equilibrium and Psychic Change. Selected Papers of Betty Joseph* (pp. 88–97). London: Routledge, 1989.

Kahneman, D., Krueger, A. B., Schkade, D., Schwartz, N., & Stone, A. (2006). Would you be happier if you were richer? *Science, 312*: 1908–1910.

Kalinich, L., & Taylor, S. (Eds.) (2008). *The Dead Father*. London: Routledge.

Kaplan, L. (1977). *Oneness and Separateness: From Infant to Individual*. New York: Simon and Schuster.

Kernberg, O. F. (1970). A psychoanalytic classification of character pathology. *Journal of the American Psychoanalytic Association, 18*: 800–822.

Kernberg, O. F. (1974b). Mature love: prerequisites and characteristics. *Journal of the American Psychoanalytic Association, 22*: 743–768.

Kernberg, O. F. (1975). *Borderline Conditions and Pathological Narcissism*. New York: Jason Aronson.

Kernberg, O. F. (1976). *Object-Relations Theory and Clinical Psychoanalysis*. New York: Jason Aronson.

Kernberg, O. F. (1980). *Internal World and External Reality: Object Relations Theory Applied*. New York: Jason Aronson.

Kernberg, O. F. (1984). *Severe Personality Disorders: Psychotherapeutic Strategies*. New Haven, CT: Yale University Press.

Kernberg, O. F. (1991). Sadomasochism, sexual excitement, and perversion. *Journal of the American Psychoanalytic Association, 39*: 333–362.

Kernberg, O. F. (2009). The concept of the death drive: a clinical perspective. *International Journal of Psychoanalysis, 90*: 1009–1023.

Kernberg, O. F., Selzer, M. A., Koenigsberg, H. W., Carr, A. C., & Appelbaum, A. H. (1990). *Psychodynamic Psychotherapy of Borderline Patients*. New York: Basic Books.

Khan, M. M. R. (1962). Dream psychology and the evolution of the psychoanalytic situation. In: *The Privacy of the Self* (pp. 27–41). London: Hogarth Press, 1974.

Khan, M. M. R. (1979). From masochism to psychic pain. In: *Alienation in Perversions* (pp. 210–218). New York: International Universities Press.

Kierkegaard, S. (1957). *The Concept of Dread*. Princeton, NJ: Princeton University Press.

Killingmo, B. (1989). Conflict and deficit: implications for technique. *International Journal of Psychoanalysis, 70*: 65–79.

Klauber, J. (1968). The psychoanalyst as a person. In: *Difficulties in the Analytic Encounter* (pp. 123–139). New York: Jason Aronson, 1976.

Kleeman, J. A. (1967). The peek-a-boo game. *Psychoanalytic Study of the Child, 22*: 239–273.

Klein, G. (1976). *Psychoanalytic Theory*. New York: International Universities Press.

Klein, M. (1923). Zur fruhanalyse. *Imago, 9*: 222–259.

Klein, M. (1930). The importance of symbol-formation in the development of the ego. *International Journal of Psychoanalysis, 11*: 24–39.

Klein, M. (1933). The early development of conscience in the child. In: *Love, Guilt and Reparation and Other Works - 1921–1945* (pp. 262–289). New York: Free Press, 1984.

Klein, M. (1935). A contribution to the psychogenesis of manic depressive states. In: *Love, Guilt and Reparation and Other Works—1921–1945* (pp. 262–289). New York: The Free Press, 1975.

Klein, M. (1937). Love, guilt, and reparation. In: *Love, Guilt and Reparation and Other Works—1921–1945* (pp. 306–343). New York: Free Press, 1975.

Klein, M. (1940). Mourning and its relation to manic–depressive states. *International Journal of Psychoanalysis, 21*: 125–153.

Klein, M. (1946). Notes on some schizoid mechanisms. In: *Envy and Gratitude and Other Works—1946–1963* (pp.1–24). New York: Free Press, 1975.

Klein, M. (1948). On the theory of anxiety and guilt. In: *Developments in Psychoanalysis*. London: Hogarth Press.

Klein, M. (1952a). Some theoretical conclusions regarding the emotional life of the infant. In: *Envy and Gratitude and Other Works 1946–1963* (pp. 61–93). New York: Free Press, 1975.

Klein, M. (1952b). On observing the behaviour of young infants. In: *Envy and Gratitude and Other Works 1946–1963* (pp. 94–121). New York: Free Press, 1975.

Klein, M. (1957). Envy and gratitude. In: *Envy and Gratitude and Other Works - 1946–1963* (pp. 176–235). New York: Free Press, 1975.

Klein, M. (1960). On mental health. *British Journal of Medical Psychology, 33*: 237–241.

Klein, M. (1963). On the sense of loneliness. In: *Envy and Gratitude and Other Works—1946–1963* (pp. 300–313). New York: Free Press, 1975.

Kogan, I. (1990). A journey to pain. *International Journal of Psychoanalysis, 71*: 629–640.

Kohlberg, L. (1984). *The Psychology of Moral Development: the Nature and Validity of Moral Stages*. San Francisco, CA: Harper and Row.

Kohut, H. (1977). *Restoration of the Self*. New York: International Universities Press.

Kohut, H. (1980). *Self Psychology and the Humanities*. New York: W. W. Norton.

Kohut, H. (1982). Introspection, empathy, and the semi-circle of mental health. *International Journal of Psychoanalysis, 63*: 395–407.

Kramer, K. (1988). *The Sacred Art of Dying*. New York: Paulist Press.

Kramer, S., & Akhtar, S. (1988). The developmental context of preoedipal internalized object relations: clinical applications of Mahler's theory of symbiosis and separation–individuation. *Psychoanalytic Quarterly, 42*: 547–576.

Kretschner, E. (1925). *Physique and Character*. New York: Harcourt Brace.

Kris, E. (1956). On some vicissitudes of insight in psychoanalysis. *International Journal of Psychoanalysis, 37*: 445–455.

Kubler-Ross, E. (1970). *On Death and Dying*. New York: Macmillan.

Kundera, M. (1990). *Immortality*. New York: HarperCollins.

Langs, R. (1997). *Death Anxiety and Clinical Practice*. London: Karnac.

Langs, R. (2004). Death anxiety and the emotion-processing mind. *Psychoanalytic Psychology, 21*: 31–53.

Lear, J. (2000). *Happiness, Death, and the Remainder of Life*. Cambridge, MA: Harvard University Press.

Lemma, A. (2000). *Humour on the Couch*. London: Whurr.

Lemma, A. (2009). Commentary on "Humour". In: S. Akhtar (Ed.), *Good Feelings: Psychoanalytic Reflections on Positive Emotions and Attitudes* (pp. 297–302). London: Karnac.

Levine, S. (2007). Nothing but the truth: self-disclosure, self-revelation, and the persona of the analyst. *Journal of the American Psychoanalytic Association, 55*: 81–104.

Levy, S. T. (1987). Therapeutic strategy and psychoanalytic technique. *Journal of the American Psychoanalytic Association, 35*: 447–466.

Lewin, B. (1932). Analysis and structure of a transient hypomania. *Psychoanalytic Quarterly, 1*: 43–58.

Lewin, B. (1937). A type of hypomanic reaction. *Archives of Neurology and Psychiatry, 37*: 111–123.

Lewin, B. (1941). Comments on hypomanic and related states. *Psychoanalytic Review, 28*: 86–91.

Lewin, B. (1950). *The Psychoanalysis of Elation*. New York: W. W. Norton.

Lewin, R., & Schulz, C. (1992). *Losing and Fusing: Borderline Transitional Object and Self Relations*. Northvale, NJ: Jason Aronson.

Lichtenstein, H. (1963). The dilemma of human identity: notes on self-transformation, self-objectivation, and metamorphosis. *Journal of American Psychoanalytic Association, 11*: 173–223.

Loewald, E. (1987). Therapeutic play in space and time. *Psychoanalytic Study of the Child, 42*: 173–192.

Loewald, H. (1960). On the therapeutic action of psychoanalysis. *Journal of the American Psychoanalytic Association, 41*: 16–33.

Loewald, H. (1970). Psychoanalytic theory and psychoanalytic process. *Psychoanalytic Study of the Child, 25*: 45–68.

Lopez-Corvo, R. (2003). *The Dictionary of the Work of W. R. Bion*. London: Karnac.

Lowenstein, R. M. (1958). Remarks on some variations in psychoanalytic technique. *International Journal of Psychoanalysis, 39*: 202–210.

McClelland, D. (1964). The harlequin complex. In: R. White (Ed.), *The Study of Lives* (pp. 94–120). New York: Atherton.

Madow, L. (1997). On the way to a second symbiosis. In: S. Akhtar & S. Kramer (Eds.), *The Seasons of Life: Separation–Individuation Perspectives* (pp. 157–170). Northvale, NJ: Jason Aronson.

Mahler, M. S. (1971). A study of the separation–individuation process and its possible application to borderline phenomena in the psychoanalytic situation. In: *The Selected Papers of Margaret S. Mahler, Vol. II* (pp. 169–187). New York: Jason Aronson, 1979.

Mahler, M. S., Pine, F., & Bergman, A. (1975). *The Psychological Birth of the Human Infant: Symbiosis and Individuation*. New York: Basic Books.

Mahon, E. J. (2004). Playing and working through: a neglected analogy. *Psychoanalytic Quarterly, 73*: 379–413.

Marmor, J. (1955). The psychodynamics of realistic worry. In: *Psychiatry in Transition: Selected Papers of Judd Marmor, M.D.* New York: Brunner/Mazel.

Masson, J. M. (Ed.) (1985). *The Complete Letters of Sigmund Freud to Wilhelm Fleiss*. Cambridge, MA: Harvard University Press.

Masur, C. (2001). Can women mourn their mothers? In: S. Akhtar (Ed.), *Three Faces of Mourning: Melancholia, Manic Defense, and Moving On* (pp. 33–46). Northvale, NJ: Jason Aronson.

Maugham, W. S. (1915). *Of Human Bondage*. New York: Random House, 1999.

May, R. (1950). *The Meaning of Anxiety*. New York: W. W. Norton, 1996.

Meissner, W. (1996). *The Therapeutic Alliance*. New Haven, CT: Yale University Press.

Meissner, W. (2007). *Time, Self, and Psychoanalysis*. Lanham, MD: Jason Aronson.

Menninger, R. (1932). Poor little good child. In: B. H. Hall (Ed.), *A Psychiatrist's World: The Selected Papers of Karl Menninger* (pp. 556–559). New York: Viking Press, 1959.

Meyers, H. (2001). Does mourning become Electra?: oedipal and separation–individuation issues in a woman's loss of her mother. In: S. Akhtar (Ed.), *Three Faces of Mourning: Melancholia, Manic Defense, and Moving On* (pp. 13–31). Northvale, NJ: Jason Aronson.

Mills, J. (2005). On moral countertransference. *International Journal of Applied Psychoanalytic Studies, 2*: 236–248.

Mistral, G. (1914). Sonnets of death. In: V. B. Price (Ed.), U. K. LeGuin (Trans.), *Selected Poems of Gabriela Mistral* (pp. 144–162). Albuquerque, NM: University of New Mexico Press.

Modell, A. (1965). On aspects of the superego's development. *International Journal of Psychoanalysis, 46*: 323–331.

Moody, R. (1975). *Life After Life: The Investigation of a Phenomenon—Survival of a Bodily Death*. New York: Harper Collins.

Moran, G. S. (1987). Some functions of play and playfulness—a developmental perspective. *Psychoanalytic Study of the Child, 42*: 11–29.

Myers, D. G. (2000). The funds, friends, and faith of happy people. *American Psychologist, 55*: 45–67.

Nagera, H. (1970). Children's reactions to the death of important objects. *Psychoanalytic Study of the Child, 25*: 369–392.

Natterson, J., & Knudson, A. (1965). Observations concerning fear of death in fatally ill children and their mothers. In: R. Fulton (Ed.), *Death and Identity* (pp. 235–278). New York: John Wiley.

Newstock, S. (2009). *Quoting Death in Early Modern England: The Poetics of Epitaphs Beyond the Tomb*. New York: Palgrave Macmillan.

Niederland, W. (1968). Clinical observations on the survival syndrome. *International Journal of Psychoanalysis, 49*: 313–315.

Norton, J. (1963). The treatment of a dying patient. *Psychoanalytic Study of the Child, 18*: 541–560.

Olinick, S. L. (1982). Meanings beyond words: psychoanalytic perceptions of silence and communication, happiness, sexual love and death. *International Review of Psychoanalysis, 9*: 461–472.

Orgel, S. (1965). On time and timelessness. *Journal of the American Psychoanalytic Association, 13*: 102–121.

Ostow, M. (1987). Play and reality. *Psychoanalytic Study of the Child, 42*: 193–203.

Pacella, B. (1980). The primal matrix configuration. In: R. F. Lax, S. Bach, & J. A. Burland (Eds.), *Rapprochement: The Critical Subphase of Separation–Individuation* (pp. 117–131). New York: Jason Aronson.

Parens, H. (2010). Thoughts on children's understanding of death. In: S. Akhtar (Ed.), *The Wound of Mortality: Fear, Denial, and Acceptance of Death* (pp. 37–50). Lanham, MD: Jason Aronson.

Parker-Pearson, M. (2001). *The Archeology of Death and Burial*. College Station, TX: Texas A&M University Press.

Parkes, C. M. (1964). The effects of bereavement on physical and mental health. *British Medical Journal, 2*: 274–279.

Parkes, C. M. (1972). *Bereavement: Studies of Grief in Adult Life*. New York: International Universities Press.

Parsons, M. (2000). *The Dove That Returns, The Dove That Vanishes: Paradox and Creativity in Psychoanalysis*. London: Routledge.

Peller, L. E. (1954). Libidinal phases, ego development, and play. *Psychoanalytic Study of the Child, 9*: 178–198.

Perez-Foster, R., Moskowitz, M., & Javier, R. A. (1996). *Reaching Across Boundaries of Culture and Class*. Northvale, NJ: Jason Aronson.

Pine, F. (1979). The separation–individuation process. *International Journal of Psychoanalysis, 60*: 225–242.

Pine, F. (1998). *Diversity and Direction in Psychoanalytic Technique*. New Haven, CT: Yale University Press.

Poe, E. A. (1846). The cask of Amontillado. In: *Collected Works of Edgar Allan Poe* (pp. 150–159). New York: Vintage Books, 1975.

Poe, E. A. (1850). The premature burial. In: *Collected Works of Edgar Allan Poe* (pp. 210–263). New York: Vintage Books, 1975.

Poland, W. (1990). The gift of laughter: on the development of a sense of humour in clinical analysis. *Psychoanalytic Quarterly, 49*: 197–225.

Poland, W. (1996). *Melting the Darkness*. Northvale, NJ: Jason Aronson.

Pollock, G. H. (1961). Mourning and adaptation. *International Journal of Psychoanalysis, 42*: 341–361.

Pollock, G. H. (1970). Anniversary reactions, trauma, and mourning. *Psychoanalytic Quarterly, 39*: 347–371.

Pollock, G. H. (1975). On mourning, immortality, and utopia. *Journal of the American Psycho-analytic Association, 23*: 334–362.

Pontalis, J. B. (1981). *Frontiers in Psychoanalysis: Between the Dream and Psychic Reality*. New York: International Universities Press.

Rank, O. (1924). *The Trauma of Birth*. New York: Robert, Brunner, 1952.

Reik, T. (1948). *Listening with the Third Ear: The Inner Experience of a Psychoanalyst*. New York: Grove Press.

Ren, R., Yan, K., & Su, Y. (1991). The reconciliation behavior of golden monkeys in small breeding groups. *Primates, 32*: 321–327.

Renik, O. (1990). Comments on the clinical analysis of anxiety and depressive affect. *Psychoanalytic Quarterly, 59*: 226–248.

Renik, O. (1996). The perils of neutrality. *Psychoanalytic Quarterly, 65*: 495–517.

Riviere, J. (1937). Hate, greed, and aggression. In: A. Hughes (Ed.), *The Inner World and Joan Riviere: Collected Papers 1920–1958* (pp. 168–205). London: Karnac.

Roach, M. (2003). *Stiff: The Curious Lives of Human Cadavers*. New York: W. W. Norton.

Roazen, P. (1989). Introductory note. *International Journal of Psycho-analysis, 70*: 715–716.

Roland, A. (1988). Indians in American: adaptation and the bicultural self. In: P. H. Elovitz & C. Khan (Eds.), *Immigrant Experiences: Personal Narrative and Psychological Analysis* (pp. 148–157). Cranbury, NJ: Associated University Press.

Rosenfeld, H. (1971). A clinical approach to the psychoanalytic theory of the life and death instincts: an investigation into the aggressive aspects of narcissism. *International Journal of Psycho-analysis, 52*: 169–178.

Russell, B. (1930). *The Conquest of Happiness*. New York: Horace Liveright.

Russell, R. (2000). *The Famous Ghalib*. New Delhi: Roli Books.

Sachs, H. (1941). Psychotherapy and the pursuit of happiness. *American Imago, 2*: 356–364.

Sandler, J., & Sandler, A.-M. (1998). *Internal Objects Revisited*. London: Karnac.

Sartre, J. (1956). *Being and Nothingness*. New York: Citadel Press.

Schachter, J. (1990). Post-termination patient–analyst contact: analyst's attitudes and experience. *International Journal of Psychoanalysis, 71*: 475–486.

Schachter, J. (1992). Concepts of termination and post-termination. Patient–analyst contact. *International Journal of Psychoanalysis, 73*: 137–154.

Schafer, R. (2002). Defences against goodness. *Psychoanalytic Quarterly, 71*: 5–20.

Schmidt-Hellerau, C. (2006). Surviving in absence: on the preservative and death drives and their clinical utility. *Psychoanalytic Quarterly, 75*: 1057–1095.

Searles, H. (1960). *The Non-Human Environment in Normal Development and Schizophrenia*. New York: International Universities Press.

Seelig, B., & Rosof, L. (2001). Normal and pathological altruism. *Journal of the American Psychoanalytic Association, 49*: 933–959.

Seligman, M. E. (2002). *Authentic Happiness*. New York: Free Press.

Sen, A. (1999). *Development as Freedom*. New York: Anchor Books.

Settlage, C. (2001). Defenses evoked by early childhood loss: their impact on life-span development. In: S. Akhtar (Ed.), *Three Faces of Mourning: Melancholia, Manic Defense, and Moving On* (pp. 47–94). Northvale, NJ: Jason Aronson.

Shengold, L. (1988). Some notes on play and playfulness. *Bulletin of the Anna Freud Centre, 11*: 146–151.

Shengold, L. (1991). *Father, Don't You See I'm Burning?* New Haven, CT: Yale University Press.

Shields, R. (1964). The "too good" mother. *International Journal of Psychoanalysis, 45*: 85–88.

Shneidman, E. (2008). *A Commonsense Book of Death*. Lanham, MD: Rowman and Littlefield.

Silberer, H. (1914). *Problem der Mystik und ihrer Symbolik*. Leipzig: Hugo Heller.

Silbermann, I. (1985). On "happiness". *Psychoanalytic Study of the Child, 40*: 457–472.

Silk, J. B. (1998). Making amends: adaptive perspectives on conflict remediation in monkeys, apes, and humans. *Human Nature, 9*: 341–368.

Silverman, P., & Worden, J. (1993). Children's reactions to the death of a parent. In: M. Stroebe, W. Stroebe, & R. Hansson (Eds.),

Bereavement, A Sourcebook of Research and Intervention (pp. 41–59). Cambridge: Cambridge University Press.

Sloan, C. (2002). *Bury the Dead: Tombs, Corpses, Mummies, Skeletons, and Rituals*. New York: Scholastic.

Smolar, A. (2002). Reflections on gifts in the therapeutic setting: the gift from patient to therapist. *American Journal of Psychotherapy, 56*: 27–45.

Smolar, A. (2003). When we give more: reflections on 'gifts' from therapist to patient. *American Journal of Psychotherapy, 57*: 300–323.

Solnit, A. (1987). A psychoanalytic view of play. *Psychoanalytic Study of the Child*, 42: 205–219.

Solnit, A. (1998). Beyond play and playfulness. *Psychoanalytic Study of the Child, 53*: 102–110.

Sperling, O. (1963). Exaggeration as a defense. *Psychoanalytic Quarterly, 32*: 533–548.

Spitz, R. (1946). Anaclitic depression: an inquiry into the genesis of psychiatric conditions in early childhood. *Psychoanalytic Study of the Child*, 2: 313–342.

Spitz, R. (1950). Anxiety in infancy: a study of its manifestations in the first year of life. *International Journal of Psychoanalysis, 31*: 138–143.

Spitz, R. (1965). *The First Year of Life*. New York: International Universities Press.

Stein, M. (1985). Irony in psychoanalysis. *Journal of the American Psychoanalytic Association, 33*: 35–58.

Stepansky, P. (Ed.) (1988). *The Memoirs of Margaret S. Mahler*. New York: Free Press.

Stern, D. (1977). *The First Relationship: Mother and Infant*. Cambridge, MA: Harvard University Press.

Sternbach, O. (1974). The pursuit of happiness and the epidemic of depression. *Psychoanalytic Review, 61*: 283–293.

Stevenson, I., & Greyson, B. (1979). Near-death experiences: relevance to the question of survival after death. *Journal of the American Medical Association, 242*: 265–267.

Stoller, R. (1973). *Perversion: the Erotic Form of Hatred*. New York: Pantheon Books.

Stolorow, R. D. (1973). A note on death anxiety as a development achievement. *American Journal of Psychoanalysis, 34*: 351–353.

Stone, L. (1961). *The Psychoanalytic Situation: an Examination of its Development and Essential Nature. Freud Anniversary Lecture*. New York: International Universities Press, 1977.

Stone, L. (1971). Reflections on the psychoanalytic concept of aggression. *Psychoanalytic Quarterly, 40*: 195–244.

Stone, M. H. (2001). Serial sexual homicide: biological, psychological, and sociological aspects. *Journal of Personality Disorders, 15*: 1–18.

Stryk, L., & Ikemoto, T. (Eds.) (1963). *Zen: Poems, Prayers, Sermons, Anecdotes and Interviews*. New York: Doubleday.

Sudilovsky, J. (2010). LOL (laugh out loud): an Ethiopian 'laugh master' tells Israelis and Palestinians to laugh their way to peace. *The Jerusalem Report* (pp. 8–9), 18 January, 2010.

Suzuki, D. T., Fromm, E., & de Martino, R. (1963). *Zen Buddhism and Psychoanalysis*. New York: Evergreen Press.

Symington, N. (2008). How belief in God affects my clinical work. In: M. K. O'Neil & S. Akhtar (Eds.), *On Freud's 'The Future of an Illusion'* (pp. 237–252). London: Karnac.

Tahka, V. (1993). *Mind and Its Treatment: A Psychoanalytic Approach*. Madison, CT: International Universities Press.

Target, M., & Fonagy, P. (1996). Playing with reality, II: the development of psychic reality from a theoretical perspective. *International Journal of Psychoanalysis, 77*: 459–479.

Taylor, C. (1989). *Sources of the Self: The Making of the Modern Identity*. Cambridge, MA: Harvard University Press.

The Philadelphia Inquirer (2009). Sideshow: your daily dose of gossip. Monday 2 November, p. E-4.

Thoma, H., & Kachele, H. (1994). *Psychoanalytic Practice, Volume 2: Clinical Studies*. Northvale, NJ: Jason Aronson.

Thompson, M. G. (2004). Happiness and chance: a reappraisal of the psychoanalytic conception of suffering. *Psychoanalytic Psychology, 21*: 134–153.

Thoreau, H. D. (1854). *Walden: Or, Life in the Woods*. Boston, MA: Ticknor and Fields.

Treurniet, N. (1997). On an ethnic of psychoanalytic technique. *Psychoanalytic Quarterly, 66*: 596–627.

Tustin, F. (1980). Autistic objects. *International Review of Psychoanalysis, 7*: 27–39.

Vallabheneni, M. (2005). Advaita Vedanta, psychoanalysis and the self. In: S. Akhtar (Ed.), *Freud Along the Ganges: Psychoanalytic Reflections on the People and Culture of India* (pp. 359–393). New York: Other Press.

Volkan, V. D. (1971). A study of a patient's re-grief work through dreams, psychological tests, and psychoanalysis. *Psychiatric Quarterly, 45*: 255–273.

Volkan, V. D. (1981). *Linking Objects and Linking Phenomena: A Study of the Forms, Symptoms, Metapsychology, and Therapy of Complicated Mourning*. New York: International Universities Press.

Volkan, V. D., Cilluffo, A. F., & Sarvay, T. L. (1975). Re-grief therapy and the function of the linking object as a key to stimulate emotionality. In: P. T. Olsen (Ed.), *Emotional Flooding* (pp. 179–224). New York: Human Sciences Press.

Waelder, R. (1933). The psychoanalytic theory of play. *Psychoanalytic Quarterly*, 2: 208–224.

Wahl, C. W. (1965). The fear of death. In: R. Fulton (Ed.), *Death and Identity* (pp. 136–160). New York: John Wiley.

Webster's Collegiate Dictionary (1998). Springfield, MA: Merriam Webster.

Weigert, E. (1967). Narcissism: benign and malignant terms. In: R. W. Gibson (Ed.), *Crosscurrents in Psychiatry and Psychoanalysis* (pp. 222–238). Philadelphia: J. B. Lippincott Company.

Weiss, E. (1934). Bodily pain and mental pain. *International Journal of Psychoanalysis*, *15*: 1–13.

Weissman, A. D. (1972). *On Dying and Denying*. New York: Behavioral Publications.

Wheelis, A. (1966). *The Illusionless Man*. New York: Harper Colophon.

Wheelis, A. (1975). *On Not Knowing How to Live*. New York: Harper and Row Publishers.

Winnicott, C., Shepherd, R., & Davis, M. (1989). *Psychoanalytic Explorations: D. W. Winnicott*. Cambridge, MA: Harvard University Press.

Winnicott, D. (1935). The manic defense. In: *Collected Papers: Through Paediatrics to Psychoanalysis* (pp. 129–144). New York: Basic Books, 1958.

Winnicott, D. (1939). Early disillusion. In: C. Winnicott, R. Shepherd & M. Davis (Eds.), *Psychoanalytic Explorations: D. W. Winnicott* (pp. 21–23). Cambridge, MA: Harvard University Press, 1989.

Winnicott, D. (1941). The observation of infants in a set situation. *International Journal of Psychoanalysis*, *22*: 229–249.

Winnicott, D. (1947). Hate in the countertransference. In: *Through Paediatrics to Psychoanalysis: Collected Papers* (pp. 194–203). New York: Brunner/Mazel, 1992.

Winnicott, D. (1953). Transitional objects and transitional phenomena. *International Journal of Psycho-Analysis*, *34*: 89–97.

Winnicott, D. (1956). The anti-social tendency. In: *Through Paediatrics to Psychoanalysis: Collected Papers* (pp. 306–316). New York: Brunner/Mazel, 1992.

Winnicott, D. (1960). Ego distortion in terms of true and false self. In: *Maturational Processes and the Facilitating Environment* (pp. 140–152). New York: International Universities Press, 1965.

Winnicott, D. (1962). Ego integration in child development. In: *Maturational Processes and the Facilitating Environment* (pp. 45–53). New York: International Universities Press.

Winnicott, D. (1971). *Playing and Reality*. London: Penguin.

Wolf, E. (1994). Selfobject experiences: developmental, psychopathology, treatment. In: S. Kramer & S. Akhtar (Eds.), *Mahler and Kohut: Perspectives on Development, Psychopathology, and Technique* (pp. 65–96). Northvale, NJ: Jason Aronson.

Wolfenstein, M. (1966). How is mourning possible? *Psychoanalytic Study of the Child, 21*: 93–123.

Yevtushenko, Y. (1960). Pasternak's grave. In: *Collected Poems of Yevgeny Yevtuskenko, 1939–1990* (pp. 83–84). New York: Henry Holt and Company.

Zetzel, E. (1968). The so-called 'good hysteric'. *International Journal of Psychoanalysis, 49*: 256–260.

Zilboorg, G. (1938). The sense of immortality. *Psychoanalytic Quarterly, 7*: 171–199.

Zilboorg, G. (1943). Fear of death. *Psychoanalytic Quarterly, 12*: 465–475.

INDEX